The (Not So) Surprising Longevity of Identity Politics

This book assesses the underpinning role 'references to identity' played and continue to play as the powerful mobilising force in domestic politics across the East European region stretching from Estonia to Bulgaria.

The EU membership of postcommunist states was to ensure stability, prevent conflict and eventually guarantee equality of all citizens regardless of their political preferences or ethnic identities. However, the promotion of such norms and values has been secondary to consolidation of state institutions and the societies they serve around ethnocentric narratives of states' core ethnic groups. The sequel of financial, then 'refugee' crises has further dented the appeal of the EU's norms across the region. Even the rhetoric commitment to respect cultural diversity and human rights has been promptly replaced with references to identity and interests of politically relevant groups. Yet, nativist and populist rhetoric has been the staple of politics since before the EU accession.

The chapters in this edited volume zoom in on politics which forge and live-off their societies' preoccupation with ethnocentric narratives, vesting national identity with persistent relevance and considerable weight across the postcommunist region.

The chapters in this book were originally published in the journal, *East European Politics*.

Timofey Agarin teaches Comparative Politics at Queen's University Belfast, where he is also the Director of the Centre for the Study of Ethnic Conflict. His research interests are ethnic politics and their impact on societal transition, including majority-minority relations, non-discrimination, migration and civil society, with a particular focus on postcommunist states in Central Eastern Europe.

The (Not So) Surprising Longevity of Identity Politics

Contemporary Challenges of the State-Society Compact in Central Eastern Europe

Edited by
Timofey Agarin

LONDON AND NEW YORK

First published 2022
by Routledge
4 Park Square, Milton Park, Abingdon, Oxon OX14 4RN

and by Routledge
605 Third Avenue, New York, NY 10158

Routledge is an imprint of the Taylor & Francis Group, an informa business

Introduction, Chapters 2 and 4–7 © 2022 Taylor & Francis
Chapter 1 © 2019 Daniel Bochsler and Andreas Juon. Originally published as Open Access.
Chapter 3 © 2019 Robert Sata and Ireneusz Pawel Karolewski. Originally published as Open Access.

With the exception of Chapters 1 and 3, no part of this book may be reprinted or reproduced or utilised in any form or by any electronic, mechanical, or other means, now known or hereafter invented, including photocopying and recording, or in any information storage or retrieval system, without permission in writing from the publishers. For details on the rights for Chapters 1 and 3, please see the chapters' Open Access footnotes.

Trademark notice: Product or corporate names may be trademarks or registered trademarks, and are used only for identification and explanation without intent to infringe.

British Library Cataloguing in Publication Data
A catalogue record for this book is available from the British Library

ISBN: 978-1-032-22262-2 (hbk)
ISBN: 978-1-032-22263-9 (pbk)
ISBN: 978-1-003-27184-0 (ebk)

DOI: 10.4324/9781003271840

Typeset in Myriad Pro
by Newgen Publishing UK

Publisher's Note
The publisher accepts responsibility for any inconsistencies that may have arisen during the conversion of this book from journal articles to book chapters, namely the inclusion of journal terminology.

Disclaimer
Every effort has been made to contact copyright holders for their permission to reprint material in this book. The publishers would be grateful to hear from any copyright holder who is not here acknowledged and will undertake to rectify any errors or omissions in future editions of this book.

Contents

	Citation Information	vi
	Notes on Contributors	viii
	Introduction: The (not so) surprising longevity of identity politics: contemporary challenges of the state-society compact in Central Eastern Europe *Timofey Agarin*	1
1	Authoritarian footprints in Central and Eastern Europe *Daniel Bochsler and Andreas Juon*	21
2	Weak pluralism and shallow democracy: the rise of identity politics in Bulgaria and Romania *Kiril Kolev*	42
3	Caesarean politics in Hungary and Poland *Robert Sata and Ireneusz Pawel Karolewski*	60
4	In Europe's Closet: the rights of sexual minorities in the Czech Republic and Slovakia *Petra Guasti and Lenka Bustikova*	80
5	Nation before democracy? Placing the rise of the Slovak extreme right into context *Erika Harris*	101
6	Latgale and Latvia's post-Soviet democracy: the territorial dimension of regime consolidation *Geoffrey Pridham*	121
7	Consolidated technocratic and ethnic hollowness, but no backsliding: reassessing Europeanisation in Estonia and Latvia *Licia Cianetti*	144
	Index	164

Citation Information

The following chapters were originally published in various issues of the journal, *East European Politics*. When citing this material, please use the original citations and page numbering for each article, as follows:

Chapter 1
Authoritarian footprints in Central and Eastern Europe
Daniel Bochsler and Andreas Juon
East European Politics, volume 36, issue 2 (2020), pp. 167–187

Chapter 2
Weak pluralism and shallow democracy: the rise of identity politics in Bulgaria and Romania
Kiril Kolev
East European Politics, volume 36, issue 2 (2020), pp. 188–205

Chapter 3
Caesarean politics in Hungary and Poland
Robert Sata and Ireneusz Pawel Karolewski
East European Politics, volume 36, issue 2 (2020), pp. 206–225

Chapter 4
In Europe's Closet: the rights of sexual minorities in the Czech Republic and Slovakia
Petra Guasti and Lenka Bustikova
East European Politics, volume 36, issue 2 (2020), pp. 226–246

Chapter 5
Nation before democracy? Placing the rise of the Slovak extreme right into context
Erika Harris
East European Politics, volume 35, issue 4 (2019), pp. 538–557

Chapter 6
Latgale and Latvia's post-Soviet democracy: the territorial dimension of regime consolidation
Geoffrey Pridham
East European Politics, volume 34, issue 2 (2018), pp. 194–216

Chapter 7
Consolidated technocratic and ethnic hollowness, but no backsliding: reassessing Europeanisation in Estonia and Latvia
Licia Cianetti
East European Politics, volume 36, issue 2 (2018), pp. 317–336

For any permission-related enquiries please visit:
www.tandfonline.com/page/help/permissions

Notes on Contributors

Timofey Agarin teaches Comparative Politics at Queen's University Belfast, where he is also the Director of the Centre for the Study of Ethnic Conflict. His research interests are ethnic politics and their impact on societal transition, including majority-minority relations, non-discrimination, migration and civil society, with a particular focus on postcommunist states in Central Eastern Europe.

Daniel Bochsler, PhD (2008), political scientist at Central European University (CEU) and the University of Belgrade, where he studies political systems in heterogeneous societies. He was the co-project leader of the Democracy Barometer.

Lenka Bustikova is Associate Professor in the School of Politics and Global Studies at Arizona State University and visiting researcher at the Czech Academy of Sciences, Institute of Sociology. Her research focuses on party politics, voting behaviour, clientelism, and state capacity, with special reference to Eastern Europe.

Licia Cianetti is Lecturer in Political Science and International Studies and Leverhulme Early Career Fellow at University of Birmingham. Her research focuses on questions of inclusion and exclusion in democratic policymaking, at national and local levels. She is an area expert in Central and Eastern Europe, and she is the author of *The Quality of Divided Democracies: Minority Inclusion, Exclusion and Representation in the New Europe* (2019) and co-editor of *Rethinking 'Democratic Backsliding' in Central and Eastern Europe* (2019).

Petra Guasti is Associate Professor of Democratic Theory at the Faculty of Social Sciences, Charles University in Prague and a Senior Research Fellow at the Institute of Sociology, Czech Academy of Sciences. Between 2016 and 2021 she served as a senior researcher, an Interim Professor at the Goethe University Frankfurt, where she completed her habilitation "Democracy Disrupted" in April 2021. Her research focuses on the reconfiguration of the political landscape and evolves around three themes – populism, democratisation, and representation.

Erika Harris is Professor of Politics and director of the "Europe and the World Centre" at the University of Liverpool. She is the author of *Nationalism Theories and Cases* (2009), *Democracy in the New Europe* (with C. Lord, 2006) and *Nationalism and Democratisation Politics of Slovakia and Slovenia* (2002).

Andreas Juon, is a postdoc in the ETH Fellows Program, based at the International Conflict Research Group at ETH Zurich. He obtained his PhD from University College London in

2020 and his dissertation was awarded the ECPR Jean Blondel Prize for the best dissertation in politics in 2021. He also holds an MA degree in Comparative and International Studies from ETH Zurich.

Ireneusz Paweł Karolewski is Professor of Political Theory and Democracy Research at the University of Leipzig, Germany. His recent publications include European Identity Revisited (2016).

Kiril Kolev is Associate Professor of Politics and International Relations at Hendrix College in Conway, AR, USA. His research interests focus on electoral integrity, electoral systems, party finance regulations and political clientelism.

Geoffrey Pridham is Emeritus Professor and Senior Research Fellow, University of Bristol, UK. He has written widely on problems of democratic transition and consolidation over several decades. His books include *The Dynamics of Democratisation: A Comparative Approach* (2000) and *Designing Democracy: EU Enlargement and Regime Change in Post-Communist Europe* (2005).

Robert Sata is Associate Research Fellow at the Political Science Department, Central European University. His latest publications include the edited volume *Migration and Border-Making: Reshaping Policies and Identities* (2020).

The (not so) surprising longevity of identity politics: contemporary challenges of the state-society compact in Central Eastern Europe

Timofey Agarin

ABSTRACT

The EU accession marked the end of postcommunist institutional transition, yet the nature of relations between state institutions with their societies was far from settled. The chapter argues that across the East European region continuous uncertainty about the nature of the state–society compact was central to maintaining the relevance of identity in politics. This compact is best understood from the distinct perspective on who owns the state and who benefits from the current form of the state. Since, postcommunist nation-state-building was as much about the exclusion of some groups of residents from the political community as it was about limiting states' reliance on thick political ideologies similar challenges persist across the region over time. The exclusion at the foundation of the states placed "national identity" at the heart of postcommunist politics and offers considerable insights for comparison of the causes, effects and challenges of identity politics in wider Europe.

It is widely agreed that the dynamics of state–society relations across the wider European region are up for revalidation. In the EU, and particularly in Central Eastern European (CEE) Member States, the trajectory of political development has been uneven and the record of democratic consolidation patchy. While the democratic idea remains close to non-negotiable across Europe and the world more broadly (Shapiro 2003, 1; Schimmelfennig, Engert, and Knobel 2006), the situation is peculiar in Central Eastern Europe as ordinary people there perceive it to be rather different from what many anticipated would come about after the end of non-democratic communist regimes (Rose, Mishler, and Haerpfer 1998). Over the three decades of EU accession, integration, and membership, East European citizens have generally learnt to appreciate democracy over the regimes previously in place: for what it does best, disengage from citizens' lives. Constrained by both, commitments to legal corpus as EU Member States and pressures of global political economy, Eastern Europe's democratic regimes have delivered well on this hope of their citizens. But CEE states' limited ability to provide public service and support to their citizens and offer opportunities for improving their own lives continues to pose a challenge for the ongoing consolidation of the relationship between the state and society in postcommunist Member States. This sets the CEE region apart from other countries in the EU. Whether it is states that ought to serve citizens, or it is citizens that should be satisfied that their states assume the role of "night watchman" is still up for debate in the region that emerged from behind the Iron Curtain to join the EU 15 years later. Thus, the starting contention of this chapter – and the volume – is that the EU accession marked the end of institutional transition and restructuring; however, the question of who and how the institutions of the state ought to serve, has not been settled then and, as we continue to witness in the ongoing contestation by Poland and Hungary of EU Treaties primacy over domestic law, it is far from agreed upon to this day.

In the nearly three decades of (liberal) democratic politics in the region, citizens have primarily experienced the absence of state support when needed. They have accepted the prohibition of discrimination, rather than the promotion of citizens' individual and group rights, and the "lean state" rather than a responsive partner of society (Bohle and Greskovits 2012). It is thus no surprise that postcommunist citizens see the essence of a liberal democracy in state non-interference in private lives (Tismaneanu 2002). Licia Cianetti refers to popular disaffection with democracy as an effect of "stunned interactions between democratic institutions and the populations these serve" (Cianetti 2018). As such, today more than before the EU accession, citizens of postcommunist Member States appreciate contemporary political regimes not for what they do, but for what they do not do (see also, Mishler and Rose 1999).

This situation is not unique to Central Eastern Europe: Re-negotiations of the state–society compact are ongoing across the EU. Whereas over the past three decades references to a gamut of identities have played a central role in politics across the postcommunist region, the increased allusion to nativist tropes, populist rhetoric and radical right ideology in the "old" Member States makes the CEE region a useful context to reflect on such Europe-wide dynamics (Pirro 2015; Minkenberg 2013). Yet, setting postcommunist countries in opposition to the rest of the "Europe" obscures diversity within and between the "new" Member States (Agarin and Regelmann 2011). It also obfuscates similarity in the institutional appeal of nation-bound ideologies across the whole of the EU, which, despite the apparently different expressions in East and West, allows political elites to peddle identity-focussed rhetoric (Agarin and Cordell 2016). In both regions, the phenomena of a *surge in nativism* and a *rise of populism* often coexist, but their root causes and consequences are distinct: *Populism* is both an ideology and a rhetorical strategy, it has long been a tool for elected or aspiring political elites to lure electorates into the aspiration of society where the "likes are ruled by the likes" (Wimmer 2008), both in East and West. At the same time, *nativism* appeals to citizens' and elites' preferences to maintain the coherence of ethnonational political community and avert institutional change that challenges the (perceived) homogeneity of and within the national citizenry. This process has been part of postcommunist transition, since all postcommunist nation-states were established to challenge the shortcomings of the past regime and to share a similar foundational dynamic of accounting only for the interests of the local and/or dominant "people". Across the Eastern European region, we observe that the states originally designed as bulwarks of (ethno-) national sovereignty have over decades normalised the domination of groups that fit easily into the narrative of a homogeneous national community and gradually shifted categories of "others" to exclude anyone with "spurious" links to the ethno-national community: minorities, migrants and refugees, LGBT people, etc.

Our volume looks at the CEE region as an ideal lab to study these Europe-wide phenomena that facilitate, encourage, and sponsor politicisation of identities (see, Hanley and Sikk 2016). We focus on causes for successful mobilisation of identity in politics and the identities' sustained salience across the CEE over the past decades. Given the limited capacity of the EU to enforce and oversee the rule of law across the entire CEE region, identity politics challenge the view that (market) liberalisation and European integration are the vehicles of democratisation and bring improvement to state–society relations by default. In this context, identity politics are a form of societal cohesion advanced by state institutions and political elites that commit to serve one (national majority) constituency above all others. In ensuring that the outcomes of political process are preferentially distributed to that community alone, they undermine perceptions of equality in representation and participation of those groups who perceive themselves as excluded from accessing the political, economic, social and cultural opportunities of liberal democracies. And, since questioning the value of pluralism underpinning liberal democratic politics folds into preference for politics focussing on identity, increasing numbers of CEE citizens doubt that their states serve them well. Additionally, they feel that EU membership has not brought the (vaguely defined, yet expected) benefits they have anticipated two decades earlier, while many perceive that the membership in this supra-national, quasi-state organisation is eroding the national fabric of societies.

This volume focusses on the ongoing renegotiation of the state–society compact in the light of the continuous salience of "identity" across the postcommunist Member States Poland, the Czech Republic, Slovakia, Latvia, Estonia, Hungary, Romania, and Bulgaria. Societies in all these states share three key elements: the consolidation of an anti-pluralist political establishment dominated by parties, personalities, and networks that command control over formally liberal democratic politics; scepticism of the role EU's equality and non-discrimination legislation has been playing to ensure lasting societal stability and peace across the wider Europe; suspicion of minorities, particularly the racialised "others" (such as Russians in the Baltic, Muslims in Bulgaria, and Roma everywhere) and of groups perceived to challenge the received gender "norms". The following chapters examine the dynamic role references to the homogenised identity of the "people" continue to play in the politics of CEE nation-state-bound societies.

Eastern Europe's people's democracies

Observers suggest that despite the fundamental redesign of Eastern Europe's political institutions and policies during the EU accession phase, majoritarian politics and plebiscitary politicking have been rather persistent both before and after joining the EU (Stroschein 2019; Enyedi and Linek 2008; Pirro 2014). Most notably, the political project of nation-state-building constricted the debate on issues of identity and belonging, affecting which members of society are considered as part of the "politically relevant communities". Over time, the voice of the numeric majority emphasised that the aspiration to join the EU was a "national" priority, consolidating this "ethnonational" approach that entails the political representation of some, but explicitly not of all residents of the state. The unanimous support for and virtual absence of an opposition to nation-state-building throughout the 1990s have allowed political entrepreneurs to successfully capitalise upon public ascent to facilitate speedy EU accession. As the aspiration of EU membership was widely shared across all states and segments of Eastern European societies, political contestation of the accession process was a non-issue; this in itself has justified the political elites' technocratic approach to political decision-making and made it acceptable.

Arguably, the notion that there is "no alternative to joining the EU" has consolidated the so-called "vacuum effect": Eastern European societies are acknowledged to have equivocally supported the transition from communism to shed institutions of non-democratic political regimes. While (almost) every citizen was open to their country joining the EU, few had a clear sense of what the EU membership entailed for their country's domestic political process or their personal engagement with democratic politics. There was far less consensus about the remit of postcommunist institutions, such as the rule of law, checks and balances on institutions, rights for minorities, and active participation of all people affected by the political process; and, almost no debate on the content of postcommunist democracy. During the postcommunist phase, the central concern in the accession states was the survival of state founding nations, forming the political objective to join the EU. It was anticipated that membership in the EU would bring positive trade-offs for national ethnopolitics, assuage regional security concerns and offset the constraints of global political economy (Petsinis 2019).

The transition of the region away from socialism towards market-oriented liberal democracies was central for the region's "return to Europe" (Mikkel and Pridham 2004) and states willingly undertook "self-orientalisation" in order to "once again" become European (Krastev 2002; Bunce 2005; Bideleux 2015). This focus on the transition *from* communism has empowered political elites who, "by capturing state institutions and resources and employing them for electoral gain, […] weaken[ed] democratic institutions" (Dimitrova 2018, 262). Examining the shortfall in the EU's democratic conditionality, some point to the "Leninist" legacies of the past, specifically to the aversion of debate about alternatives and preference for "getting on with the homework" (Jowitt 1993; Agarin 2013). Others, acknowledge that the inevitability of EU membership has discouraged engagement with issues of politics in societies that have not had much experience of democratic deliberation under socialism (Horvat and Stiks 2015; Anduiza, Guinjoan, and Rico 2019), while privileging politics focused on affirming and consolidating the newly acquired identities (Donskis 1999; Laitin 2002; Huszka 2014).

The individualising thrust of EU's liberal politics during the accession phase had allowed ample space for political leaders to thrive on concerns over national identity and state sovereignty, consolidating the earlier pre-accession embryonic national identity-politics. As the contributions to this volume demonstrate, for many postcommunist citizens, EU membership failed to deliver on original expectations, such as economic stability, the primacy of domestic over external, i.e. European decision-making, and to dispel concerns over national security. This happened despite the concerted efforts of competing fractions among the political elites who appeased electorates with a penchant for strong leadership to exploit consensus over the EU accession (McGann and Kitschelt 2005). In turn, this fused political and electoral contestation with concerns over form, rather than content of democratic politics.

By 2013, most postcommunist states have been holding free and fair elections on a regular basis, satisfying the Schumpeterian ideal of competitive democracy (Schumpeter 1947: 269; Huntington 1991). There is no doubt that all postcommunist Member States are electoral democracies, which allow their people to express consent or to contest decisions of their representatives, while enjoying broad political and civil rights, freedom of speech and association (Dahl 1972). Unlike in the past, when political competition and citizens' enjoyment of individual rights were either circumscribed, or non-existent, the mere opportunity for citizens to input political process is often taken as evidence for successful postcommunist democratisation across the region.

The experience of the accession to the EU, the establishment of market economy and liberal democratic governance are all but a comparable institutional background to understand the ongoing renegotiations of state–society relationship across the continent. But whereas formal democratic institutions are similar across the EU, the CEE citizens remarkably often choose to avoid interacting with these institutions in their states unless they need to. The absence of public participation in political decision-making has been central to criticism of the formally democratic postcommunist democracies (Howard 2003; Agarin 2016). In these regimes, structural inequalities and uneven distribution of the state's socioeconomic assets, particularly between majorities and minorities (Rueschemeyer, Rueschemeyer, and Wittrock 1998; Morlino and Quaranta 2016), have, over time, consolidated the limited advancement of rights and protections for minority groups (Brosig 2010; Haughton 2007) and undermined public debates on the ultimate purpose of democratic governing, government, and governance (Dryzek 2000; Hurrelmann 2015).

In many postcommunist states elites are not committed to stepping aside (Hale 2014; Shaw and Wiener 2000), nor do many postcommunist elites resolve differences on policy preferences in a consensual manner (Bochsler and Kriesi 2013). Unsurprisingly, political leadership across the region has been said to poorly reflect the interests of the publics, as during their term in office, the elites oftentimes predatorily continue to extract benefits for their own networks, rather than serving their broadly defined constituencies (Kitschelt and Wilkinson 2007).

No doubt, Eastern Europe's Member States have all the hardware of liberal democracies in place (Rose, Mishler, and Haerpfer 1998), yet it remains uncertain whether the version of its software pivoted on "Washington Consensus" runs to the satisfaction of postcommunist citizens. As Geoffrey Pridham cautioned in 2002,

> the EU strengthening executive and bureaucratic power without active popular engagement [...] creates a potential for widening the gap between political elites and masses, already a problem in many post-communist democracies; and, hence, for creating disillusionment when democratic attitudes have not fully taken root. (2002, 954)

Somewhat more recently, Dorothee Bohle and Bela Greskovits have argued that postcommunist democracies have been marred by low quality (2007), later adding that these had but a shell of liberal democratic institutions and procedures, poorly understood and only conditionally accepted by citizens (2012).

Postcommunist transitions started with an aspiration to bring democracy to "the people", but political transformations remained focussed on the nation-state. Who owned the state and who was to benefit from the "national optic" on societies varied considerably across the CEE region and over time, depending on historical legacies, the respective socio-economic situation, and geopolitical factors. Yet, the everyday perception of the "people" translated into the political jargon via the familiar, "national" trope of "a historically constituted, stable community of people, formed on the basis of a common language, territory, economic life, and psychological make-up manifested in a common culture" (Stalin 1936 [1913]). This marked polities as confounding the nation, establishing non-negotiable narratives that permeated the public debate, shaped preferences for economic and public policies, and geopolitical orientations. Since 2004, all countries in the region have, to some extent, engaged in dismantling the acceptance of societal pluralism underpinning liberal democratic politics (Bustikova and Guasti 2017; Hanley and Vachudova 2018), fostered public disaffection with the political process by capitalising on communist socialisation (Howard 2003; Ekman, Gherghina, and Podolian 2016), evacuating the "political" out of politics (Dawson 2016; Cianetti, Dawson, and Hanley 2018), or failing to provide positive experiences of participation in decision-making (Kolstø and Melberg 2002).

It is open to debate whether such government without consensus merely got worse over the past decade or did not evolve in the first place (Harris 2019; Braghiroli and Petsinis 2019). Some suggest that the parties' failure to gauge people's opinions (Mair 2006), institutional complacency and backsliding (Greskovits 2015), and technocratic abuse of power (Cianetti 2018; Buštíková and Guasti 2018) have marked politics in the Eastern Europe throughout the period of transition. Over the past decade, dominant groups in nation-states have rediscovered the powerful role that identity can play in mobilising the "people" against "minorities", to scale back the "benefits" afforded to these at the expense of the constitutionally enshrined rights of the ethno-nation that owns the state. In doing so, most postcommunist Member States, not only Poland and Hungary, and more recently, Slovenia and Czechia, have reneged on some of their commitments made under the Copenhagen Criteria: These criteria clearly established the requirements for liberal, non-majoritarian democracies, which limits significantly the type of policies, politics, and, indeed, politicking that the members of the Council of Europe and of the EU ought to pursue. However, since the accession, political process gradually returned to the original postcommunist people's centred politicking advocating both the majoritarian and plebiscitary decision-making. Taking this mandate of the "people" to protect the majorities' interests, states became stand-ins for the "nation", normalising the "national optic" on domestic politics and eroding deeper commitment to the equality of all citizens of the EU.

The chapters in this volume recount a story of *un*changed political preferences across the CEE region, not because of the fading legitimacy of the EU, but rather due to the continuous and growing appeal of a nation-state–majority compact. While the aspiration to join the EU was shared across postcommunist populations, in practice, little knowledge about the concrete effects of membership allowed publics to invest whatever their elites promised it would *not* be. Isolating the "people" from their past experiences justified bowing down to both the acquis and political conditionality if only to secure national sovereignty in a Europe of "free nations". Primarily, this included the view that the EU would not interfere in national politics, protect Member States' nations from the economic hardship and countenance geopolitical volatility – all the aspirations at the heart of the Eastern European national movements' emancipatory appeal of the late 1980s. Following accession, however, a somewhat more cynical attitude towards membership made itself present: "European" was no longer self-evidently perceived of as something desirable, as the sceptics have increasingly become intent on portraying the "liberal European agenda" as antithetical to, or even a threat to the peoples', "national values". In sum, as we have witnessed in the recent address by the Polish Prime Minister to the European Parliament (Morawiecki 2021), the payoff of membership has now become negligible for accepting the encroachments on the decision-making capacity of one's "own" nation-state.

Postcommunist state-society compact

Over the nearly three decades, postcommunist political elites have been smiting alliances with variant ideologies with – in part contradictory – economic, political, cultural, and religious connotations, effortlessly coming and leaving the political office without major shifts in polities' overall EU-oriented rhetoric. Yet, critical references to the Soviet/communist "Other" have been persistently marking only a "thin ideological commitment" to consensus-based decision-making, whilst invoking the "interest of the people" (Stanley 2008). Political elites shoring up their support base and mobilising identity-focussed constituencies have all been nested in the narrative of the state serving the ethno-nation, and, as such, demanding compliance, not challenges from the "people". Rather than a case of "sharp political conflict" between the "people" and the elites observed elsewhere in the EU (Plattner and Diamond 2007, 5), the spread of the so-called populist political forces in the East of Europe marks continuity rather than change in the state-society, more specifically in the nation-state–majority compact established at the beginning of transition.

At the beginning of transition, the long-term "national priorities" credibly justified that some – in the short term impalpable – decisions were made in the interest of "the people" and commanded popular deference to choices, however misguided, of people's representatives. Earlier exclusionary practices targeted those not part of the majority of the population, whether in regard to ethnicity, language, tradition, civilizational or party identity, but following the EU accession the challenges to the established status quo come from other quarters. The "people-centred" democracies have since seen a weakening of the democratic process as publics have brought feelings of dejection into the open, polarising public opinions and pitting the "people" against those "running the state" (Buštíková and Guasti 2018; Agarin 2013).

Many established democracies currently experience the decline in public support for the political establishment, but the accompanying decline in the quality of democratic institutions and of a state's ability to cater to the needs of its society, that are of particular worry to observers. This rise of "people versus elites" ideologies has been acknowledged to affect most, if not all European states, and scholars studying populism often start by recognising the increasing dis-identification of publics from their elected political representatives (March and Mudde 2005). This shift is expressed in the attitudinal change from *dejection* to *rejection* of democratically elected political leaders, of consensus based political decision-making and, even in the formally established democracies, of guarantees for citizen equality.

The dismal state of popular engagement with the democratic process as well as a lack of feedback mechanisms between political elites and publics on issues of electoral salience are made responsible for the erosion of trust in representatives, institutions, and regimes as a whole. The "downhill trend" in these is often contrasted with more intensive interactions that citizens (are believed to have) had with the governing elites, governments and processes of governance in the past. One could speak about the outright "populist explosion", both as a political phenomenon and as an object of study (Judis 2016). While some state that populism is on a "global rise" (Rooduijn and Pauwels 2011), going as far as asking "is everyone a populist now?" (Müller 2016, 7), others remain more sceptical about the analytic weight of such distinctions (Kessel 2015), or wonder whether we are dealing with an epiphenomenon at all (Pappas 2016; March 2017). Focussing on populism as an antidote to democracy, as many do, suggests a zero-sum game between the two, a view that has been thoroughly discredited long before the transition from communism began (Canovan 1983). Criticism of obsession with the "rise of populism" mount from the left and right, indicating that the term obstructs more than it is able to explain (Cannon 2018). If, as Margaret Canovan claims, "the sources of populism […] are to be found in the tensions at the heart of democracy" (Canovan 1999, 2), we ought to identify liberal democracy as the context most prone to the rise of "people versus elites" ideological alternatives.

The answer to the question, why populists' gain of political ground in the (still so-called) "new" Member States causes particular dismay in observers, points to the heart of the problem of ill-defined state–society relations in the postcommunist area (Bustikova and Kitschelt 2009; Rupnik 2007; Minkenberg 2002). For one, it is because "people centred" politics have a much longer history in the region. The dynamic relationship between liberal democratic institutions of postcommunist Member States, political elites operating these institutions, and the publics that confirm the appropriateness of the political process with their expectations at regular intervals via the ballot box, are highly comparable with those in the wider Europe and beyond (Sandel 2018; Ayyangar 2017; Bugaric 2008; Buštíková and Guasti 2018). And while the people-centrism in domestic politics constricts and constrains the "real existing" diversity to be represented in the liberal democratic political process, states are uncritically accepted to serve the (purposefully vaguely-defined) "majority" that pivots on experiences of ethno-cultural, language, religious, civilisational, territorial and historical homogeneity. In practice this allows postcommunist citizens to view their elected elites as "natives" dancing to the tune of the European (and other situationally significant) "aliens" (see, Mudde 2009, chapter 1).

The compact between the "people's majority" and the political elites speaking on their behalf justified the technocratic approach to solving challenges during the EU accession. And, this broad societal consensus about the desirability of the EU membership prevented Eastern European societies from engaging with the compromise-based, rather than majoritarian forms of decision-making in publics and among their elected representatives. Along the way, the instruments available to the nation-state to exercise cohesion over its entire citizenry foreclosed the debates about alternatives to the overall direction of political, economic, and social transitions to unfold once the EU membership was achieved. The emphasis on majoritarian and plebiscitary democratic decision-making facilitated acceptance of painful reforms during the critical period of transition; it has also delegitimised (nearly all) legacies of the communist past as being made in the interest of the ideology, party, or bureaucracy, not in the name of the "people" (Cordell 2013; Karolewski 2016). Yet, the nature of the EU accession and membership did little to reform populations' acquiescence to decisions made by political elites representing them as one "people", not as citizens with diverging interests. Regular executive and legislative elections continue to keep politicians and politics in check, the (unelected) representatives in the judiciary continue to balance legislators and presidents keen to roll back democracy, but sufficient numbers of the electorate are yet to show enthusiasm for a challenge to the experts making decisions for the people (Barnes and Simon 1998; Orenstein 2009).

The EU's Eastern enlargement has been widely perceived not only to promise a departure from non-democratic political regimes for good; in co-opting the view that "Europeanisation equals democratisation", it increased the stakes for both the elites and the people in the accession states to cooperate in the short term to benefit from governance closer to "the people" in the long run (Agarin and Yilmaz 2016; Noutcheva 2016; Keil 2013; Schwellnus 2006). As such, the EU accession only facilitated the consolidation of "the people" around the putatively homogeneous "nation". National identity retained it prominence in Eastern European politics because the EU accession process foregrounded the democratic consolidation of states in their existing national form, assuming (mistakenly) that all residents – majorities alongside other groups originally marginalised from political decision-making – would have their lot improved once liberal democracy, that is, non-intrusive political regime settles in. The hard-to-stomach outcomes of the EU membership, such as those of commitment to joint decision-making, economic cooperation, and obligations to prevent discrimination, paved the way for more restrictive views on who owns the state, who is entitled to run it and who is to profit from its current configuration (Agarin and Cordell 2016).

A technical view of the EU accession process, therefore, has compromised the underpinnings of postcommunist states' European integration at large, and questioned the EU's objective of forging a functioning political community of interdependent states, not sovereign national communities (Scicluna and Auer 2019; Kochenov, Ridder, and Eline 2011). In the past, the EU's promotion of citizen equality has gone beyond a shared view of financial discipline and economic cooperation, ensuring independence of political and judicial institutions. This has also allowed the EU to tame mutual distrust between Member States and their peoples, to balance the centrifugal nationalisms across the continent and to forge a semblance of European polity (Plattner and Diamond 2007; Sedelmeier 2017). But, and once EU membership was guaranteed, the political institutions that were shoring up national identities had already formed the experiential background for "political entrepreneurs" to pursue politicking around exclusive societal categories. This hailed the ascent of concerns over *national* identity into politics as soon as political, economic, and cultural exchanges within the EU have made clear that the identity of nation, people, and their elites did not map well onto one another. Identity politics of "the people" were reinvigorated becoming identity politics of "the (ethno-)nation".

The single-issue politics that defined the accession phase have returned under the guise of identity politics in the post-accession phase, allowing voters to easily ascertain their preferences in an uncertain political landscape. Issues that once were recipes for political success – fighting corruption, guaranteeing welfare, addressing environmental concerns, catering the regional or ethnic cleavages, and tackling immigration – eased the arrival of parties mobilising around the interests hard to place on the "traditional" ideological spectrum between left and right. As it turned out, nation-state building successfully appeased the "demos", promoting ethnocentric views and shifting the overall political dynamics from concerns over issues to politicising markers of identity.

The central role played by identity in Eastern European politics has laid bare the tension at the heart of transition from communism to democracy. Where little experience of consensus-based politics was to be found, politics of identity offered institutional opportunities to vent public anger, challenge "outward looking" political agendas and leadership. At the same time, the prevalence of institutions serving discrete interests of "national communities" encouraged political entrepreneurs to talk-up the social salience and relevance of identity in politics. The fact that many postcommunist states were reconstructed as polities serving designated ethnic majority groups reflected closely on the nation-focussed political ideologies in a volatile geopolitical environment (Agarin 2017). The notion of the national community under threat from global political, economic, and cultural forces sat at the heart of late socialist popular movements for emancipation from external, usually Russian, dominance. Today, similar narratives barrage "Europe" as the last vestige of oppression.

The salience of identity politics

The demise of socialism has quickly become embodied by the vision of an "end of history": The initial diagnosis that publics' ideological commitments to socialism were low, while affinity for the Western style democracy high, seemed accurate enough due to the fact that postcommunist citizens defected to market economy and liberal democracy en mass. However, acquis conditionality over the "short decade of accession" only entrenched laws and institutions to guarantee CEE states the ability to assume rights and duties as Member States, with little attention paid to benchmarking norms of liberal and pluralist, democratic politics. And too little attention was given to reforming other, more salient aspects of societal acquiescence with the political process: For many postcommunist citizens, the falling away of socialism meant just the end of external patronage and the ability to take politics into one's own hands.

The disengagement of publics from politics has been a persistent feature across Central Eastern Europe since early 1990s. Despite turning up in (considerably) higher numbers to cast ballots on landmark decisions, such as on the composition of the first postcommunist governments, to join the EU, or more recently to oppose the EU's refugee quotas, the populace has mainly been approving, rather than rejecting governments' proposals throughout. However, the recent protests across the region bare continuous witness that the debate between those favouring elite- or citizen-centred politics is still outstanding. The "people" taking to the streets of Bucharest and Budapest, Warszawa and Bratislava all marked the return of extra-parliamentary debates on politics out of sync with public expectations. These send mixed messages about citizens' preferred changes and come from pro- and anti-government groups, some coming out in favour of greater liberalisation and more technocratic politics, others for the protection of the "national" from global political, economic, and cultural challenges. The nature of public disaffection thus expressed indicates that politics responding to citizens' interests are currently being replaced by politics concerned with identity of the "people" across the wider region.

In response, the elites representing the increasingly polarised electorates have taken on to redefine what it means to belong to, identify with and gain from the resources managed by "their" states (Kopecký and Mudde 2000). As earlier EU enthusiasm is being replaced by criticisms of Europe's contribution to democratisation (Lendvai 2004; Vachudova and Hooghe 2009), economic liberalisation (Berman 2003; Đurašković 2016) and cultural changes (Urbinati 2014), question whether Europeanization and democratization possibly pull Member States in different directions have become louder throughout Europe (Bideleux 2001; Kochenov and De Ridder 2011; Ágh 2018).

The limited past involvement of the public in the process of governing has been made responsible for the EU's democratic deficit (Rohrschneider 2002; Kelemen and Blauberger 2017; Blatter, Schmid, and Blättler 2017), and it explains why citizens have been seeking to "take back control" after the European crises. Yet, little, if any, debate takes place about who the "people" are, or what is the shared aspiration by these putative "people". However, the new style of politics makes wide use of the rhetoric of responsibility and responsiveness to the electorate, promising better politicking by and outcomes for the "people". Yet, referencing the "people" is "tailor-made for catch-all politics, and analysis of its use can easily turn into a study in the pathology of modern democratic politics, or how to talk nonsense to the greatest political effect" (Canovan 1984, 322).

The Eastern European Member States offer a unique set of cases in this regard: European crises not only polarised their domestic electorates, but also equally marked the region as comparative laggard of political, economic, and social transitions. Because citizens of postcommunist states envisaged that their countries' membership in the EU would improve their personal, social, and economic wellbeing, European crises have dented the optimism of the infallibility of the EU's model of governance. While the benefits of the regional as geopolitical alignment with the EU are still cherished by most states in the region, their many citizens are increasingly reluctant to accept other parts of the bargain. Stretching Claus Offe's (1991) analogy comparing postcommunist transitions to building a ship at high sea to consider the challenges of consolidating the market economy, democracy and the nation-state simultaneously, we can see that as soon as the storm gathered on the horizon, some of the original aspirations, particularly pluralist democracy, went overboard.

Some observers underline the view that democracy failed to crystalize at least in parts of Central Eastern Europe (as yet); this is an unhelpful shortcut in reasoning showcasing an "unacknowledged bias equating democracy with its liberal variant" (Cannon 2018). We ought to acknowledge that several views on what democracy is have coexisted peacefully over half a century of communism in the Eastern European societies, but only one of these versions has persisted during postcommunist transition and became the norm during the EU accession phase. Assorted left and right populist challengers to contemporary models of governance point out that East European citizens continue to vest "democracy" with a rather different meaning than the one favoured by the EU (Rueschemeyer 2015; Ágh 2016). Thus, labelling political movements, that challenge the political status quo regardless of their ideological positions or programmatic proposals, does not only stifle the debate about any potential for reform, but ought to be welcome as democratic contestation of meaning, content and form of governance. Absent in the past, alternative visions of democracy seem to emerge across the region seeking to engage wider segments of society in political debate and appease the "people", much like other postcommunist political elites have done so over the three decades of transition.

In part, the effects of nation-state building across the region have caught up on domestic politics following the EU accession when external leverage could no longer be applied to correct the "nationalising" aspirations of the states (Brubaker 1996). In some postcommunist Member States, politics by and for the national majority brought societies divided over ideological principles together into one political community. In all cases, however, the putative majorities were united in their commitment to the democratically expressed (read: plebiscitary) will of the "people" delivered upon by the elite-enforced decision-making. Particularly in the countries that originally grappled to defend the "national sovereignty" from external and domestic ethnic challengers, all types of non-dominant groups found themselves objects of marginalisation, and ultimately securitisation, by the formally liberal democratic institutions 30 years after the start of transition from communism.

Similar strategies are widely deployed by political entrepreneurs often boxed together into the "populist" camp. But the reason for the regional drift towards populist politics has been similar in so far as most of the Eastern European states have either been established as or have entrenched the commitment to *national* identity over the decades. A crucial feature of these references to the nation is that they have normalised the view of a putative national homogeneity vis-à-vis equally homogeneous "others" across the region. These ever-changing "others" are perceived to challenge, and more often threaten security and, ultimately, stability of, one's own group's hold on power, regardless how minimal it is. This in turn showcases the persistence of identity-based mobilization in diverse postcommunist societies that are served by polities that have been exclusionary by design from the start. Against this background, our volume looks at EU integration as an opportunity missed to demobilise (national) identity-focussed politicking, politics and policies favouring majorities across postcommunist CEE societies. The following contributions particularly focus on how concerns over the coherence of political and national communities across the region have remained a constant feature of national politics and how the majority's identity retained salience in such politics.

Contributions of the volume

Our chapters address developments across the region over a considerable period of time. Contextualising the concerns of each country at the time of accession to the EU that have remained salient, the chapters revisit three aspects of politics in the region since accession: Public disengagement from discussions of political ideology and about the direction of political, economic, social-cultural change in their societies; the continuous tutelage by political elites over public perception of programmatic issues, shaping and manipulating opinions of the largely dejected citizenry; the obstinate resonance of nation-focussed ideologies in the absence of other ideological commitments to underpin the "political community" across the entire spectrum of postcommunist Member States.

The chapters of this volume rely upon and contribute to three discrete debates in scholarship on Eastern European politics and societies: First, we engage in discussions on the current response of CEE citizens to the consolidation of political regimes that many believe do not serve their interests. Though some of the cases broach the theme of "populist revolution", this collection makes clear that the tentative "democratic malaise" of populism has been a feature of the region for a long while. The chapters do suggest that the "weakest link" of the region's democracy are its publics, the "demos". The limited consensus among the citizens about the identity of the "demos" has been repeatedly mobilised by competing forces for the exploit of their own version of "kratos", the "power to" that is particularly attracted to majoritarian politics. Concerns over identity of the public with their state, nation, and belonging to European civilisation have been systematically manipulated to consolidate the exclusionary logic of nation-state building.

Second, the contributions assess the impact of the EU's technocratic implementation of (liberal) democracy with market economy as the "only game in town". All chapters take stock of discussions on the impact EU membership had on the formal quality of democracy across the region; in all countries this pushed the debates about the nature and the purpose of governance into the background. This has undermined the original commitment of postcommunist publics to participatory democracy and allowed the consolidation of nation-state institutions serving predominantly the putatively homogeneous "collectivities of fate" (Dahrendorf 2003). The political entrepreneurs underlined that departure *from* communism equals functioning market economy *as well as* liberal democracy for the designated majorities. Opinions that did not receive institutional support were side-lined. In so doing, the entire set of postcommunist Member States is marked up by distinct – parallel – spaces for politicking by political entrepreneurs engaged in tutelage of publics increasingly questioning elite commitment to people's democracy (Petsinis 2019).

Third, our chapters signal that the EU's inability to sanction the equivalence established between the identity of a person, a people, citizenry, and a nation in the postcommunist region has kept identity politics on its steady course over 30 years. Estonia, Latvia, Lithuania, Poland, the Czech Republic, Slovakia, Hungary, Slovenia, Romania, Bulgaria, and Croatia have joined the EU in subsequent rounds of enlargement: 2004, 2007, and 2013. However, despite the different timing and conditions of their inclusion into the EU, these countries' "choice of Europe" has been justified by economic benefits trickling down, political clout and national sovereignty afforded to all EU's states qua membership. The chapters assert that as a result of EU membership much has changed in the manner of politicking across these wide geographic areas, yet the issue of *nation-centred* sovereignty that originally drove the transition from communism continues to focus the region's contemporary politics on the ethnic identity of the majority.

However, the contributions to this volume eschew the engagement with discussions on what legitimised such focal identities across the region in the first place (see, Agarin and Regelmann 2011). Such engagement would be specific to communities operating such categories, for example, state majorities will clearly have a different view from members of minorities. At the same time, the compactly settling minorities, e.g. Hungarians in Romania or Slovakia, would have their own unique views on who "owns" the territory they inhabit and consequently, who is the majority. Categories of "majority" would also inevitably change over time, e.g. the view on what makes a "real Pole" in Poland proper has undergone considerable change since *Prawo i Sprawiedliwość* (Law and Justice) ascended to power (Bill and Stanley 2020); domestic dynamics in Hungary also had a knock-on effect on the political use of identity claims by Magyars in the neighbouring states, Romania above all (Verovšek 2021; Zielonka and Rupnik 2020). Thus, each chapter tackles the question of who the majority is from their individual comparative angle, teasing out differences in cases, but above all similarities across the region.

Daniel Bochsler and Andreas Juon offer a comparative analysis of the quality of democratic institutions across the postcommunist region (Bochsler and Juon 2019). The authors conclude that though institutions of democracy might be robust across much of the region, a democracy's quality varies depending on the likelihood of political elites turning to the tools of authoritarian government. The limited capacity of the EU to benchmark democracy in its Member States and the weakening of the incentives offered by European integration after the global financial crisis form the background for public disaffection with democracy as such. The chapter explains that not in all cases where the populists have entered governments can one observe democratic de-consolidation; however, after the logic of past accession and potential membership has encouraged elites to appeal to the "power of people" in order to remain in the driving seat.

Kiril Kolev argues that the recent rise in identity politics in Bulgaria and Romania is due to a weak commitment to pluralism and the limited consolidation of publics around the idea of democratic politics (Kolev 2019). The chapter traces the evolution of societal attitudes towards pluralism before and after the EU accession process in Bulgaria and Romania. Kolev suggests that externally imposed policies sponsoring cultural pluralism and the tolerance of diversity in political opinion were not reciprocated by the populations. The analysis links the relatively more pronounced lack of subcultural pluralism in Bulgaria to a more vigorous anti-EU backlash during the current period, while deference to political elites' decisions has been reflected in the widespread anti-elite sentiment in Romania. In neither cases, however, does the chapter find public acceptance of pluralism and commitment to equality critically important for a robustly democratic political process devoid of references to national identity.

Petra Guasti and Lenka Bustikova explore the dynamics and the outcomes of a backlash against the LGBT community in the Czech Republic and Slovakia (Guasti and Bustikova

2019). The authors start by distinguishing the "old" from "new" minority groups, indicating that while ethnic minorities tend to field particularistic demands, LGBT rights are universal and hence should, in theory, facilitate coalition building and advocate policies of accommodation. The evidence from the Czech Republic and Slovakia shows that paradoxically the translation of universal claims from the LGBT discourse into policymaking faces the greatest resistance, blocking progress in respective legislations for extended periods. This, as the chapter suggests, reflects the overall dynamics on the region-wide opposition to ideas of equality concerning groups that challenge the social agendas of politics grappling with the visible erosion of a uniform identity of a national society.

Robert Sata and Ireneusz Pawel Karolewski focus on the cases of Hungary and Poland, the two states where the erosion of democratic institutions has gone in hand with the surge of identity politics (Sata and Karolewski 2019). In both countries, the weakness of national democratic institutions was used by the opportunistic leadership, who was able to extract political capital out of public disappointment with the stalling economy. The authors describe how the use of patronage and power-hoarding by the ruling elites has facilitated societal mobilisation around exclusionary identities that shifted democracy towards, what they term, Caesarean politics. The concentration of decision-making power in the hands of individual leaders and its management by cartels of elites has made access to the political networks of PiS and Fidesz an essential element of democratic stasis in both Poland and Hungary. Ruling parties, therefore, have been the main generators of politics focused on identities and tilted a plebiscitary view of political participation in favour of the entrenched representatives of the "people".

The chapter by Erika Harris explores the Slovak political context (Harris 2019), mapping the role played by the normalisation of ethnonationalism during the period of accession, the discontent with the dominance of liberal norms after the country joined the EU, and governing parties' negative response to migration for the rise of parties pedalling the intolerant political ideologies throughout the 2010s. Asserting that Slovakia's political drift to the right is highly emblematic of "ethnic interpretation of the nation and increased preference for national sovereignty" observable across postcommunist region, Harris sums up that the "heightened sense of threat" to the "nation, its identity and its sovereignty" has side-lined commitment to democratic norms and principles.

In his review of liberal regime's consolidation in Latvia, Geoffrey Pridham focusses on the importance of relationship between the centre and periphery in a national state for public confidence in democratic institutions and procedures (Pridham 2018). The chapter underlines the structural difficulties for the Latvian state to manage socioeconomic disparities in its easternmost region Latgale, marked by distinct cultural, religious, and ethnic heritage. Critically, Pridham identifies central state's neglect of regional needs as the condition for persistent systemic loyalty of local multi-ethnic society, as well as the potential for anti-system exploitation by local, regional, and transborder actors. Pragmatic relationships between Riga and Latgalian periphery have been conducive to consolidation of democracy in the region, and ultimately centripetal orientation of residents, parties, and elites in the region.

Licia Cianetti's contribution to this volume uses Estonia and Latvia as illustrative cases to demonstrate the challenging balance all postcommunist EU Member States ought to recon with: between quality and stability of democracy (Cianetti 2018). The chapter is based on a strong claim that in diverse societies "technocratic" approach of political elites to policy making easily confounds explicit dominance of ethnic majority interests and implicit minority exclusion. In the two Baltic state, Cianetti argues, de-politicisation of politics and marginalisation of ethnic minority voices in political process has been the unanticipated consequence of the EU accession process. As a consequence, in the Baltic as elsewhere in the region where political regimes assume deference of their diverse publics to majorities' elites' decisions, low-quality democratic systems are likely to remain internally stable. Hollowing out the political process, make de-democratisation and backsliding unlikely; however, it might be seductive for political elites to shrink the space for public participation and debate, pushing the evolution of democratic political culture into even more distant future.

Our volume suggests to focus on the causes of nativism and the rise of populism precisely because both feed-off the same relevance of national identity in politics. The challenge of centring politics on identity is not about the type of government, or the form of governance, but about the institutionally cultivated sense of sameness of the people with their political representatives. This perception of sameness is to justify whatever decisions the elites make, overriding dissenting opinions in the name of the narrowly defined "people" to exercise their majority's mandate. Mobilising concerns over identity to bring about the consent of the affected about the yet to be disclosed benefits is the bread-and-butter of de-democratisers and populists alike. As can be vividly observed in Austria, Denmark, Greece, France, Finland, Italy, Spain, the Netherlands and the UK (Nordensvard and Ketola 2014; Kovras and Loizides 2014; Lees 2018; Pirro and Van Kessel 2017; Usherwood 2019), questioning institutional checks and balances on the majoritarian decision-making in the name of the "people" is not limited to the postcommunist region.

To illustrate the similarity between "East" and "West", the chapters of this volume put the state–society relations at the centre of their analysis. All of them suggest that rather than galvanised by the notions of pluralism and liberal democracy, postcommunist publics coalesced around the notion of exclusion, upheld by the institutions of the nation-state and by the national political elites. The form and speed of accession to the EU, rather than its content, paved the way for, rather than challenged the salience of identity in politics across the CEE region. All chapters look at how the "national self" has been constructed first in deference to, then in opposition to a notional "Europe", but at all times as antagonistic to external regional and domestic "others" who violate the perceived perceptions of national homogeneity of the in-group. This group, usually an ethnic nation, is (thought of as being) both perennial and homogeneous, upholding the idea propping up the nation-state majority's claims to state ownership.

The volume as such speaks of state–society relations, that are still negotiated in the region and of which the outcome is not yet clear. Whereas similar processes are currently taking place across the board of the EU Member States, political regimes in CEE two decade since the EU accession have settled on the overtly idealised image of the "nation" for which states exercise decision-making. In some parts of the region, the initial mass disenfranchisement from citizenship (as was the case in Estonia, Latvia, and Slovenia) added a clearer component of ethnic exclusion. But everywhere, the inclusion of only a part of the citizens into the category of a socially salient and strategically relevant political community is what explains the persistent contestation of the state–society compact and salience of national identity in postcommunist Member States' politics.

Acknowledgements

I am very grateful to Daniel Bochsler, Petra Guasti, Ireneusz Pawel Karolewski, Lenka Bustikova, and Andrea Pirro for invaluable comments on the earlier drafts of this contribution. Also, thanks to all the authors contributing to this special section, and the participants of ECPR General Conference, Hamburg 2018, as well as of the colloquium of the International Political Studies Association, Research Committee 14 "Politics and Ethnicity", Sarajevo 2019.

References

Agarin, Timofey, and Ada-Charlotte Regelmann. 2011. "Status Quo Multiculturalism: The Crux of Minority Policies in Central Eastern Europe's EU Member-States". *Journal of Minority Studies* 5 (3): 69–98.

Agarin, Timofey, and Gözde Yilmaz. 2016. "Talk the Talk, or Walk the Walk? Changing Narratives in Europeanization Research". *Südosteuropa: Journal of Politics and Society* 65 (1): 149–69.

Agarin, Timofey, and Karl Cordell. 2016. *Minority Rights and Minority Protection in Europe*. Rowman & Littlefield.

Agarin, Timofey. 2013. "Resident Aliens? Explaining Minority Disaffection with Democratic Politics in the Baltic States". *Ethnopolitics* 12 (4): 331–51. https://doi.org/10.1080/17449057.2012.748247.

Agarin, Timofey. 2013. "The Dead Weight of the Past? Institutional Change, Policy Dynamics and the Communist Legacy in Minority Protection". In *Institutional Legacies of Communism: Change and Continuities in Minority Protection*, edited by Karl Cordell, Timofey Agarin, and Alexander Osipov, 14–30. London: Routledge.

Agarin, Timofey. 2016. "Citizens' Participation in Post-Communist Europe". *Communist and Post-Communist Studies*, 49 (3): 201–6. https://doi.org/10.1016/j.postcomstud.2016.06.008.

Agarin, Timofey. 2017. "Nation-States into Nationalising States". *Intersections. East European Journal of Society and Politics* 3 (4). http://intersections.tk.mta.hu/index.php/intersections/article/view/393.

Ágh, Attila. 2016. "The Decline of Democracy in East-Central Europe: Hungary as the Worst-Case Scenario". *Problems of Post-Communism* 63 (5–6): 277–87.

Ágh, Attila. 2018. "The Dual Crisis and 'Regionalization' in the Visegrád States: The Identity Politics of East-Central Europe in the New World Order". In *Central and Eastern Europe in the EU*, 177–89. London: Routledge.

Anduiza, Eva, Marc Guinjoan, and Guillem Rico. 2019. "Populism, Participation, and Political Equality". *European Political Science Review* 11 (1): 109–24. https://doi.org/10.1017/S1755773918000243.

Ayyangar, Srikrishna. 2017. *The Promise and Perils of Populism: Global Perspectives*. Lexington: University of Kentucky Press.

Barnes, Samuel H., and Janos Simon. 1998. *Popular Conceptions of Democracy in Postcommunist Europe*. Budapest: Erasmus Foundation.

Berman, Jacqueline. 2003. "(Un) Popular Strangers and Crises (Un) Bounded: Discourses of Sex-Trafficking, the European Political Community and the Panicked State of the Modern State". *European Journal of International Relations* 9 (1): 37–86.

Bideleux, Robert. 2001. 'Europeanization and the Limits to Democratization in East–Central Europe'. In *Prospects for Democratic Consolidation in East-Central Europe*, edited by Geoffrey Pridham and Attila Ágh, 25–53. Manchester: Manchester University Press.

Bideleux, Robert. 2015. "The 'Orientalization" and 'de-Orientalization" of East Central Europe and the Balkan Peninsula". *Journal of Contemporary Central and Eastern Europe* 23 (1): 9–44.

Blatter, Joachim, Samuel D. Schmid, and Andrea C. Blättler. 2017. "Democratic Deficits in Europe: The Overlooked Exclusiveness of Nation-States and the Positive Role of the European Union". *JCMS: Journal of Common Market Studies* 55 (3): 449–67.

Bochsler, Daniel, and Andreas Juon. 2019. "Authoritarian Footprints in Central and Eastern Europe". *East European Politics* 36 (2): 167–187. https://doi.org/10.1080/21599165.2019.1698420.

Bochsler, Daniel, and Hanspeter Kriesi. 2013. 'Varieties of Democracy'. In *Democracy in the Age of Globalization and Mediatization*, edited by Kriesi, Hanspeter, Sandra Lavenex, Frank Esser, Jörg Matthes, Marc Bühlmann, and Daniel Bochsler, 69–102. Houndmills: Palgrave Macmillan.

Bohle, Dorothee, and Bela Greskovits. 2007. "Neoliberalism, Embedded Neoliberalism and Neocorporatism: Towards Transnational Capitalism in Central-Eastern Europe". *West European Politics* 30 (3): 443–66.

Bohle, Dorothee, and Bela Greskovits. 2012. *Capitalist Diversity on Europe's Periphery*. Ithaca: Cornell University Press.

Braghiroli, Stefano, and Vassilis Petsinis. 2019. "Between Party-Systems and Identity-Politics: The Populist and Radical Right in Estonia and Latvia". *European Politics and Society*, 1–19.

Brosig, Malte. 2010. "The Challenge of Implementing Minority Rights in Central Eastern Europe". *Journal of European Integration* 32 (4): 393–411. https://doi.org/10.1080/07036331003797539.

Bugaric, Bojan. 2008. "Populism, Liberal Democracy, and the Rule of Law in Central and Eastern Europe". *Communist and Post-Communist Studies* 41 (2): 191–203.

Bunce, Valerie. 2005. "The National Idea: Imperial Legacies and Post-Communist Pathways in Eastern Europe". *East European Politics and Societies* 19 (3): 406–42.

Bustikova, Lenka, and Herbert Kitschelt. 2009. "The Radical Right in Post-Communist Europe. Comparative Perspectives on Legacies and Party Competition". *Communist and Post-Communist Studies* 42 (4): 459–83.

Bustikova, Lenka, and Petra Guasti. 2017. "The Illiberal Turn or Swerve in Central Europe?" *Politics and Governance* 5 (4): 166–76. https://doi.org/10.17645/pag.v5i4.1156.

Buštíková, Lenka, and Petra Guasti. 2018. "The State as a Firm: Understanding the Autocratic Roots of Technocratic Populism". *East European Politics and Societies*, https://doi.org/10.1177/0888325418791723.

Bustikova, Lenka. 2009. "The Extreme Right in Eastern Europe: EU Accession and the Quality of Governance". *Journal of Contemporary European Studies* 17 (2): 223–39.

Cannon, Barry. 2018. "Must we talk about populism? Interrogating populism's conceptual utility in a context of crisis". *New Political Science* 40 (3): 477–96.

Canovan, Margaret. 1983. "A case of distorted communication: a note on Habermas and Arendt". *Political Theory* 11 (1): 105–16.

Canovan, Margaret. 1984. "'People', Politicians and Populism 1". *Government and Opposition* 19 (3): 312–27.

Canovan, Margaret. 1999. "Trust the People! Populism and the Two Faces of Democracy". *Political Studies* 47 (1): 2–16. https://doi.org/10.1111/1467-9248.00184.

Cianetti, Licia, James Dawson, and Seán Hanley. 2018. "Rethinking "Democratic Backsliding' in Central and Eastern Europe – Looking beyond Hungary and Poland". *East European Politics* 34 (3): 243–56.

Cianetti, Licia. 2018. "Consolidated Technocratic and Ethnic Hollowness, but No Backsliding: Reassessing Europeanisation in Estonia and Latvia". *East European Politics* 34 (3): 317–36.

Cordell, Karl. 2013. "The Ideology of Minority Protection during the Post-Communist Transition in Europe'. In *Institutional Legacies of Communism, Change and Continuities in Minority Protection*, edited by Karl Cordell, Timofey Agarin, and Alexander Osipov, 77–89. Routledge.

Dahl, Robert A. 1972. *Polyarchy: Participation and Opposition*. New Haven: Yale University Press.

Dahrendorf, Ralf. 2003. "The Challenge for Democracy'. *Journal of Democracy* 14 (4): 101–14.

Dawson, James. 2016. *Cultures of Democracy in Serbia and Bulgaria: How Ideas Shape Publics*. Routledge.

Dimitrova, Antoaneta L. 2018. "The Uncertain Road to Sustainable Democracy: Elite Coalitions, Citizen Protests and the Prospects of Democracy in Central and Eastern Europe'. *East European Politics* 34 (3): 257–75.

Donskis, Leonidas. 1999. "Between Identity and Freedom: Mapping Nationalism in Twentieth-Century Lithuania'. *East European Politics & Societies* 13: 474–500.

Dryzek, John S. 2000. *Deliberative Democracy and Beyond: Liberals, Critics, Contestations*. Oxford: Oxford University Press.

Đurašković, Stevo. 2016. "National Identity-Building and the 'Ustaša-Nostalgia" in Croatia: The Past That Will Not Pass". *Nationalities Papers* 0 (0): 1–17.

Ekman, Joakim, Sergiu Gherghina, and Olena Podolian. 2016. "Challenges and Realities of Political Participation and Civic Engagement in Central and Eastern Europe". *East European Politics* 32 (1): 1–11.

Enyedi, Z., and L. Linek. 2008. "Searching for the Right Organization: Ideology and Party Structure in East-Central Europe". *Party Politics* 14 (4): 455.

Greskovits, Béla. 2015. "The Hollowing and Backsliding of Democracy in East Central Europe". *Global Policy* 6: 28–37.

Guasti, Petra, and Lenka Bustikova. 2019. "In Europe's Closet: The Rights of Sexual Minorities in the Czech Republic and Slovakia". *East European Politics* 0 (0): 1–21. https://doi.org/10.1080/21599165.2019.1705282.

Hale, Henry E. 2014. *Patronal Politics: Eurasian Regime Dynamics in Comparative Perspective*. Cambridge University Press.

Hanley, Seán, and Allan Sikk. 2016. "Economy, Corruption or Floating Voters? Explaining the Breakthroughs of Anti-Establishment Reform Parties in Eastern Europe". *Party Politics* 22 (4): 522–33.

Hanley, Seán, and Milada Anna Vachudova. 2018. "Understanding the Illiberal Turn: Democratic Backsliding in the Czech Republic". *East European Politics* 34 (3): 276–96.

Harris, Erika. 2019. "Nation before Democracy? Placing the Rise of the Slovak Extreme Right into Context". *East European Politics* 35 (4): 538–57. https://doi.org/10.1080/21599165.2019.1667770.

Haughton, Tim. 2007. "When Does the EU Make a Difference? Conditionality and the Accession Process in Central and Eastern Europe". *Political Studies Review* 5 (2): 233–46. https://doi.org/10.1111/j.1478-9299.2007.00130.x.

Horvat, Srecko, and Igor Stiks. 2015. *Welcome to the Desert of Post-Socialism: Radical Politics after Yugoslavia*. Verso Books.

Howard, Marc Morjé. 2003. *The Weakness of Civil Society in Post-Communist Europe*. Cambridge: Cambridge University Press.

Hurrelmann, Achim. 2015. "Demoi-Cratic Citizenship in Europe: An Impossible Ideal?" *Journal of European Public Policy* 22 (1): 19–36.

Huszka, Beáta. 2014. "Framing National Identity in Independence Campaigns: Secessionist Rhetoric and Ethnic Conflict". *Nationalism and Ethnic Politics* 20 (2): 153–73.

Jowitt, Ken. 1993. *New World Disorder: The Leninist Extinction*. Berkley: University of California Press.

Judis, John B. 2016. *The Populist Explosion: How the Great Recession Transformed American and European Politics*. Columbia Global Reports New York.

Karolewski, Ireneusz Paweł. 2016. "Protest and Participation in Post-Transformation Poland: The Case of the Committee for the Defense of Democracy (KOD)". *Communist and Post-Communist Studies* 49 (3): 255–67. https://doi.org/10.1016/j.postcomstud.2016.06.003.

Keil, Soeren. 2013. "Europeanization, State-Building and Democratization in the Western Balkans". *Nationalities Papers* 41 (3): 343–53.

Kelemen, R. Daniel, and Michael Blauberger. 2017. "Introducing the Debate: European Union Safeguards against Member States' Democratic Backsliding". *Journal of European Public Policy* 24 (3): 317–20.

Kessel, Stijn van. 2015. *Populist Parties in Europe: Agents of Discontent?* Springer.

Kitschelt, Herbert, and Steven I. Wilkinson. 2007. *Patrons, Clients and Policies: Patterns of Democratic Accountability and Political Competition*. Cambridge University Press.

Kochenov, Dimitry, and Eline De Ridder. 2011. "Democratic Conditionality in Eastern Enlargement: Ambitious Window Dressing". *European Foreign Affairs Review* 16 (5): 589–605.

Kolev, Kiril. 2019. "Weak Pluralism and Shallow Democracy: The Rise of Identity Politics in Bulgaria and Romania". *East European Politics* 0 (0): 1–18. https://doi.org/10.1080/21599165.2019.1700954.

Kolstø, Pål, and Hans Olav Melberg. 2002. "Integration, Alienation, and Conflict in Estonia and Moldova at the Societal Level: A Comparison". In *National Integration and Violent Conflict in Post-Soviet Societies: The Cases of Estonia and Moldova*, edited by Pål Kolstø. Oxford: Roman and Littlefield.

Kopecký, Petr, and Cas Mudde. 2000. "What Has Eastern Europe Taught Us about the Democratization Literature (and Vice Versa)?" *European Journal of Political Research* 37 (4): 517–39.

Kovras, Iosif, and Neophytos Loizides. 2014. "The Greek Debt Crisis and Southern Europe: Majoritarian Pitfalls?" *Comparative Politics* 47 (1): 1–20. https://doi.org/10.5129/001041514813623164.

Krastev, Ivan. 2002. "The Balkans: Democracy without Choices". *Journal of Democracy* 13 (3): 39–53.

Laitin, David D. 2002. "Culture and National Identity: The East' and European Integration". *West European Politics* 25 (2): 55–80.

Lees, Charles. 2018. "The 'Alternative for Germany': The Rise of Right-Wing Populism at the Heart of Europe". *Politics* 38 (3): 295–310.

Lendvai, Noémi. 2004. "The Weakest Link? EU Accession and Enlargement: Dialoguing EU and Post-Communist Social Policy". *Journal of European Social Policy* 14 (3): 319–33.

Lijphart, Arend. 1997. "Unequal Participation: Democracy's Unresolved Dilemma". *The American Political Science Review* 91 (1): 1–14.

Mair, Peter. 2006. "Ruling the Void: The Hollowing of Western Democracy". *New Left Review* 42: 25–51.

March, Luke, and Cas Mudde. 2005. "What's Left of the Radical Left? The European Radical Left after 1989: Decline and Mutation". *Comparative European Politics* 3 (1): 23–49.

March, Luke. 2017. "Left and Right Populism Compared: The British Case". *The British Journal of Politics and International Relations* 19 (2): 282–303.

McGann, Anthony J., and Herbert Kitschelt. 2005. "The Radical Right in the Alps: Evolution of Support for the Swiss SVP and Austrian FPÖ". *Party Politics* 11 (2): 147–71.

Mikkel, Evald, and Geoffrey Pridham. 2004. "Clinching the 'Return to Europe': The Referendums on EU Accession in Estonia and Latvia". *West European Politics* 27 (4): 716–48.

Minkenberg, Michael. 2002. "The Radical Right in Postsocialist Central and Eastern Europe: Comparative Observations and Interpretations". *East European Politics & Societies* 16 (2): 335–62.

Minkenberg, Michael. 2013. "From Pariah to Policy-Maker? The Radical Right in Europe, West and East: Between Margin and Mainstream". *Journal of Contemporary European Studies* 21 (1): 5–24.

Mishler, William, and Richard Rose. 1999. "Five Years After the Fall: Trajectories of Support for Democracy in Post-Communist Europe". In *Critical Citizens: Global Support for Democratic Governance*, edited by Norris Pippa, 78–99. Oxford: Oxford University Press.

Morawiecki, Mateusz. 2021. "Statement by Prime Minister Mateusz Morawiecki in the European Parliament". *The Chancellery of the Polish Prime Minister*. 19 October. www.gov.pl/web/primeminister/statement-by-prime-minister-mateusz-morawiecki-in-the-european-parliament.

Morlino, Leonardo, and Mario Quaranta. 2016. "What Is the Impact of the Economic Crisis on Democracy? Evidence from Europe". *International Political Science Review* 37 (5): 618–33.

Mudde, Cas. 2009. *Populist Radical Right Parties in Europe*. Cambridge: Cambridge University Press.

Müller, Jan-Werner. 2016. *What Is Populism*. Philadelphia: University of Pennsylvania Press.

Nordensvard, Johan, and Markus Ketola. 2014. "Nationalist Reframing of the Finnish and Swedish Welfare States – The Nexus of Nationalism and Social Policy in Far-Right Populist Parties". *Social Policy & Administration*, August, n/a-n/a. https://doi.org/10.1111/spol.12095.

Noutcheva, Gergana. 2016. "Societal Empowerment and Europeanization: Revisiting the EU's Impact on Democratization". *JCMS: Journal of Common Market Studies* 54 (3): 691–708. https://doi.org/10.1111/jcms.12322.

Offe, Claus. 1991. "Capitalism by Democratic Design? Democratic Theory Facing the Triple Transition in East Central Europe". *Social Research* 58 (4): 865–82.

Orenstein, Mitchell A. 2009. "What Happened in East European (Political) Economies?: A Balance Sheet for Neoliberal Reform". *East European Politics and Societies* 23 (4): 479–90.

Pappas, Takis S. 2016. "Modern Populism: Research Advances, Conceptual and Methodological Pitfalls, and the Minimal Definition". In *Oxford Research Encyclopedia of Politics*.

Petsinis, Vassilis. 2019. "Ethnopolitics in Central and Eastern Europe in a State of Flux". *Ethnopolitics*, 1–4.

Petsinis, Vassilis. 2019. "Identity Politics and Right-Wing Populism in Estonia: The Case of EKRE". *Nationalism and Ethnic Politics* 25 (2): 211–30.

Pirro, Andrea LP, and Stijn Van Kessel. 2017. "United in Opposition? The Populist Radical Right's EU-Pessimism in Times of Crisis". *Journal of European Integration* 39 (4): 405–20.

Pirro, Andrea LP. 2014. "Populist Radical Right Parties in Central and Eastern Europe: The Different Context and Issues of the Prophets of the Patria". *Government and Opposition* 49 (4): 600–629.

Pirro, Andrea LP. 2015. *The Populist Radical Right in Central and Eastern Europe: Ideology, Impact, and Electoral Performance*. Routledge.

Plattner, Marc F., and Larry Jay Diamond. 2007. "Is East-Central Europe Backsliding?" *Journal of Democracy* 18 (4): 5–6.

Pridham, Geoffrey. 2002. "EU Enlargement and Consolidating Democracy in Post-Communist States - Formality and Reality". *Journal of Common Market Studies* 40 (3): 953–73.

Pridham, Geoffrey. 2018. "Latgale and Latvia's Post-Soviet Democracy: The Territorial Dimension of Regime Consolidation". *East European Politics* 34 (2): 194–216.

Rohrschneider, Robert. 2002. "The Democracy Deficit and Mass Support for an EU-Wide Government". *American Journal of Political Science*, 463–75.

Rooduijn, Matthijs, and Teun Pauwels. 2011. "Measuring Populism: Comparing Two Methods of Content Analysis". *West European Politics* 34 (6): 1272–83.

Rose, Richard, and Neil Munro. 2003. *Elections and Parties in New European Democracies*. Washington, DC: CQ Press.

Rose, Richard, William Mishler, and Christian Haerpfer. 1998. *Democracy and Its Alternatives: Understanding Post-Communist Societies*. Baltimore, Maryland: The John Hopkins University Press.

Rueschemeyer, Dietrich, Marilyn Rueschemeyer, and Bjorn Wittrock. 1998. *Participation and Democracy, East and West: Comparisons and Interpretations*. Armonk, NY: M.E.Sharp.

Rueschemeyer, Dietrich. 2015. *Participation and Democracy East and West: Comparisons and Interpretations: Comparisons and Interpretations*. Routledge.

Rupnik, Jacques. 2007. "From Democracy Fatigue to Populist Backlash". *Journal of Democracy* 18 (4): 17–25.

Sandel, Michael J. 2018. "Populism, Liberalism, and Democracy". *Philosophy & Social Criticism* 44 (4): 353–59.

Sata, Robert, and Ireneusz Pawel Karolewski. 2019. "Caesarean Politics in Hungary and Poland". *East European Politics* 0 (0): 1–20. https://doi.org/10.1080/21599165.2019.1703694.

Schimmelfennig, Frank, Stefan Engert, and Heiko Knobel. 2006. *International Socialization in Europe: European Organizations, Political Conditionality and Democratic Change*. Palgrave Macmillan.

Schwellnus, Guido. 2006. "Reasons for Constitutionalization: Non-Discrimination, Minority Rights and Social Rights in the Convention on the EU Charter of Fundamental Rights". *Journal of European Public Policy* 13 (8): 1265–83.

Scicluna, Nicole, and Stefan Auer. 2019. "From the Rule of Law to the Rule of Rules: Technocracy and the Crisis of EU Governance". *West European Politics* 0 (0): 1–23. https://doi.org/10.1080/01402382.2019.1584843.

Sedelmeier, Ulrich. 2017. "Political Safeguards against Democratic Backsliding in the EU: The Limits of Material Sanctions and the Scope of Social Pressure". *Journal of European Public Policy* 24 (3): 337–51.

Shapiro, Ian. 2003. *The State of Democratic Theory*. Princeton University Press.

Shaw, Jo, and Antje Wiener. 2000. "The Paradox of the European Polity". *The State of the European Union* 5: 64–88.

Sikk, Allan. 2006. "From Private Organizations to Democratic Infrastructure: Political Parties and the State in Estonia". *Journal of Communist Studies and Transition Politics* 22 (3): 341–61.

Stanley, Bill, and Ben Stanley. 2020. "Whose Poland Is It to Be? PiS and the Struggle between Monism and Pluralism". *East European Politics* 36 (3): 378–94.

Stroschein, Sherrill. 2019. "Populism, Nationalism, and Party Politics". *Nationalities Papers*, 1–13.

Tismaneanu, Vladimer. 2002. "Discomforts of Victory: Democracy, Liberal Values and Nationalism in Post-Communist Europe". *West European Politics* 25 (2): 81–100.

Urbinati, Nadia. 2014. *Democracy Disfigured*. Cambridge, MA: Harvard University Press.

Usherwood, Simon. 2019. "Shooting the Fox? UKIP's Populism in the Post-Brexit Era". *West European Politics*, 1–21.

Vachudova, Milada A, and Liesbet Hooghe. 2009. "Postcommunist Politics in a Magnetic Field: How Transition and EU Accession Structure Party Competition on European Integration". *Comparative European Politics* 7 (2): 179–212.

Verovšek, Peter J. 2021. "Caught between 1945 and 1989: Collective Memory and the Rise of Illiberal Democracy in Postcommunist Europe". *Journal of European Public Policy* 28 (6): 840–57.

Wimmer, Andreas. 2008. "Elementary Strategies of Ethnic Boundary Making". *Ethnic and Racial Studies* 31 (6): 1025–55. https://doi.org/10.1080/01419870801905612.

Zielonka, Jan, and Jacques Rupnik. 2020. "From Revolution to "Counter-Revolution": Democracy in Central and Eastern Europe 30 Years On". *Europe-Asia Studies* 72 (6): 1073–99. https://doi.org/10.1080/09668136.2020.1784394.

Authoritarian footprints in Central and Eastern Europe

Daniel Bochsler and Andreas Juon

ABSTRACT
Central and Eastern Europe is the last world region to transition towards democracy. Today, it shows alarming signs of de-consolidation, most prominently in Hungary, Poland, and Serbia. This article assesses whether these observations form part of a systematic pattern across the region. It relies on newly-updated objective data from the Democracy Barometer for the period between 1990 and 2016. It revisits evidence for the three most prominent explanations of democratic backsliding in the region: the rise of populist parties, the incapacity of the European Union to secure democracy once pre-accession incentives weaken, and the global financial crisis.

1. Introduction

Never before in history has a greater extent of the world been under democratic rule than today. In spite of this, political observers are deeply concerned with the global state of democracy (Merkel 2015). In particular, many accounts highlight problems in the last regional cluster of countries to democratise: the post-communist countries in Central and Eastern Europe (CEE). After an initially rapid transition towards democracy in the 1990s, the region has shown worrying signs of de-consolidation, and has, in recent years, even been diagnosed as being on the edge of an authoritarian backlash.

Recent political developments have further stoked fears about democratic backsliding[1] in the CEE region, even resulting in assessments that they may herald the beginning of a new, reversed wave of democratisation (Diamond 2015; Levitsky and Ziblatt 2018; Mounk 2018; Snyder 2018). In particular, political parties with illiberal programmes have entered government not only in Poland, Hungary, and Serbia, but also in Bulgaria, Slovakia, and most recently in the Czech Republic (Rupnik 2007, 2018; Enyedi 2016; Kelemen 2017; Mounk 2018). In some cases, they have subsequently exploited the weakness of the media and judiciary to strengthen partisan control over the state, for example in Macedonia and Serbia (e.g. Esen and Gumuscu 2016; Bieber 2018). The region's international and economic environment further reinforce these warnings: While external actors – in particular the European Union – have been important for promoting democracy in the region in

---

This is an Open Access article distributed under the terms of the Creative Commons Attribution License (http://creativecommons.org/licenses/by/4.0/), which permits unrestricted use, distribution, and reproduction in any medium, provided the original work is properly cited.

the past (Schimmelfennig and Sedelmeier 2004; Agarin, 2020), they seem unable to guarantee the same incentives in the long run (Carothers 2015). In addition, the repercussions of the global financial crisis have weakened both democracy at home, as well as the capacity of external actors to implement their democracy agenda (Armingeon and Guthmann 2014; Morlino and Quaranta 2016).

Many of these pessimistic accounts are based on qualitative assessments of single countries (e.g. Enyedi 2016; Krekó and Enyedi 2018; Pehe 2018) or on the observation of trends across small sets of cases. These often include the same set of cases: Mečiar and Fico in Slovakia, Orbán in Hungary, and the Kaczynskis in Poland (Brusis 2016; Bustikova and Guasti 2017; Grzymala-Busse 2017; Kelemen 2017; Luce 2017; Rupnik 2018; but see Cianetti, Dawson, and Hanley 2018). In contrast, the few existing quantitative investigations of recent democratic developments have either focused on Latin America (Huber and Schimpf 2016b) or they include only a few EU members from Central and Eastern Europe (Huber and Schimpf 2016a; Huber and Ruth 2017).[2] Studies with global samples face difficulties of distinguishing between potentially strongly diverging processes such as the entrenchment of authoritarian systems or backsliding in the quality of democracy (e.g. Lührmann et al. 2018).

Contributing to this debate, we identify and assess the state of the quality of democracy in all 19 democracies in Central and Eastern Europe.[3] In addition to taking stock of recent changes, we assess their associations with the most prominently-cited explanatory factors behind purported democratic backsliding in the region. In particular, we investigate three widely-cited explanations: first, the increasing role of anti-elite, populist parties in government; second, the European Union's fatigue with efforts to sustain improvements in the quality of democracy once an applicant state has joined the Union; and, third, the financial crisis of 2008, which has deeply affected the economies of CEE countries and which has had serious repercussions not only for their political systems, but also for the capacity of the European Union and its democratic agenda.

Our regional focus on Central and Eastern Europe offers three advantages: First, as earlier research has found important differences in the effect of populism on democracy between consolidated and weak democracies (Mudde and Rovira Kaltwasser 2012a, 18–26, 2012b), the recent transition of the region towards democracy offers a set of similar cases for comparison. Second, it also offers crucial variance for the most prominent explanations for the purported backsliding. On the one hand, Central and Eastern European democracies have experienced a strong influence of populist actors (Grzymala-Busse 2017) from all ideological families, thus enabling a more systematic assessment of their relationship with democracy than regions dominated by populists of the right (Western Europe) or the left (Latin America). On the other, it also offers the opportunity to assess the role of external factors, in a region where EU accession processes are linked to a political agenda of promoting liberal democracy (Schimmelfennig 2005). Third, the investigation of gradual changes in the quality of democracy enables us to focus on the most crucial process in the region, leaving aside inter-regime transitions that are more relevant in other contexts.

For our analysis, we rely on the Democracy Barometer dataset. This has two advantages, First, it is based overwhelmingly on objective or survey data and thus allows us to avoid the known problems of expert surveys (e.g. Silva and Littvay 2019) – often recruited among academics with strong liberal-democratic norms. Second, it is suited for an assessment of the Quality of Democracy in a fine-grained, disaggregated fashion, along nine principles. We have extended the data to cover the period until 2016 across 70 democracies, including 19 in Central and Eastern Europe (Merkel et al. 2018).

Our results indicate that the widespread public perception of a deep crisis of democracy in Central and Eastern Europe may be exaggerated. While improvements in the quality of democracy that started in the 1990s have indeed faltered, and while some democratic functions are under threat in some countries, this does not appear to constitute a general trend towards the deterioration of democratic quality across the region. However, according to our data, in several countries authoritarian leaders or governing parties have left a significant mark on two functions of democracy: the rule of law and the freedom of the press. In particular, concern seems appropriate about press freedom, transparency, competition, and the rule of law in Moldova, Bulgaria, the Czech Republic, Slovakia, Ukraine, and Hungary. Vice-versa, European integration has been able to foster some principles of democracy in the course of the EU accession process, but the EU has no powers in preventing post-accession backsliding under populist governments.

In the rest of this paper, we proceed as follows. First, we introduce the term "quality of democracy", discussing both its conceptualisation and operationalisation with the newly-updated Democracy Barometer dataset. Second, we use this dataset to empirically trace recent trends in the quality of democracy in all 19 countries in Central and Eastern Europe, identifying both countries displaying major transformations, as well as the democratic functions most strongly affected. Third, we take advantage of a large set of new data sources to trace the importance of the three suspected drivers behind recent democratic reversals in the countries of the region: populist actors in and outside government, post-EU accession fatigues, and the 2008 financial crisis. In our last section, we conclude and compare our findings to the results of expert-based assessments.

2. The quality of democracy

Central to our purpose of tracing recent democratic developments in Central and Eastern Europe is the concept of quality of democracy. Before starting our empirical endeavour, this section introduces its conceptualisation and subsequently presents how we operationalise it using a newly-updated version of the Democracy Barometer.

The *concept of quality of democracy* only applies to political regimes which fulfil minimal democratic criteria. It allows us not only to distinguish to what degree these regimes fulfil ideals established in democratic theory, but also to identify potential democratic deficits (cf. Diamond and Morlino 2004; Morlino 2004). Hybrid regimes, which at best display only a democratic facade, do not fulfil the minimal democracy criteria, rendering the concept of quality of democracy inappropriate in these cases. This caveat is especially important for our study period – after the end of the Cold War – as it brought about the rise of political regimes which conduct regular elections, but are only superficially democratic (Diamond 2002). These countries – regional cases thereof are Belarus or Russia – are not captured by our concept of the quality of democracy and *a priori* excluded from all analyses.

Merkel's (2004) and Diamond and Morlino's (2004) concepts of "quality of democracy" build on mid-range concepts of democracy which go beyond the electoral principle and also incorporate further liberal functions of democracy, such as the rule of law or an active political society. This more extensive, yet procedural concept explicitly foresees a number of trade-offs between the realisation of different functions of democracy found in specific types of democracy. For example, while majoritarian democracies put an emphasis on stable governments and the responsiveness of democracy to the median voter, consensus democracies emphasise a broad and inclusive system of representation (see, for instance Lijphart 1999; Powell 2000; Bochsler and Kriesi 2013).

The specific concept of quality of democracy which we use in this paper is based on an encompassing set of operationalizable functions of democracy. At its core, it relies on the functions of *democratic control and decision-making*. These include institutions which make the government accountable to citizen preferences (through competitive elections), which make this process inclusive (for example, through universal suffrage and inclusive representation), and which encourage broad participation in it. These, in turn are embedded in *democratic rights and freedoms*, as well as *checks and balances,* including assurances of free political debate, basic civil rights (personal liberty, freedom of expression and of information, freedom of religion, economic and social rights), the rule of law, limitations to the power of governments, provisions for transparent government procedures, and horizontal checks on government (parliamentary procedures, independent courts, bicameralism, federalism, central bank independence). A further indispensable function is provided by *pluralist intermediaries* between state and society, including the media, the public sphere, and civil society. Finally, to maximise the quality of democracy, governments should not be subject to extra-constitutional actors, such as the military, but should have actual *power to govern*. All functions combine both formal constitutional rules (establishing the legal environment for democracy), and democratic practices (for example, effective electoral competition, or the absence of state-based or private repression of journalists).

Most of the existing literature on democratic backsliding relies on *measures of democracy* that broadly differentiate between democracies, authoritarian regimes, and intermediate cases on one or two dimensions. The most commonly-used measures are the Polity IV, the Freedom House, and the V-Dem index of democracy (Freedom House 2018; Lührmann et al. 2018), although a small number of articles rely on other sources (Morlino and Quaranta 2016; Börzel and Schimmelfennig 2017). On all of these indices, Central and Eastern European democracies usually obtain stable ratings at the top end of the scale and, with few exceptions, were already doing so years before EU accession. This article aims for a more nuanced assessment which allows us to incorporate specific transformations of the quality of democracy into our study.

In order to identify such changes in the quality of democracy, we rely on the Democracy Barometer dataset (Bühlmann et al. 2012). Mirroring our concept, the Democracy Barometer conceives of democracy as based on individual freedom, equality, and actual degree of control the government possesses over the state. It builds on a total of 105 indicators primarily from objective sources and representative surveys rather than expert assessments. They are grouped along nine primary functions of democracy: individual liberties, rule of law, the public sphere, competition, mutual constraints, governmental capabilities, transparency, participation, and representation. Each indicator is coded so that the majority of its values, and the aggregate scores for each function, lie between 0 and 100 (see Bühlmann et al. 2012; Merkel et al. 2018, for details).

3. Trends in the quality of democracy in Central and Eastern Europe, 1990–2016

We start our empirical analysis with a descriptive assessment of the quality of democracy in the 19 countries of Central and Eastern Europe, beginning with the year of democratisation (usually 1990 or shortly thereafter), up to 2016. Except for Belarus and Russia, all Central and Eastern European countries can be considered democracies, according to Polity IV (minimal Polity IV score of 6).[4]

Figure 1 plots the overall trends for democracy in Central and Eastern Europe by democratic function. There is a clear positive trend since the 1990s, with the region making advances with regards to competition, transparency, and the public sphere. However, this upwards trend has slowed down markedly since around 2000, with some democratic functions even appearing to show decreases. Furthermore (similar to the new democracies in Latin America (cf. Bochsler and Juon 2018)) the countries in Central and Eastern Europe clearly have not attained a similarly high level of democratic quality as the established democracies in Western Europe. Most remarkably, there is a deep crisis of the rule of law (and to a somewhat lesser degree, the public sphere) in Central and Eastern Europe. However, to the extent that these reversals can be captured by our indicators, relying on objective data rather than expert-coding, our findings contradict recent claims by academics and political analyses of a widespread backsliding against the quality of democracy in the region (Bustikova and Guasti 2017; Rupnik 2018). Indeed, no such general trend can be observed on any of the nine functions of democracy which we assess, at least as regards the time period until 2016 which is included in our analysis.

Figure 2 unpacks these regional averages to reveal country-specific trajectories, showing separate trends for each of the 18 Central and Eastern European countries for which we have data (excluding Kosovo, due to missing data).[5] Reflecting the regional average, the quality of democracy has remained stable or improved on most functions of democracy in most countries, in particular in two Baltic States (Latvia, Lithuania), in Poland, and in Slovenia – though in each of the countries with significant (enduring) weaknesses.[6] However, there are temporary fluctuations in some of the indicators (especially those measuring government capacity – this is partly related to measurement issues).

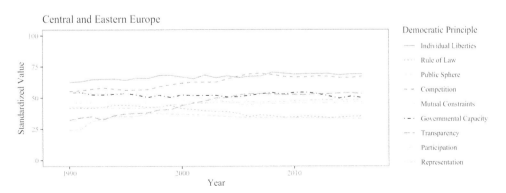

Figure 1. The development of the quality of democracy by region (mean values).

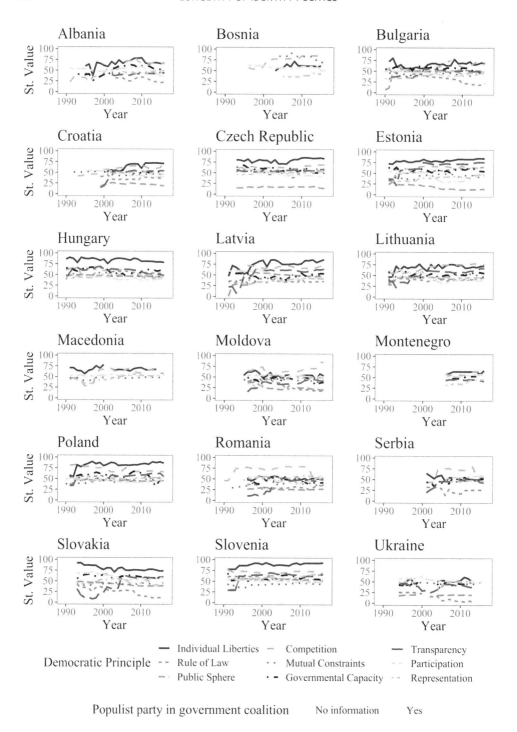

Figure 2. The development of the quality of democracy in Central and Eastern Europe, by countries.

The subsequent analysis focuses primarily on important instances of backsliding, rather than on persistent democratic shortcomings.

As regards particular democratic functions, the most systematic development, observable in several countries, is the erosion of the *rule of law*. Our measure for the rule of law reached its peak in the late 1990s, with several countries establishing a truly independent judiciary and with landmark judgments signalling to governments that the courts constituted a genuine limit to government power (Bugarič and Ginsburg 2016), though suffering from significant informal infringements elsewhere (e.g. Bugarič and Kuhelj 2015). However, since the 2000s, we observe a erosion of the rule of law in countries such as Slovakia, Ukraine, Bulgaria (since 2000), Romania (around 2012–2013), and in Albania (since 2011). The underlying reasons for this are not only institutional changes, but also government infringements on the judiciary in practice, including replacements of members of the judiciary with party loyalists (Bugarič and Ginsburg 2016). Other symptoms of this process are significant backlashes against judicial independence and an immense drop in public confidence in the judiciary and police.

A further noteworthy development is the drastic reduction of political *competition* in three countries in the 2010s. In all three, this was related to the surge of a new, dominant leader and political party. In Hungary, Viktor Orbán and his Fidesz-KDNP alliance won a landslide election victory in 2010, gaining a 68% supermajority in parliament (cf. Sata and Karolewski 2020). In Romania, the Romanian Social Liberals of Victor Ponta became dominant after the 2012 elections (59% of the seats). In Serbia, the Serbian Progress Party won 29% of the seats in 2012 and has dominated politics since 2014 with a 63% majority in parliament. While the changes in these countries are suggestive, they clearly do not represent an overall regional trend.

On other democratic functions, the developments are even more heterogeneous, with recent decreases appearing to reflect country-specific circumstances rather than a regional trend: First, there has been a recent drop in *participation* in several countries, in particular in the Czech Republic after 2001 and in Hungary after 2014, driven by the curtailing of suffrage through new electoral rules. Second, there has been an erosion of *transparency* in Hungary since 2009 and in Serbia since 2015. Both countries have reduced press freedom (Huszka 2018). In Hungary the transparency of government communication has also suffered. Third, *individual liberties* deteriorated in Ukraine and in Moldova in 2014, culminating in riots. They have also been under threat in Slovakia since 2005 with de-facto violations of political liberties and reported cases of torture. Fourth, the *public sphere* has deteriorated in several countries. Croatia experienced an erosion of its civil society and of economic interest groups in the 2010s (as indicated by declining membership numbers). In Estonia, the press has become increasingly politically unbalanced since 2002.

Overall, our analysis finds both parallels and differences in the development of the quality of democracy in the countries of Central and Eastern Europe. It does not support the notion of an overall regional deterioration in the quality of democracy, however. On the one hand, the upwards trend of the 1990s has certainly stopped, and, as regards several specific countries in the region, has reversed direction. However, the general trend of democratic backsliding, alleged by country experts, is not reflected across countries and functions, at least not in the objective indicators on which the Democracy Barometer dataset relies and at least not in the time period we are able to consider (until 2016). In other parts of the region, the quality of democracy has even improved, although this process was usually similarly limited to some democratic functions. While our data thus contradicts pessimistic judgements for the whole region, the time period covered does not allow us to consider more recent alleged impairments of checks and balances and the liberal rights regime through constitutional changes and non-constitutional infringements of individual and minority rights between 2017 and 2018 (Sandurski 2019).

4. The three processes behind democratic changes in CEE

Having mapped the heterogeneous democratic developments in the CEE region, we now proceed to analyse the processes behind them. In particular, we consider the three most prominently-cited factors behind purported democratic backsliding in the region: first, populist-authoritarian parties in government and in opposition; second, reduced incentives to uphold liberal democratic principles after EU accession; and, third, political repercussions of the global financial crisis of 2008. In order to do so, we have collected data for each of these three factors and descriptively investigate their associations with democratic changes in our sample. In our main text, we focus on the four functions of democracy for which our data show the highest variance: Individual liberties, rule of law, competition, and transparency.[7] While sample limitations prevent us from conducting a causal investigation and from considering interrelated effects, our systematic bivariate investigation nevertheless enables us to trace patterns and serves as a plausibility test for the three explanations. The discussion highlights the most influential cases driving these developments, as well as the heterogeneity between individual countries.

4.1. Process 1: authoritarian-populist governments

The first widely-cited regional driver of democratic changes, especially of recent erosions of the quality of democracy, are authoritarian leaders, linked to the emergence of strong populist parties. In Central and Eastern Europe, they played an important role long before populism spread over the continent. Some of these parties were populist with an emphasis on identity politics, in particular the nationalist parties in the Western Balkans (e.g. the Croatian Democratic Union, HDZ, in Croatia; the Serbian Radical Party, SRS, in Serbia; or the Internal Macedonian Revolutionary Organisation, VMRO, in Macedonia). In other countries, authoritarian leaders were political entrepreneurs combining populist ideology with centrist or mainstream political positions. Some rose quickly and became the new political elites, such as the former Bulgarian king Simeon Sakskoburgotski (prime minister 2001–2005), or newcomer political parties in several of the Baltic states (Sikk 2012; Hanley and Sikk 2016). However, it was only after the transformation of Viktor Orbán's Fidesz into a populist-authoritarian party in Hungary and its rise to power in the 2010 elections that populism was discussed as a threat to liberalism and democracy.

We define populism as a "thin ideology": populists juxtapose a supposedly "homogeneous people" with an elite class they portray as corrupt and as dominating politics, the economy, society in general and/or the media (Mudde 2004). This defining feature of populism can be combined with diverse "thick" ideologies (e.g. identity politics/nationalism, socialism, conservative thought) or issue positions, for example those of the far-left

Figure 3. Populists in opposition (left), in government (middle), and in dominant governments (right) and trends in the quality of democracy.

(March 2011), the far-right (Mudde 2011; Huber and Schimpf 2016a), and the political centre (van Kessel 2015). Thereby, the defining features of populism are anti-liberal, anti-pluralist and anti-democratic, and it can transform or damage democracy (Mudde and Rovira Kaltwasser 2012a). Furthermore, it also closes the door to external actors promoting democracy (Carothers 2015).[8]

To identify populist parties, and in line with our definition of populism, we relied on existing sources[9] (Hawkins 2009, 2013; March 2011; Mudde 2011; van Kessel 2015; Hawkins and Silva 2016; Huber and Schimpf 2016b, 2016a), and combine them to maximise coverage,[10] partly using temporal extrapolation.[11] Based on an underlying party-level coding (which included all parties with at least 2% of the seat share in the first chamber of parliament), we then created our country-level variables for populist parties in government and opposition, discarding country years where we could not account for the populism status of a significant share of parties.[12]

Figure 3 identifies the footprints of populists in opposition (left panel), in government as partners or majority parties (middle), and in electorally dominant governments (right).[13] It shows the trends for (uninterrupted) years of populist activity, with the number of years that populist actors have been in government or in opposition on the X-axis. Multiple populist time spans within the same country are included as separate cases. The trend estimates in Figure 3 and all subsequent figures (in red) are based on bivariate models with period-fixed effects; we interpret them when they show a substantially important change.[14] Populist governments with at least two-thirds of parliamentary seats have a particularly dominant role, which in many countries corresponds to the threshold for changing the constitution.

Populist footprints leave three observable marks on the quality of democracy. First, we find a drop in the *rule of law* in four countries right after populist administrations enter office. This is the case for Vasile Tarlev (Moldova, 2001), Mirek Toplánek (Czech Republic, 2006), Robert Fico (Slovakia, 2006), and Boyko Borisov (Bulgaria, 2009). In Ukraine, the rule of law is already extremely weak at the beginning of the second Timoshenko administration in 2007, and only drops slightly further (see Figure 1). However, as the comparative analysis also shows, there does not appear to be a homogeneous relationship between populist governments and developments of the rule of law. Instead, there is considerable fluctuation in the trend, and the presence of pure downward trends is rather the exception than the rule.

Second, under some populist cabinets, *transparency* deteriorates. This is the case for Ivo Sanader in Croatia (2003), Robert Fico in Slovakia (2006), Viktor Orbán in Hungary (2010) and Beata Szydło in Poland (2014). Again, this authoritarian footprint is not homogeneous. Other populist administrations, have boosted, rather than weakened the transparency of rule, e.g. the right-wing populist cabinets of Adrian Năstase and Călin Popescu-Tăriceanu in Romania (2000-2007). This goes back to a period when the Romanian government's primary agenda was access to EU membership.

Third, *competition* drops sharply when populist governments take office in Hungary (after 2010), Bulgaria (after 2009 and in 2015) and Moldova (in 2001). In Hungary, the victory of the Fidesz was accentuated by an electoral system with partly majoritarian features, which created a huge discrepancy in the representation of the governing party and the opposition – the Fidesz party won 68% of the seats with only 53% of the votes. In all these cases, the drop in our measure of competition is partly due to the effective dominance over the party system by populist parties, and partly because of changes to electoral rules and rules on party funding.

While the populist critique of the state of liberal democracies aims to strengthen vertical accountability at the expense of strong horizontal checks and balances, we find that this critique in some of the countries disguises the real impact of populists on democracy. When populist governments do change the institutional setup of democracy, they also target aspects of democracy which are crucial for citizen control over their government, such as party funding rules or freedom of the press.

However, in our sample, populism is neither a sufficient, nor a necessary condition for any of the erosion in the quality of democracy: the rule of law is also seen to suffer under some of the non-populist governments, e.g. Albania (2010-2016) or Hungary (1999-2002). Freedom of the press and government transparency can similarly also suffer in non-populist politics, e.g. Poland (1996-1999) or Hungary (1999-2001). For all other functions of the quality of democracy, the trends under populist governments are even more heterogeneous. The same applies for periods where populist governments govern with a two-thirds majority in parliament, or for those where populists emerge as viable opposition forces.[15]

These patterns do not allow us to reject the explanation that populist rule has transformed democracy in Central and Eastern Europe. However, they show that populist governments differ significantly with regards to our research question, and that the relationships between populist rule and the quality of democracy are strongly context-dependent (cf. Agarin 2020). Across countries, the targets of populist governments vary, and in several contexts our data has not picked up alterations in democratic practices, at least not yet. In particular, the populist-authoritarian backslides remain limited to countries with only weak EU membership perspectives (Moldova, Ukraine), or to periods after CEE countries have acceded to the European Union.

4.2. Process 2: EU political integration and post-accession backsliding

According to a second line of argument, declines in the quality of democracy in Central and Eastern Europe are directly related to processes occurring in post-EU-accession periods. In this reasoning, before granting membership, the EU is able to render any deepening of European integration conditional on political criteria. Among other factors, the Union demands that prospective members improve their democratic, human rights, and minority protection credentials, and that they enshrine the rule of law (Pevehouse 2002; Dimitrova and Pridham 2004; Freyburg and Richter 2010; Kolev 2020). While these effects might be less important for liberal political parties, with a democratisation agenda, EU conditionality could play a peculiar role in countries with a mixed government between liberal and authoritarian parties (Schimmelfennig 2005). Once a country has achieved membership, as is the case for 11 countries in the region, this conditionality mechanism vanishes. While the Union has a limited range of sanctions at its disposal, they are not very effective, politically costly, and difficult to activate, requiring a unanimous decision after a lengthy procedure.

Recent regional developments illustrate this reasoning. The EU disciplinary proceedings against Poland and Hungary, activated in 2017 and 2018 due to their systemic threats to the rule of law, have remained largely ineffective. As long as the two countries' governments back each other, the necessary unanimity for disciplinary sanctions cannot be reached. In addition, the financial crisis of 2008 has put the success story of democratisation, European integration, and liberal markets into question, especially in Central and Eastern Europe. There, popular hopes that democracy would also deliver economic welfare gave way to disappointment, also spawning doubt in democracy as a political system (Mishler and Rose 1996; Brusis 2016; Bochsler and Hänni 2019).

As regards previous evidence, several qualitative studies come to the conclusion that the EU cannot prevent the erosion of democracy and the deterioration of the rule of law, media and academic freedom in some of its new member states (Kelemen 2017; Enyedi 2018). However, there is no systematic evidence for a drastic anti-liberal turn after countries access the European Union. Börzel and Schimmelfennig (2017) do not find any significant and systematic trends in the level of democracy, once new member states have accessed the Union, although other studies indicate that after this crucial moment, the speed at which new members implement pro-democratic reforms slows down (Levitz and Pop-Eleches 2010). However, Levitz and Pop-Eleches' analysis only includes two post-accession years, and stops before the global financial crisis of 2008, while Börzel and Schimmelfennig rely on means across countries in the region, assuming homogeneity in the pre – and post-accession effects.

Different from these analyses, we employ our new multi-dimensional measure of the quality of democracy, tracing heterogeneous developments, and distinguish between periods of conditionality and post-accession. In particular, we assume that conditionality is in play only before countries make the step towards a higher level of integration, while post-accession fatigue only becomes a factor after countries have reached a more intensive degree of integration. To assess the role of conditionality and EU accession,

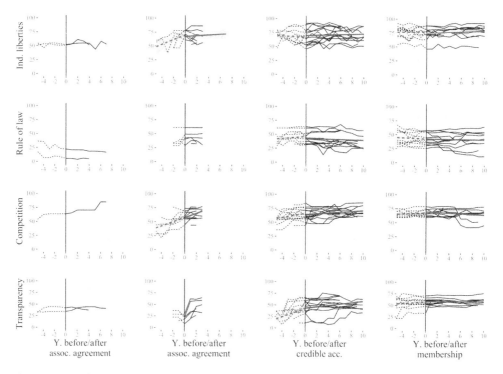

Figure 4. EU political integration and trends in the quality of democracy (selected functions) (For all 9 functions, see appendix, figure B2).

we use the four levels of integration identified by Börzel and Schimmelfennig (2017): Association Agreements, weakly credible accession perspectives, credible accession perspectives, and EU membership.[16]

Figure 4 assesses the development of democratic functions in the time period including the 5 years before and the 10 years after the four steps of EU integration, focusing again on the most volatile dimensions of the quality of democracy (see appendix B2 for a full assessment). In brief, it indicates that EU integration is a success story for the quality of democracy before membership is achieved, although the trajectories become heterogeneous thereafter.

A first insight is that significant advances in democratic qualities occur *right before* countries are offered *weakly credible accession perspectives*, which is due to important reforms passed at these crucial points in time. These advances are related to several democratic functions. One case, which drives this effect in particular, in the field of *competition*, is Croatia. It has reformed its electoral system, while Albania improved its rules on party funding in 2000. Competition also *de facto* improved in Romania in 1992, in Macedonia in 1998, and in Albania and Croatia in 2000-2001. In the fields of *individual liberties*, the *rule of law* and the *public sphere*, the three Baltic States (Estonia, Latvia, Lithuania) passed their post-Soviet constitutions in 1992/1993, or reinforced pre-Soviet constitutions with more expansive provisions. In particular, they introduced or reinstated constitutional rules concerning the protection of individual liberties, and rights and liberties related to public communication, the independence and professionalism of the justice system and public trials. Albania experienced a significant improvement in the area of law and order in 1998, after public security was reformed in 1997. In contrast, *transparency* improved in several countries (Croatia, Estonia, Latvia, Serbia and Montenegro, Slovenia) right after they were granted weakly credible accession perspectives, rather than before.

A second major improvement across multiple cases and dimensions occurs in the years *before* countries are offered *credible accession perspectives*: Representation became more *inclusive* in Poland in 1993, in Albania in 2001, and in Macedonia in 2002. *Political competition* intensified in Romania in 1993, in Latvia in 1996, in Lithuania 1997, and in Bosnia–Herzegovina in 2001. In many places, constitutions were also amended at these points in time, guaranteeing freedoms related to the *public sphere*. This concerned, in particular freedoms of association, assembly speech and/or of the press, for example in Latvia in 1997, in Lithuania and Poland in 1993, and in Slovenia in 1994. Furthermore, the public sphere improved *de facto* in Croatia in 2002. Similarly, *transparency* increased due to improvements in press freedom (legally and de facto), and due to party finance disclosure rules in several countries (Poland in 1991 and 1993, in Slovenia in 1994, Estonia and Latvia around 1993-1995, and Lithuania by 1997). Hungary lifted legal restrictions on freedom of information between 1990 and 1992. Croatia lifted restrictions on freedom of information around 2000-2003, and introduced effective press freedom, both legally and in practice. In neighbouring Serbia-Montenegro, this step occurred simultaneously, but was less successful: in 2003, press freedom was under threat, and corruption prevailed.

In contrast to advances due to accession perspectives, *EU membership* itself is not systematically associated with improvements in the quality of democracy, with our measures failing to pick up any homogeneous trend. Three governments became more *transparent* in the years before their countries became EU members. Slovakia in 2001 and Poland in 2002 lifted restrictions on freedom of information. Slovakia also improved the legal environment for press freedom and Romania introduced legislation for transparent party financing in 2003.

In addition to these improvements, we also find evidence for several instances of democratic erosion occurring at different stages of the EU accession process. Some countries experienced important relapses in some of their democratic functions in the aftermath of EU accession, for example the aforementioned cases of Hungary, Slovakia, Bulgaria, and of the Czech Republic. However, such backslides on some democratic functions occur not only in EU members, but also in countries with Association Agreements (e.g. Moldova, Ukraine) and those with future membership perspectives (Albania, Serbia). Among EU member states, they occur in those governed by populist governments (e.g. rule of law and individual liberties in Bulgaria, Slovakia), as well as in those by non-populists (same functions, in Poland, 2009, or Romania, 2010-2012). Hence, while association agreements are often associated with an improvement in some of the democratic functions analysed, EU membership is neither a sufficient, nor a necessary condition, not even in conjunction with further factors analysed in this article, for changes in any of our functions of democracy. Once countries become EU members, their pathways are very heterogeneous.

In sum, on the ladder of European integration, the most important positive steps for the quality of democracy occur in the initial stages where countries aim for either weak or strong commitments in order to achieve integration into the Union. Less important is the last step – EU membership – as well as other forms of association, which do not come with the promise of later membership. The improvements are based on the logic of conditionality: reforms with regards to individual liberties, minority protection, rule of law, transparency, etc. occur *before*, and not *after* reaching a new stage of integration. Once a new step of integration is reached, the EU instruments provide little leverage, unless the EU in in a position to reward democratic progress with even further integration.

4.3. Process 3: the consequences of the financial crisis

A third factor that is an often-cited driver of alleged regional erosion of the quality of democracy is the global financial crisis of 2008. In particular, it has spawned significant concerns about how young democracies can cope with economic turmoil (Bermeo and Bartels 2014; Kriesi and Pappas 2015). The severe economic consequences which a number of democracies in the region have suffered in the wake of the financial crisis have direct and indirect implications for political regimes. First, they can lead to a collapse

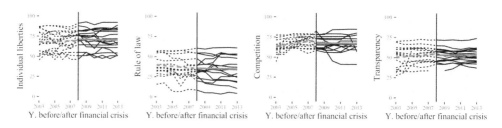

Figure 5. The financial crisis of 2008 and the quality of democracy (selected functions) (For all 9 functions, see appendix, figure B3)

of trust in political institutions and dissatisfaction with democracy (Armingeon and Guthmann 2014). Second, social unrest can precipitate the collapse of governments. Third, the preoccupation of European Union institutions with stabilising the financial sector and the common currency reduces the Union's capacity to deal with democracy-related issues and precipitates enlargement fatigue, thus curtailing the enlargement effect on the quality of democracy in not-yet member states.

In order to assess these arguments, Figure 5 plots four democratic functions before and after 2008. However, we do not find a reversal of the regional trends after the crisis for any of the nine functions (see also appendix, figure B3). Four countries (Bosnia and Herzegovina, Bulgaria, Croatia, Hungary) experienced important backslides in individual liberties after the financial crisis, partly because of civil and political rights violations by states, reported by Amnesty International and US State Department reports. In two countries (Bulgaria, Slovakia), the rule of law suffered, and in Moldova the pre-existing crisis of rule of law deepened further. In Albania and in Hungary, competition deteriorated, and the governing parties became more dominant. However, beyond these individual cases, our more systematic assessment of political developments across the region corroborates Ekiert's (2013) observation that the financial crisis has not initiated an illiberal turn in Central and Eastern Europe. Instead, this occurred only where authoritarian parties in power managed to channel the grievances against the liberal institutions.

5. Discussion

Since the 1990s, the countries of Central and Eastern Europe have seen an unusually fast transition towards, and a consolidation of, democracy. Has this trend now started to reverse and has the region moved into a period of de-consolidation of democratic rule, a period of defective democracies with illiberal features? Both the academic and the public debate have centred around such a purported anti-liberal backslide (Rupnik 2018). Prominent explanations for the perceived erosion in the quality of democracy include the rise of populist-authoritarian parties that dominate the national governments in several countries of Central and Eastern Europe (Brusis 2016; Bustikova and Guasti 2017), the inability of the European Union to enforce democratic standards after countries have been granted membership (Sedelmeier 2014; Kelemen 2017), and the economic and political consequences of the global financial crisis of 2008 (e.g. Bermeo and Bartels 2014; Brusis 2016).

This paper offers a new, systematic assessment of this alleged illiberal turn of Central and Eastern European democracies. It compares the trajectory of the quality of democracy across all democracies in Central and Eastern Europe, relying on a newly extended dataset covering nine dimensions of the quality of democracy, which is based on objective indicators. It examines the trends in the quality of democracy in light of the three above-mentioned explanations, analysing both the overall regional trend as well as subsets of countries. In brief, while it finds correlational evidence consistent with purported democratic effects of populist governments and the EU accession process, it does not detect any systematic changes associated with the financial crisis.

As regards the former, the rise of populist actors, the article finds that Central and Eastern Europe has seen the meteoric rise of newcomer political parties long before this trend spread to Western Europe (Sikk 2012). Some of these parties ran with a populist programme, and by 2016, every one of the 17 countries of the region for which we have measures of populism available experienced at least one episode of a populist party in government. Populists view themselves as correctors of democracy. In their eyes, the institutions of horizontal accountability, and some liberal rights are tools in the hands of corrupt elites. They decry what they perceive to be the excessive protection of minority rights, weakening the majoritarian principle of democracies (Houle and Kenny 2018). Instead, they want to strengthen vertical accountability, strictly following the "will of the people" – a combination of majoritarian and plebiscitary ideas.

The analysis of the quality of democracy in Central and Eastern Europe finds mixed evidence for these purported effects of populists in government. In some cases, they are clearly associated with changes in the quality of democracy: The most important patterns thereof which the Democracy Barometer reports are a reduction of political competition and moves towards less transparent governments during populist rule. While our objective indicators identify, to a considerable extent, the same backsliding democracies as expert-based data (Lührmann et al. 2018, 1327), the insights gained from our analysis (limited to 2016) rebuff the alarmist view of a deep and widespread crisis of democracy. Different from studies of other regions (Huber and Schimpf 2016b), we identify several populist governments that have not left any mark on the quality of democracy, while others have even made changes that reduce future opportunities to exert popular control. However, our empirical assessment is also not in line with the view of populists as a corrective (Huber and Ruth 2017). Developments in the quality of democracy are not uniform in the region, and the observable footprints of populist-authoritarian governments on the quality of democracy appear highly context-dependent.

As regards the process of European integration, the article overall confirms the assessment that it advances the quality of democracy in the region. This appears to occur right before the countries take steps on the ladder of European integration, in particular in the earlier stages of the process of European integration, when countries are aiming for either weak or strong commitments for integration into the Union. However, after countries have taken steps towards European integration, they can de-consolidate, owing to a lack of disciplinary instruments. Such steps backwards have occurred in EU member states (Hungary, Slovakia, Bulgaria, and of the Czech Republic), but not only there. In many ways, the deterioration of the public sphere and of transparency of government action under the Vučić presidency in Serbia (outside the EU), closely resembles the deterioration of press freedom under the Orbán administration in Hungary. In Macedonia and Serbia, governments have profited from the fragility of the political and legal institutions and the media system. They have used democratic weaknesses to consolidate their partisan control of the state, while dismantling liberties and horizontal controls (e.g. Esen and Gumuscu 2016; Bieber 2018). Political pluralism in Serbia and Hungary has been erased by dominant ruling parties, which have further consolidated their rule through changes to electoral laws and rules on party funding.

In spite of indicating a crucial role for both populism and the EU accession process, the article cannot confirm an overall regional trend that is attributable to the two. While drastic cases, such as Hungary and, more recently, Poland, that highlight both the influence of populist actors and the weakness of EU instruments are given extensive media and academic spotlight, they do not seem representative for the region. Our assessment indicates that there is relatively limited backsliding until 2016, which can be observed by relying on objective quantitative data (though some important anti-constitutional moves have taken place since, esp. in Poland, cf. Sata and Karolewski 2020). They are counterbalanced by improvements to the quality of democracy in other cases.

None of the three explanations this article has investigated is either sufficient or necessary on its own to explain erosions in the quality of democracy. If the quality of democracy in Central and Eastern Europe is understood as a competition between the European Union and populist-illiberal leaders, then the score remained undecided as of 2016: The accession of CEE democracies to the EU means that the EU loses its trump card – conditionality. However, the quality of democracy remains stable in most of the new EU member states. While the global financial crisis of 2008 slowed down enlargement, and therefore weakened the power of the conditionality card regarding non-members, it was not followed by a genuine backslide. The incapacity of the Union to prevent major backsliding in member-states (Hungary, Poland) and non-members (Serbia, Ukraine) might, however, be read as a green light to populist-authoritarian governments across Europe to take authoritarian measures and compromise the EU's capacity to sustain the quality of democracy. In this way, rather than only exhibiting unsystematic, localised impacts, the authoritarian footprints left by populist actors may be felt more strongly across the region in the years to come.

Notes

1. We define "democratic backsliding" or "erosion of the quality of democracy" as a gradual deterioration of democracy or some democratic principles (Waldner and Lust 2018), i.e. changes within a political regime of democracy. Authoritarian backlashes are understood as a process of de-democratisation.
2. But see Börzel and Schimmelfennig (2017), who study post-accession dynamics. However, their analysis of regional and sub-regional means does not allow the identification of heterogeneous country developments.
3. Albania, Bosnia and Herzegovina, Bulgaria, Croatia, Czech Republic, Estonia, Hungary, Latvia, Lithuania, Macedonia, Moldova, Montenegro (2006–2016), Poland, Romania, Serbia (2006–2016), Serbia and Montenegro (2001–2005), Slovakia, Slovenia, the Ukraine. As for Kosovo many indicators are missing, it is only included in parts of the analysis.
4. We also include Bosnia and Herzegovina, which Polity IV does not rate as a democracy due to the international supervision active there. We do so because Bosnia and Herzegovina has fully developed domestic institutions.
5. In addition, the figure also shows periods of populist parties in governing cabinets. The operationalization for this factor is discussed in section 4.1 below.
6. For instance, Latvia suffers from a lack of inclusive participation and representation. A weak civil society, and informal practices and a deteriorating public confidence in the justice system weaken the rule of law in Latvia, Lithuania and Slovenia. (Bugarič and Kuhelj 2015).
7. In our supplementary material, appendix A provides corresponding results for all nine functions.
8. Alternatively, populism is seen as a "corrective" to the current state of democracy, eliminating allegedly corrupt elites' control of the state (through horizontal accountability, and some of liberal rights), simultaneously freeing it from the grip of minorities, and instead strengthening vertical accountability (Ruth and Hawkins 2017), revitalising participation, including the participation of lower classes (Anduiza, Guinjoan, and Rico 2019).
9. Where the sources coded presidential candidates (in particular, Huber and Schimpf 2016b) or chief executives (in particular, Hawkins 2009, 2013), we first looked up these individuals' party affiliations with a quick web-based search.

10. The sources differ slightly in their definition of populism, and we combine sources that identify the populist left, right, and the centre. Where several sources exist for the same party, we accept a single identification as populist as sufficient. Most sources directly code political parties in a dichotomous way. Where previous sources used a continuous measure of populism, we define a cut-off point (0.5 for the measures provided by (Hawkins 2009, 2013; Hawkins and Silva 2016).
11. We extrapolated the eight sources for each party in our dataset across the maximum time period (1990–2016), regardless of their time coverage. Following our sources, our aggregated measure allows for changes in a particular party's populism status over time. We did not extrapolate across a party year if at least one source codes a change in the populist status at that point. For example, van Kessel (2015) codes the Hungarian Fidesz party as populist only from 2006 (and as not populist before). Consequently, we did not extrapolate any other source's measure (for which some of the election periods were missing) across this time period.
12. Even though we combined a large number of sources to obtain as broad a coverage as possible, we were still unable to code populist status for a number of mostly smaller or more recently-emerged parties. In order to keep a maximum of information in, we kept country years where at least one governing party is populist (and where, according to our measure, the maximum degree of populist power access is thus already achieved, no matter how any missing parties are coded), and country years for which we have populist status data of at least two-thirds of the governing coalitions' seats (i.e., if we lacked data on a small coalition partner. If the size of the uncoded coalition partner was at least 33% of the total seat share of the governing coalition, we discarded the country-year). Out of a total of 988 parties that form the basis of the country years in our analysis, we have populism data for 861.
13. Defined as governments with a seat share of 67% or larger in parliament, under participation of populists. We follow Huber & Schimpf's argument according to which the presence of at least one populist party in government suffices to decisively influence policy outcomes. For simplicity's sake we do not consider the special case of surplus cabinets where populist government parties have an arguably smaller influence (Huber and Schimpf 2016a).
14. See model results reported in Online Appendix B, calculated for all functions with at least ten separate periods.
15. We find significant coefficients for populist governments or oppositions in our full models (appendix, tables B1a and B1b), e.g. on competition or constraints, or representation. Where these coefficients are minuscule and are attained in specifications without controls for time-variant confounders, we do not consider them as sufficient evidence for a discussion in the paper.
16. We omit Neighbourhood Policy. Our sample contains too few country years for this weakest form of integration.

Acknowledgments

We are very grateful to Michelle Roos for invaluable coding assistance. We thank Sascha Kneip, Timofei Agarin, and participants at ECPR General Conference, Hamburg 2018, the annual meeting of the Serbian Political Science Association 2018, Belgrade, and seminars at the University Kyiv/Molhya Academy for helpful comments. We have received generous financial support from the Swiss National Science Foundation (NCCR Democracy) and the Centre for Democracy Studies Aarau (ZDA).

Disclosure statement

No potential conflict of interest was reported by the authors.

ORCID

Daniel Bochsler http://orcid.org/0000-0001-6423-5560
Andreas Juon http://orcid.org/0000-0003-1803-6688

References

Agarin, Timofey. 2020. "The (not so) Surprising Longevity of Identity Politics: Contemporary Challenges of the State–Society Compact in Central Eastern Europe." *East European Politics* 36 (3).
Anduiza, Eva, Marc Guinjoan, and Guillem Rico. 2019. "Populism, Participation, and Political Equality." *European Political Science Review* 11 (1): 109–124
Armingeon, Klaus, and Kai Guthmann. 2014. "Democracy in Crisis? The Declining Support for National Democracy in European Countries, 2007–2011." *European Journal of Political Research* 53 (3): 423–442.
Bermeo, Nancy, and Larry M. Bartels. 2014. *Mass Politics in Tough Times: Opinions, Votes and Protest in the Great Recession.* Oxford: Oxford University Press.
Bieber, Florian. 2018. "Patterns of Competitive Authoritarianism in the Western Balkans." *East European Politics* 34 (3): 337–354.
Bochsler, Daniel, and Miriam Hänni. 2019. "The Three Stages of the Anti-Incumbency Vote: Retrospective Economic Voting in Young and Established Democracies." *European Journal of Political Research* 58 (1): 30–55.
Bochsler, Daniel, and Andreas Juon. 2018. "*Authoritarian Footprints: The Transformation of Democracy, 1990–2016.*" Paper presented at the ECPR General Conference, Hamburg, 22–25 August.
Bochsler, Daniel, and Hanspeter Kriesi. 2013. "Varieties of Democracy." In *Democracy in the Age of Globalization and Mediatization*, edited by Hanspeter Kriesi, Sandra Lavenex, Frank Esser, Jörg Matthes, Marc Bühlmann, and Daniel Bochsler, 69–102. Hondmills: Palgrave.
Börzel, Tanja A., and Frank Schimmelfennig. 2017. "Coming Together or Drifting Apart? The EU's Political Integration Capacity in Eastern Europe." *Journal of European Public Policy* 24 (2): 278–296.
Brusis, Martin. 2016. "Democracies Adrift? How the European Crises Affect East-Central Europe." *Problems of Post-Communism* 63 (5): 263–276.
Bugarič, Bojan, and Tom Ginsburg. 2016. "The Assault on Postcommunist Courts." *Journal of Democracy* 27 (3): 69–82.
Bugarič, Bojan, and Alenka Kuhelj. 2015. "Slovenia in Crisis: A Tale of Unfinished Democratization in East-Central Europe." *Communist and Post-Communist Studies* 48: 273–279.
Bustikova, Lenka, and Petra Guasti. 2017. "The Illiberal Turn or Swerve in Central Europe?" *Politics and Governance* 5 (4): 166–176.
Bühlmann, Marc, Wolfgang Merkel, Lisa Müller, and Bernhard Weßels. 2012. "The Democracy Barometer: A New Instrument to Measure the Quality of Democracy and its Potential for Comparative Research." *European Political Science* 11 (4): 519–536.
Carothers, Thomas. 2015. "Democracy Aid at 25: Time to Choose." *Journal of Democracy* 26 (1): 59–73.
Cianetti, Licia, James Dawson, and Seán Hanley. 2018. "Rethinking 'Democratic Backsliding' in Central and Eastern Europe - Looking Beyond Hungary and Poland." *East European Politics* 34 (3): 243–256.
Diamond, Larry. 2002. "Thinking About Hybrid Regimes." *Journal of Democracy* 13 (2): 21–35.
Diamond, Larry. 2015. "Facing Up to the Democratic Recession." *Journal of Democracy* 26 (1): 141–155.
Diamond, Larry, and Leonardo Morlino. 2004. "The Quality of Democracy. An Overview." *Journal of Democracy* 15 (4): 20–31.
Dimitrova, Antoaneta, and Geoffrey Pridham. 2004. "International Actors and Democracy Promotion in Central and Eastern Europe: The Integration Model and its Limits." *Democratization* 11 (5): 91–112.

Ekiert, Grzegorz. 2013. "The Illiberal Challenge in Post-Communist Europe. Surprises and Puzzles." *Taiwan Journal of Democracy* 8 (2): 63–77.

Enyedi, Zsolt. 2016. "Populist Polarization and Party System Institutionalization. The Role of Party Politics in De-Democratization." *Problems of Post-Communism* 63 (4): 210–220.

Enyedi, Zsolt. 2018. "Democratic Backsliding and Academic Freedom in Hungary." *Perspectives on Politics* 16 (4): 1067–1074.

Esen, Berk, and Sebnem Gumuscu. 2016. "Rising Competitive Authoritarianism in Turkey." *Third World Quarterly* 37 (9): 1581–1606.

Freedom House. 2018. *Democracy in Crisis - Freedom in the World 2018*. Washington, DC: Freedom House.

Freyburg, Tina, and Solveig Richter. 2010. "National Identity Matters: The Limited Impact of EU Political Conditionality in the Western Balkans." *Journal of European Public Policy* 17 (2): 263–281.

Grzymala-Busse, Anna. 2017. "Global Populisms and Their Impact." *Slavic Review* 76 (S1): S3–S8.

Hanley, Seán, and Allan Sikk. 2016. "Economy, Corruption or Floating Voters? Explaining the Breakthroughs of Anti-Establishment Reform Parties in Eastern Europe." *Party Politics* 22 (4): 522–533.

Hawkins, Kirk A. 2009. "Is Chávez Populist? Measuring Populist Discourse in Comparative Perspective." *Comparative Political Studies* 42 (8): 1040–1067.

Hawkins, Kirk A. 2013. "Measuring Populism in Comparative Perspective." In Paper presented at the XXXI International Congress of the Latin American Studies Association, Washington, DC, May 29–June 1.

Hawkins, Kirk A., and Bruno Castanho Silva. 2016. *A Head-to-Head Comparison of Human-Based and Automated Text Analysis for Measuring Populism in 27 Countries*. Provo, UT: Brigham Young University.

Houle, Christian, and Paul D. Kenny. 2018. "The Political and Economic Consequences of Populist Rule in Latin America." *Government and Opposition* 53 (2): 256–287.

Huber, Robert A., and Saskia P. Ruth. 2017. "Mind the Gap! Populism, Participation and Representation in Europe." *Swiss Political Science Review* 23 (4): 462–484.

Huber, Robert A., and Christian H. Schimpf. 2016a. "A Drunken Guest in Europe? The Influence of Populist Radical Right Parties on Democratic Quality." *Zeitschrift für Vergleichende Politikwissenschaft* 10: 103–129.

Huber, Robert A., and Christian H. Schimpf. 2016b. "Friend or Foe? Testing the Influence of Populism on Democratic Quality in Latin America." *Political Studies* 64 (4): 872–889.

Huszka, Beáta. 2018. "Human Rights on the Losing End of EU Enlargement: The Case of Serbia." *JCMS: Journal of Common Market Studies* 56 (2): 352–367.

Kelemen, R. Daniel. 2017. "Europe's Other Democratic Deficit: National Authoritarianism in Europe's Democratic Union." *Government and Opposition* 52 (2): 211–238.

Krekó, Péter, and Zsolt Enyedi. 2018. "Orban's Laboratory of Illiberalism." *Journal of Democracy* 29 (3): 39–51.

Kriesi, Hanspeter, and Takis S. Pappas. 2015. "Populism in Europe During Crisis: An Introduction." In *European Populism in the Shadow of the Great Recession*, edited by Hanspeter Kriesi, and Takis S. Pappas, 1–19. Colchester: ECPR Press.

Levitsky, Steven, and Daniel Ziblatt. 2018. *How Democracies Die*. New York: Crown.

Levitz, Philip, and Grigore Pop-Eleches. 2010. "Why No Backsliding? The European Union's Impact on Democracy and Governance Before and After Accession." *Comparative Political Studies* 43 (4): 457–485.

Lijphart, Arend. 1999. *Patterns of Democracy. Government Forms and Performance in Thirty-Six Countries*. New Haven: Yale University Press.

Luce, Edward. 2017. *The Retreat of Western Liberalism*. New York: Atlantic Monthly Press.

Lührmann, Anna, Valeriya Mechkova, Sirianne Dahlum, Laura Maxwell, Moa Olin, Constanza Sanhueza Petrarca, Rachel Sigman, Matthew C. Wilson, and Staffan I. Lindberg. 2018. "State of the World 2017: Autocratization and Exclusion?" *Democratization* 25 (8): 1321–1340.

March, Luke. 2011. *Radical Left Parties in Europe*. Abingdon: Routledge.

Merkel, Wolfgang. 2004. "Embedded and Defective Democracies." *Democratization* 11 (5): 33–58.

Merkel, Wolfgang. 2015. *Demokratie und Krise. Zum schwierigen Verhältnis von Theorie und Empirie*. Wiesbaden: Springer.

Merkel, Wolfgang, Daniel Bochsler, Karima Bousbah, Marc Buhlmann, Heiko Giebler, Miriam Hänni, Lea Heyne, et al. 2018. "Democracy Barometer. Methodology. Version 5." Zentrum für Demokratie. www.democracybarometer.org.

Mishler, William, and Richard Rose. 1996. "Trajectories of Fear and Hope. Support for Democracy in Post-Communist Europe." *Comparative Political Studies* 28 (4): 553–581.

Morlino, Leonardo. 2004. "What is a 'Good' Democracy?" *Journal of Democracy* 11 (5): 10–32.

Morlino, Leonardo, and Mario Quaranta. 2016. "What is the Impact of the Economic Crisis on Democracy? Evidence From Europe." *International Political Science Review* 37 (5): 618–633.

Mounk, Yasha. 2018. *The People vs. Democracy*. Cambridge, MA: Harvard University Press.

Mudde, Cas. 2004. "The Populist Zeitgeist." *Government and Opposition* 39 (4): 542–563.

Mudde, Cas. 2011. *Populist Radical Right Parties in Europe*. Cambridge: Cambridge University Press.

Mudde, Cas, and Cristóbal Rovira Kaltwasser. 2012a. "Populism and (Liberal) Democracy." In *Populism in Europe and the Americas. Threat or Corrective for Democracy?*, edited by Cas Mudde, and Cristóbal Rovira Kaltwasser, 1–26. Cambridge: Cambridge University Press.

Mudde, Cas, and Cristóbal Rovira Kaltwasser. 2012b. "Populism: Corrective and Threat to Democracy." In *Populism in Europe and the Americas. Threat or Corrective for Democracy?*, edited by Cas Mudde, and Cristóbal Rovira Kaltwasser, 205–222. Cambridge: Cambridge University Press.

Pehe, Jiri. 2018. "Czech Democracy Under Pressure." *Journal of Democracy* 29 (3): 65–77.

Pevehouse, Jon C. 2002. "With a Little Help from My Friend? Regional Organizations and the Consolidation of Democracy." *American Journal of Political Science* 46 (3): 611–626.

Powell, G. Bingham Jr. 2000. *Elections as Instruments of Democracy. Majoritarian and Proportional Visions*. New Haven/London: Yale University Press.

Rupnik, Jacques. 2007. "From Democracy Fatigue to Populist Backlash." *Journal of Democracy* 18 (4): 17–25.

Rupnik, Jacques. 2018. "The Crisis of Liberalism." *Journal of Democracy* 29 (3): 24–38.

Ruth, Saskia P., and Kirk A. Hawkins. 2017. "Populism and Democratic Representation in Latin America." In *Handbook on Political Populism*, edited by R. Heinisch, Oskar Mazzoleni, and C. Holtz-Bacha, 255–273. Baden-Baden: Nomos.

Sandurski, Wojciech. 2019. *Poland's Constitutional Breakdown*. Oxford: Oxford University Press.

Sata, Robert, and Pawel Ireneusz Karolewski. 2020. "Caesarean Politics in Hungary and Poland." *East European Politics* 36 (3).

Schimmelfennig, Frank. 2005. "Strategic Calculation and International Socialization: Membership Incentives, Party Constellations, and Sustained Compliance in Central and Eastern Europe." *International Organization* 59: 827–860.

Schimmelfennig, Frank, and Ulrich Sedelmeier. 2004. "Governance by Conditionality: EU Rule Transfer to the Candidate Countries of Central and Eastern Europe." *Journal of European Public Policy* 11 (4): 661–679.

Sedelmeier, Ulrich. 2014. "Anchoring Democracy from Above? The European Union and Democratic Backsliding in Hungary and Romania After Accession." *JCMS: Journal of Common Market Studies* 52 (1): 105–121.

Sikk, Allan. 2012. "Newness as a Winning Formula for New Political Parties." *Party Politics* 18 (4): 465–486.

Silva, Bruno Castanho, and Levente Littvay. 2019. "Comparative Research is Harder Than we Thought: Regional Differences in Experts' Understanding of Electoral Integrity Questions." *Political Analysis* 27 (4): 599–604.

Snyder, Timothy. 2018. *The Road to Unfreedom*. New York: Tim Duggan Books.

van Kessel, Stijn. 2015. *Populist Parties in Europe: Agents of Discontent*. Basingstoke: Palgrave.

Waldner, David, and Ellen Lust. 2018. "Unwelcome Change: Coming to Terms with Democratic Backsliding." *Annual Review of Political Science* 21: 91–113.

Weak pluralism and shallow democracy: the rise of identity politics in Bulgaria and Romania

Kiril Kolev

ABSTRACT
The rise of identity politics has been surprising in two countries that have benefitted extensively from EU membership. To address the puzzle, the paper suggests that the EU vision of common and inclusive identity, grounded in a formal set of rules, had its strongest effect before and immediately after accession. Yet, its intensity was short-lived and mistaken for a popular embrace of multiculturalism. To understand this dynamic, the paper traces the interactions between citizens and elites, as well as the tradeoffs and complementarities between democracy and legitimacy in the two countries.

Introduction

Robert Dahl outlined five conditions that are conducive to sustaining democratic institutions: control of military and policy by elected officials, democratic beliefs and political culture, no strong foreign control hostile to democracy, a modern market economy, and weak subcultural pluralism (Dahl 1998). To him, a country that is missing one or more of the defining elements is a polyarchy – a term used to distinguish the ideal type of democracy from what we often observe in reality.

Three of the five criteria listed above are especially important when examining recent trends in Central and Eastern Europe (CEE): the absence of strong foreign influence hostile to democracy, weak subcultural pluralism, and the presence of democratic beliefs and political culture. This paper suggests that Romania and Bulgaria have general publics that, while committed to competitive elections and favourable of democracy in a broad sense, have not embraced the tolerance and minority rights that the subcultural pluralism criterion requires. Therefore, sustained foreign pressure from the European Union for the adoption of mechanisms and rules that protect smaller groups without infringing on their identities has been seen as foreign control that has been inconsistent with the will of the majority and is therefore undemocratic. The two countries, therefore, suggest that the five criteria by Dahl are not always compatible and public understandings of democracy might also mean minority exclusion and disillusionment with foreign pressure that is pro-liberal, but perhaps contrary to the general will.

In 1989, the non-democratic influence of the Soviet Union gave way to the liberal allure of the European Union. It is easy to classify this profound change as a pro-democratic one: after all, the new role models for the former Eastern Bloc countries were all developed and established democracies. The assumption that joining the West would bring about liberalism and democracy, however, equates liberalism with democracy. While the EU principles of accession promote certain basic rights and freedoms, their adoption can be classified as democratic only if it corresponds to a genuine popular embrace of pluralism and tolerance among the newly empowered voting citizens of each country. In many CEE countries, however, the general public retained a well-established preference for majoritarianism which assumed dominance and lack of true pluralism throughout the entire post-communist experience. As pointed out in the introduction to this special issue, elites adopted a strategy of plebiscitary rule that tried to capitalise on majoritarian sentiments while pushing technocratic EU reforms, behaving as if EU liberalism would not come into conflict with majoritarian dominance preferences.

The aftermath of this approach to governance is well catalogued by recent research that highlights the exacerbated split between the people and the state that has resulted in populism (Bustikova and Guasti 2017) or reduced media freedom and rule of law (Authors Bochsler and Juon, this issue). The concept of polyarchy reminds us that it is possible to have competitive regimes that curb certain essential rights and freedoms. What this paper suggests is that the external imposition of liberalism in polyarchical regimes can undermine the consolidation of democracy in the long term. In other words, the process of transplanting Western norms of pluralism to Central and Eastern Europe was inconsistent with popular opinion that was much more rigid and intolerant. The current political backlash in Eastern Europe should be understood within this context.

This paper employs Dahl's foundational framework of democratic pluralism to shed some light on identity politics in Bulgaria and Romania. Both countries experienced a shift from communist control to pro-liberal EU influence in the early 1990s. Their citizens have been consistently in favour of democracy. However, their commitment to reducing the political importance of cultural cleavages has been faltering, albeit in somewhat different ways. Romania faced the possibility of ethnic conflict early on in its transition and took decisive steps to appease minorities. By the time the European Union accession put pluralism front and centre, it had already grappled with some challenges of the multi-culturalism-nationalism divide.

In Bulgaria, where minorities make up a larger share of the population, the initial period of democratisation saw elites and publics that largely glossed over multicultural issues. EU accession then caught Bulgarian citizens and political elites by surprise. The haphazard attempts towards pluralism that were taken in the early 2000s caused a nationalist counter-reaction that was further amplified by the broader economic and cultural issues that Europe faced in 2008. Consequently, today Bulgaria is more divided and perhaps even less tolerant of minority issues than ever. Repressive majoritarianism has spilled over from ethnic identities to broader cultural issues, such as gender equality and LGBTQ rights. This shift is lamented by some as immoral and primitive. What is less often discussed is that this reaction is also democratic, insofar as it reflects broad dissatisfaction with external pressures and plebiscitary domestic rule that have been inconsistent with societal preferences for a long time.

A polyarchical theory of identity politics

Two aspects of Dahl's three preconditions of democracy are evident in existing explanations of democratisation. Some point out that democracy is imperfect whenever it is imposed "from above" (Bunce 2003; Janos et al. 1999; Reynolds 2005). According to this school of thought, pro-liberal external influences are not nearly as important as an embrace of democracy on behalf of the publics. The alternative "bottom up" source of democracy, however, takes much longer. As argued by Charles Tilly, more successful democratizations have happened *in spite of* political elites and have featured prolonged negotiations between the publics and the elites that have yielded gradual concessions, rather than wholesale institutional reforms (Tilly 1995).

This framework has been used by scholars of Central and Eastern Europe extensively. Some point to the imperfect commitment to democracy by domestic elites and the general publics (Dimitrova 2018; Hughes, Sasse, and Gordon 2005). Other attribute success or failure to external actors alone (Kelley 2008; Knaus and Martin 2003). Finally, some point out that international and pro-democratic domestic actors interact (Escobar 2000; Jacoby et al. 2006).

Dahl's framework of polyarchy is worth revisiting in the CEE context because is highlights two questionable assumptions. First, it shines light on the distinction between commitment to democracy and commitment to pluralism. "Weak subcultural pluralism" is particularly helpful to understand this. It suggests that minority identities should be protected and the interests that stem from them respected. This type of pluralism is "weak", insofar as it is accommodated before it could potentially lead to conflict and minority dissatisfaction that could threaten the overall integrity of the state. It assumes that the majority prefers conciliation to homogenisation of minorities and their gradual adoption to the culture and identity of the majority. However, this scenario might not always play out. When analysing the role that domestic actors play in governance, we should not conflate a desire for competitive elections and responsiveness to the will of the majority with acceptance of minority rights. It is possible that certain countries have publics that prefer a majoritarian (or even tyrannical) regime that does not pay attention to the specific preferences of smaller voter groups but does conduct elections with integrity and has a government that is responsive to the will of the majority. In Dahl's framework, such a society might exhibit commitment to democracy, but lack weak subcultural pluralism.

Second, in such illiberal but pro-democracy societies, international actors that equate liberalism and democracy could face a complicated tradeoff. On the one hand, they need to encourage the presence of free, fair and competitive elections. On the other, insofar as these elections reliably deliver governments that exclude minorities, democracy means control by majority over that might repeatedly fail to lead to weak subcultural pluralism. If international actors push towards minority empowerment, they can easily be seen as acting against the popular will and therefore undemocratic. In Dahl's framework, this will add another polyarchical element: the presence of foreign influence that is not conducive to democracy.

This paradox exemplifies the dilemma that the European Union has faced in Bulgaria and Romania. To trace the somewhat different dynamics in the two countries, this paper focuses on the interaction between three collective actors over time: the general public, the domestic political elite and the European Union elite. In Bulgaria and Romania, they have interacted during three distinct periods: early transition (1989 – late 1990s), pre-accession (late 1990s – 2007) and post accession (2007 to present).

Over time, the three actors can be analysed in terms of the extent to which they emphasise governance on the basis national identity versus pluralism. For example, an emphasis on dominant national identity represents a narrowly-defined majority in-group that has the final say in terms of political decisions. In its most extreme form, this scenario features a dominant group's monopolisation of political institutions and decisions, even when this means marginalisation and exclusion of non-dominant minorities. Alternatively, an emphasis on pluralism represents the opposite situation, whereby a dominant group does not exist either because of high levels of homogeneity or a fluid majority that features all sorts of different smaller groups over time, neither of which is seeking or able to monopolise the decision-making process permanently.

Among the three actors, the European Union has consistently embraced a pluralist view of governance, adopting regulations and ideologies that explicitly seek to avoid the tyranny of the majority. While this preference does not have to come at the expense of national identity, it inevitably undermines the most extreme dominant version of nationalism described above. Positioning the general public, however, can be quite dynamic over time. For example, the public feeling of national pride might go up and down or the ability of a majority to coopt the levers of dominance might be suppressed or bolstered. Furthermore, national identity might switch from being a salient political issue to being diminished at the expense of other more pressing concerns. During periods of low salience, the majority might be more willing to cooperate and share power with a minority, even if it ultimately does not believe in pluralistic model of governance. Paying attention to salience in such circumstances is important: just because the majority is not exerting its will on the minority does not mean that it has permanently embraced subcultural pluralism.

The third relevant actor, the domestic political elite, has to respond to the positioning of the public vis-à-vis the European Union. This could be a relatively easy task when the public is close to the EU's ideal point of pluralism and moderate nationalism. On the other hand, the elite might find it difficult to address public preferences when national identity issues are salient and diverging from the EU's ideal point. Failure to capture and track changing public sentiment could be costly to domestic politicians. They could easily be accused of being EU's puppets and challenged by nationalist parties that would be more than happy to point out the glaring discrepancy between the public and EU view on pluralism.

At the same time, domestic political elites cannot follow public opinion to any pro-nationalist extreme. This is especially true when the same elites that are facing an electorate that is embracing dominant majoritarianism have also made official commitments to the European Union during accession. In many instances, the embrace of pluralism is so deeply rooted that it is part of the ideological DNA of a party. Engaging in identarian politics, in such circumstances, will be easily detected by the EU and also interpreted as insufficient adherence to ideological commitments by the general public. The first will yield a quick resort to conditionality by the EU, whereas the second – an accusation of bait-and-switch tactics on behalf of the citizens and political opponents.

In the end, pro-EU domestic elites might lose elections and the "tyranny of the majority" might prevail. However, this does not magically undo commitments made at the supranational level as part of European accession. Inevitably, newly empowered nationalist politicians will have to manage the inherent tension between EU community principles and the domestic popular mandate that hinges on them reasserting the exclusionary will of the majority. In trying to keep sometimes extremist politicians to accession obligations, however, the EU might find out that the disciplinary tools at its disposal might be powerful, but will be viewed increasingly as contrary to the popular will and therefore undemocratic.

This framework could be applied to the shifts observed in Bulgaria and Romania. Both countries had a history of minority repression that translated to a low public commitment to subcultural pluralism. At the same time, the general publics in both countries were very supportive of democracy and were also very sensitive to pro-pluralistic pressures by the European Union. To be sure, their paths post-communist trajectories were not identical. In Romania, ethnic tensions that led to violence activated the multiculturalism-nationalism cleavage as soon as communism collapsed. They highlighted the dangers of excluding minorities systematically. Consequently, Romania adopted more conciliatory minority provisions in its first democratic constitution. It also had to work through a period that featured both nationalist and pro-minority political parties soon after democratisation. As turbulent as this initial period was, the acknowledgment of the presence of this cleavage put Romania in a somewhat better position to openly debate and adopt the European Union and Council of Europe directives in the early 2000s.

Bulgaria's approach to its more sizeable minority population in the early 1990s was to ignore its very existence. While a pro-minority party emerged and consistently received support by the ethnic Turkish population of the country, it also played by the tacit agreement to rarely frame policy issues along ethno-cultural lines and diffuse ethnic conflict via patronage and clientelism. By the early 2000s, Bulgaria had not experienced the presence of a nationalist party, but it had also made very limited progress towards minority accommodation. When the European Union and the Council of Europe exerted pressure on the country to address the poor socio-economic conditions of the minorities, the Bulgarian political elites had to adopt legislation that pleased the West in a hurry. This led to an abrupt backlash immediately after EU accession that led to seismic shifts in the political landscape, the demise of establishment parties and the rise of nationalist rhetoric that has persisted until today.

What this paper seeks to establish, therefore, is that "polyarchy" is not some imperfect intermediate type of democracy. Rather, it could be a stable equilibrium and the preferred option in contexts where there is pronounced pro-majoritarian sentiment, coupled with deep and lasting commitment to competitive elections and representative government. Such situations could, however, highlight the fact that externally imposed liberalism could lead to perceptions that see the European Union as interventionist and even undemocratic.

Towards polyarchical democracy? Romania and Bulgaria since the 1990s

The empirical analysis is divided into four sections. The first provides an overview of trends in minority political empowerment and societal attitudes over time. These trends are then elaborated on in the qualitative narrative. More specifically, the second section focuses on the post-transition period from 1989 to the late 1990s. It summarises some key decisions about institutional design and constitutional provisions for minority representation and rights to shed a light on how the majority defined democracy and whether it was consistent with Dahl's definition of polyarchy. The third section focuses on the time immediately before and after the EU accession (2000–2007). It analyses new legislation adopted as part of the pre-accession process and the extent to which it was consistent with public preferences. It also tracks how the political platforms of political parties that were in power related to public attitudes towards pluralism. The final section provides an overview of the post-accession period. It tracks public opinion towards both the EU and identity issues, as well as the protests and challenges of elites by the general public. It also describes the new actors and the ideological shifts that established elites have had to undergo in their attempts to both please the publics and honour transnational commitments made to the European Union Figure 1.

General trends over time

The citizens of Bulgaria and Romania have remained staunch proponents of democracy and electorates have also been rather centrist. Bulgarians have remained quite patriotic over time, whereas Romanians have demonstrated a sustained decline in the levels of attachment to their country. Both states have experienced very sharp drops in their level of support for the EU. In the case of Bulgaria, this trend is mirrored by a similar drop in the confidence in the country's parliament. In Romania, confidence in parliament was never high to begin with.

The relatively stable levels of support for democracy, moderate ideological predispositions and attachment to one's country are in stark contrast with the low confidence in the national parliaments and the European Union. In other words, citizens of both countries have mostly become disillusioned with their representation at the national and supranational level. This finding is consistent with an explanation that features an interaction at the domestic and EU elite level that leaves the public consistently feeling poorly

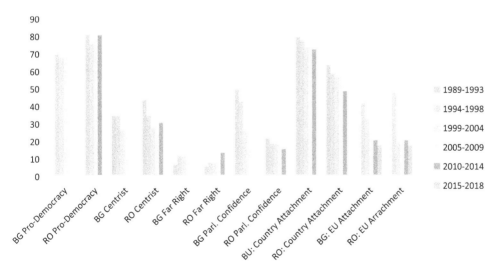

Figure 1. Public attitudes in Bulgaria and Romania over time. Source: http://ec.europa.eu/commfrontoffice/publicopinion/index.cfm/General/index. Each bar reflects levels of support or strong support.

represented. It is also consistent with the specific argument that pro-majoritarian preferences have been incompatible with EU regulations and domestic elites that have failed to achieve both EU integration and representation of public preferences Figure 2.

The two countries are also similar in terms of their consistent tendency towards exclusion of ethno-cultural minorities. The Ethnic Power Relations Dataset provides assessments of the level of political empowerment by minority groups over time (Vogt et al. 2015). The minority population of Bulgaria consists of Turkish Bulgarians (10 percent), Roma (5 percent), Pomaks (1–2 percent) and a small group of Macedonians (0.2 percent). The post-democratisation period between 1989 and the late 1990s did not bring much change to the political status of minorities. As demonstrated by Figure 1 above, both the Turkish and Roma were considered powerless by EPR: they are the two main groups that comprise 17 percent of the Bulgarian population that is considered disempowered until 2001. The early 2000s brought some positive change to the Turkish minority, however. Largely as a function of entering government coalitions, the level of empowerment for this minority shifted to junior partners and the share of politically powerless Bulgarians dropped to about 6 percent, made up of mostly Roma citizens. The Turkish minority returned to political disempowerment, according to EPR, in 2010, with the exception of the short-lived minority coalition government of 2014.

In Romania, minority groups make up slightly less than 10 percent of the population and feature primarily Hungarians (6.7 percent) and Roma (2.5 percent). Unlike their counterparts in Bulgaria, Romanian minorities enjoyed better political representation throughout the 1990s and into the early 2000s. As discussed in the next section, this had to do with constitutional provisions that were geared towards placating the Hungarian Romanians that were themselves a consequence of the threat of violence and interstate conflict. However, the dominance of ethnic Romanians returned to pre-transition levels following the 2013 elections. This suggests that, similarly to Bulgaria,

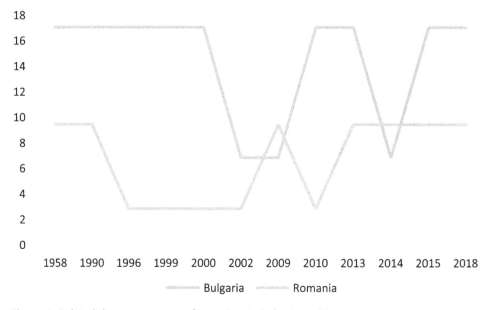

Figure 2. Political disempowerment of minorities in Bulgaria and Romania.

Romanians never quite embraced multiculturalism once the EU accession negotiations were over.

The lack of political empowerment has had significant policy consequences for both the Turkish and Roma minorities in Bulgaria and the Roma in Romania. For example, only 7.2 percent of the Roma and 26.6 percent of the Bulgarian Turks attain secondary education or higher, compared to 76.5 percent among the majority population (Tomova 1998). The level of unemployment for minority groups in Bulgaria has traditionally been estimated to be about double the rate of the majority population (Ivanov 2015). The trends are similar in Romania for the Roma: the poverty rate is about three times higher than that of the Romanian majority. However, the Hungarian minority enjoys above-average levels of education and material well-being. It is important to not attribute this to any policy decisions following 1989, however: Hungarians enjoyed high levels of human development even before the transition to communism.

Bulgaria and Romania score low on quantitative measures of social justice and equality. The two countries come in 25th and 26th out of 28 EU countries on the social cohesion and equality measure of Bertelsmann Stiftung social justice index (Shcraad-Tischler and Schiller 2016). This measure assesses the extent to which there are specific policies of social inclusion and non-discrimination for minorities.

Bulgarians and Romanians are generally distrustful of others. Romania has the lowest levels of out-group trust among European countries in Christian Welzel's study of political culture (Welzel 2013) which does not feature Bulgaria. Similarly, Bulgaria ranks last in the 2016 European Social Survey measure of trust in other people: a study that includes all EU countries, with the exception of Romania. The low ranking of Bulgaria has been consistent over seven rounds of ESS surveys, going back to 2002.

Country-specific studies of societal attitudes towards minority groups in the two countries confirm the impressions from the large-n quantitative measures. In perhaps the most comprehensive sociological study of social distance attitudes along ethnic lines in Bulgaria, Pamporov demonstrates that majority attitudes towards the Roma and Turkish have remained unfavourable and remarkably stable over the 1992–2007 period (Pamporov 2009). Only between 4 and 6 percent of respondents said they were willing to get married to someone of Roma descent and between 27 and 33 percent saw Roma as potential friends. Over the period of the study, the share of the population willing to live in the same neighbourhood as the Roma declined from 52% in 1992 to 28% in 2003 and stood at 41% in 2007. The overall favorability of people who married Roma was 11.5%, compared to 21.4% for Bulgarian Muslims, 39.5% for Russians and 44.5% for EU citizens, the highest category of potential spouses. Furthermore, across the various types of proximity measures, Bulgarians consistently demonstrated their suspicion of out-group members, even those coming from Western countries. Barely half of Bulgarians were willing to accept EU citizens in their immediate neighbourhoods or even cities (Pamporov 2009, 42) and far less than half were willing to accept a foreigner as an immediate job supervisor (Pamporov 2009, 51).

According to a government-sponsored survey, only 18.6% of Romanians supported greater autonomy for counties with predominantly Hungarian populations. This figure declined to 13.8% in 2006 (Salat 2008). Less than half of respondents supported Hungarian language education and double citizenship for Hungarian Romanians (Salat 2008, 30). In

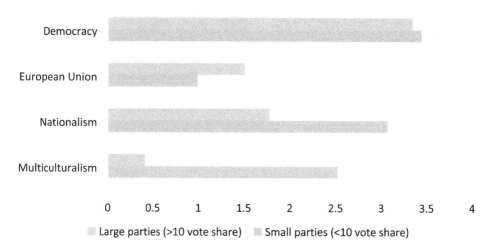

Figure 3. Relative Importance of Issues, by Party Size. Note: Variables used for comparison are: per607 (multiculturalism), per601 (nationalism), per108 (EU support), per202 (democracy support).

addition, Romanians increasingly viewed the Romanian–Hungarian relations as conflictual (Salat 2008, 31) Figure 3.

Given the strong pro-majoritarian element in public opinion, it is no surprise that political parties in both Bulgaria and Romania have not readily taken explicit positions on multicultural matters. A quick glance at the party platforms coded by the Party Manifesto Project reveals that the multiculturalism – nationalism debate has generally been reserved for the smaller parties in both countries over the 1990–2017 time period (Volkens et al. 2018). The Hungarian Democratic Alliance of Romania and the Movement for Rights and Freedoms in Bulgaria were, unsurprisingly, among the greatest supporters of multiculturalism, with 9.3 and 7.5 positive mentions of the issue in their platforms. The nationalist parties are also not surprising: the United Patriots, National Union Attack in Bulgaria made 16 and 11 mentions of the national way of life in their platforms, respectively. In Romania, the National Unity Party and the Greater Romania Party made similar reference 8 and 7 times, respectively.

This aggregate analysis paints a picture of a citizenry in favour of majority dominance and political parties that are, on the whole, reluctant to explicitly mention minority rights or take a position on nationalism in their political platforms. What it does not reveal is that, over time, the political debate on multiculturalism and nationalism became more polarising and more in favour of the latter, rather than the former.

Early transition period (1989 – late 1990s)

Both Bulgaria and Romania entered the early 1990s with a pronounced system of political dominance by the majority. In Bulgaria, this is best exemplified by the "Revival Process" of the mid-1980s, when the country's ethnic Turks had to adopt Bulgarian names and give up certain cultural traditions. Bulgaria's approach to its second-largest minority, the Roma, included segregation and economic and social discrimination. Romania's treatment of its own Roma minority did not differ much from Bulgaria's. In addition, it had a history of tensions with its Hungarian population, which formed its largest non-majority group, going back to the end of World War I. While the Hungarian Autonomous Region was formed in 1952, it never enjoyed even a semblance of self-governance from the very beginning (Šisler 2016).

As the two states adopted their post-communist constitutions in 1991, they also experienced foreign incentives to embrace tolerance of their minority populations. In the spirit of pluralism, they adopted strong parliaments elected by proportional representation. Foreign influence in the earlier period also came in the form of Council of Europe (COE) membership conditionality and featured the requirement for respect for the provisions of the Charter of the United Nations, the Final Act of Helsinki and the Charter of Paris (OECD 1995). The two countries consequently embraced constitutional provisions that, at least on paper, bolstered the rule of law, democracy and human rights, and sought to guarantee the rights of ethnic and national groups and minorities (Decaux 1992).

While Bulgaria abolished its communist-era assimilation campaigns in 1991, its constitution was nonetheless considered among the least tolerant in the region (Elster 1997). This was primarily due the lack of any recognition of the existence of minorities in the country, with the exception of the vague reference to "citizens whose mother tongue is not Bulgarian", who were nonetheless required to study in the majority language. In addition, Article 14(4) of the constitution specifically banned the formation of parties along ethnic, racial or religious lines. This article necessitated an intervention by the Constitutional Court in 1992 that ruled that the Movement for Rights and Freedoms, which had a predominantly Turkish electorate and leadership, did not violate this rule. According to some, in spite of the court ruling that allowed MRF to participate in elections, Article 14(4) has consistently limited the extent to which the party has been able to push for minority rights and protections since democratisation (Rechel 2007). In addition, Article 2(1) stated that "autonomous territorial formations" are prohibited. This provision's objective was to maintain conformity with the COE's insistence of local self-governance, while explicitly reserving control over the Turkish minority that was geographically heavily concentrated in the southeastern part of the country. In this early period of reform, Bulgaria's framework failed to even identify other minorities, ignoring the sizeable population of Roma and the less numerous Pomaks and Macedonians.

In Romania, the initial transition period was considerably more turbulent. The tension between the Romanian majority and Hungarian minority escalated into violent clashes in the town of Tirgu-Mures, the one-time administrative centre of the Hungarian Autonomous Region, in 1990. Perhaps because of the quickly escalating ethnic violence, the Romanian constitution recognised the existence of minorities explicitly and reserved seats in parliament for all national minorities that were represented by only one organisation that failed to cross the regular 5 percent electoral threshold.

The more formal recognition of the presence of minorities, however, also translated into a clear multiculturalism-nationalism split among some of the smaller political parties in the country. In 1992, the Hungarian Democratic Alliance of Romania (HDAR) ran on an explicitly multicultural platform and gained 7.5 percent of the vote. However, as many as four other parties ran on platforms that contained clear emphasis on national identity. This was perhaps most evident in the platforms of the Greater Romania and Romanian National

Unity parties, which about 10 percent of the vote altogether. In 1996, the Democratic Alliance of Hungarians in Romania (DAHR), entered the governing coalition. Consequently, the new Department for Protection of National Minorities was established in 1997, following by the institution of the Ombudsman. Both were essential in adopting legislation of restitution of property and adoption of education and language policy (Constantin 2004).

In summary, while both countries conformed to the general principles of Council of Europe membership when designing their post-communist constitutions, they did leave the door open to reserving political advantages for the respective majorities. This was particularly obvious in Bulgaria where the constitution refused to acknowledge the existence of minorities. In Romania, as a result of early ethno-cultural clashes, the constitution adopted more decisive regulations for encouraging weak subcultural pluralism, even though the primacy of the majority was never put in question either.

Pre-accession period (late 1990s – 2007)

The first post-transition period was characterised by popular excitement about democracy and moderate external influence on behalf of the Council of Europe that masked deeply rooted pro-majoritarian preferences among the citizens. The second period, which started in the late 1990s and ended in 2007, featured gradual popular disillusionment with the domestic governments' ability to provide a quick fix to the many economic problems, combined with a laser-sharp focus on European integration. In many ways, the publics saw the European Union and foreign actors more broadly as their best hope to improve their material well-being. However, the strong support for EU membership among the general public should not be conflated with a ready adoption of a pluralist European identity. More than 40 percent of Bulgarians and 18 percent of Romanians claimed the nation was the most important entity. The figures for the EU stood in the low single digits in both countries (Lubbers and Coenders 2017, 106). Consequently, Bulgaria struggled to both reaffirm its commitment to liberalism while staying true to the preference for majoritarian dominance that was evident among the electorate.

In Bulgaria, the bipolar setup between the Bulgarian Socialist Party and the Union of Democratic Forces collapsed when the National Movement Simeon the Second (NDSV) won elections in 2001, only eleven weeks after officially registering as a political party. This was Bulgaria's first populist moment: a rebellion against the elites that had alternated in power but, to many, did little to address the pressing problems of the country. NDSV deserves special attention because it symbolised an unstable equilibrium between nationalism and globalism for the sake of European integration. The party's leader, Simeon Saxe-Coburg Gotha, was Bulgaria's monarch-in-exile, who had been forced out of the country by the communists when he was six and had settled in Spain. His return symbolised anti-authoritarianism, former national glory and a link to the Western elites all at once. He was therefore able to appeal to both the nationalist sentiment and the desire of most Bulgarians to become members of the European Union. NDSV's platform was extremely thin on policy details and Saxe-Coburg Gotha became famous for responding to most questions pressing him to elaborate on his approach to governance with: "I will tell you when the time comes". Yet NDSV is the party that took care of the majority of negotiations for EU accession during its 2001–2005 mandate. Its quick rise to power and its precipitous decline after the end of its only mandate also show the impossibility of reconciling the pro-majoritarian tendencies of the publics with the liberalist requirements imposed by the EU.

Bulgaria and Romania were treated as a package enlargement deal starting in 1995 and faced an even more pronounced external influence to adopt liberal democratic rules (Phinnemore 2010). The infusion of Western norms towards national minorities is well documented by Judith Kelley, who examines at length that the project first started by the Council of Europe was amplified by the joint efforts of the EU and the OSCE in the late 1990s (Kelley 2004). Her story features conditionality prominently and suggests that, had the EU not had the prospect of full membership and a well-articulated monitoring infrastructure, socialisation and norm adoption would have failed.

In the case of minority protection, the key mechanism of reform the Council of Europe's Framework Convention for the Protection of National Minorities (FCNM) (Hofmann 2008). It utilised a multi-layer approach to implementation that originated at the Council of Europe level, but relied on within-country working groups that cooperated directly with the interest groups that represented each country's minorities. The COE's Advisory Committees visited the countries to consult with political leaders and minority representatives and explored minority-majority regions to assess the areas of progress and need. The reports were then used to produce official Advisory Committee opinions that were submitted to the national governments for comment and follow-up. The process was implemented in two monitoring cycles: the first was scheduled for 1999 in Romania and 2000 in Bulgaria; the second was supposed to occur five years later.

Romania showed relatively good responsiveness to the monitoring schedule implemented by the FCNM. It actively engaged with both reports. However, critiques of the financial and social position of the Roma in the country remained a point of emphasis, revealing that the conditions of the poorest and least tolerated minority in the country were never truly addressed in practice. The end of the first monitoring cycle in Romania occurred in 2002. In 2003, the Social Democratic Party government passed the most extensive reforms targeted at minority accommodations since the 1991 constitution that were also consistent with many of the FCNM recommendations. Article 120 of the Constitution allowed for the use of minority language in the public administration, while Article 127 provided the right to an interpreter in the Courts (Constantin 2004). Article 121 allowed minority groups to request the study of language, literature and history of the diaspora and Article 123 made arrangements for the creation of higher education institutions with Hungarian as the primary language of instruction (Constantin 2004, 6). Other arrangements were made to foster representation of the Roma minority. This included programmes for teacher training of Roma citizens and some affirmative-action style provisions for admission to schools and universities.

The responsiveness to Western pressure for minority accommodation in the early 2000s can be explained with the relatively powerful political position that the pro-minority part had. While the Democratic Alliance of Hungarians In Romania (DAHR) was not an official coalition member in 2003, its support was essential on an ad-hoc basis for the survival of the Social Democratic Party (PSD) government. This alliance was motivated, in part, by the tremendous threat that the nationalist Greater Romania Party (PRM) of Corneliu Tudor posed to the PSD: Tudor was the runner-up in the 2000 presidential election and PRM had won 37 percent of the parliamentary seats after the general election that year, becoming the second most powerful party in the legislature. The nationalist threat to the PSD and the intense negotiation phase for EU accession made the DAHR a natural ally for PSD, which opened up significant opportunities for minority accommodation in Romania. The case of Romania in the early 2000s, therefore, illustrates how, when minority parties are necessary for the survival of government and when external pressure is present, there can be progress made in terms of embracing pluralism (Kiss and Székely 2016). At the same time, the increasing influence of the nationalist bloc in Romania further demonstrated that the progress made deepened an already significant nationalism-multiculturalism divide in Romania. In other words, the presence of robust opposition to pluralism makes it difficult to claim that Romania exhibited weak subcultural pluralism and remained largely a polyarchical regime even when the EU conditionality for reform was at its highest levels.

With the exception of Latvia, Bulgaria had the worst record of compliance with the Framework Convention for the Protection of National Minorities (FCNM). After receiving its first Advisory Committee opinion in 2004, it produced a very strongly worded government response that rejected the COE statement that minorities were not served properly. This featured an explicit statement that Macedonians and Pomaks did not have sufficiently "distinctive features" to warrant minority classification. It also showed lack of responsiveness about the implementation of language and educational programmes. The second monitoring cycle never occurred in Bulgaria. This led to an increased pressure on behalf of the European Commission, in its regular 2005 pre-accession report on the country (Sobotka 2009). Faced with the hardest form of external conditionality, the Bulgarian government spurred into action and announced of Decade of Roma Inclusion (2005–2015) and the founding of the Anti-Discrimination Commission in November 2005. Similarly to Romania, however, the socio-economic status of minorities in Bulgaria did not improve over the next decade and Bulgaria remained a polyarchy (Nancheva 2007).

The eventual compliance, at least on paper, led to swift backlash in Bulgaria politically. While prior elections did not feature a nationalist party like in Romania, the 2005 election saw the rise to prominence of Ataka, which explicitly embraced majority dominance as its core ideology. This featured hateful statements against the Roma and the Turkish and emphasis on Christianity and the Bulgarian language as foundational elements of the nation-state. A more pronounced embrace of traditional Bulgarian national values was more explicit in the messaging of three other parties in 2005 too, including the Bulgarian People's Union, the United Democratic Forces and the rapidly shrinking NDSV itself. The era of identity politics was beginning in Bulgaria.

Post accession (2007 to present)

In 2007, Bulgaria and Romania became official European Union members, in spite of numerous shortcomings relative to the expectations set forth in the *acquis*. The most recent period was characterised by the end of direct EU conditionality and an increase in popular dissatisfaction both with the EU and the domestic governments in both countries. These trends were amplified by the financial and refugee crisis and the ongoing debate about the viability and sustainability of the common European project Table 1.

Bulgaria continued to experience a much higher incidence of pronouncedly anti-minority and pro-nationalist rhetoric among its electorally viable parties. In 2009 and 2013, the

Table 1. Distribution of nationalist and minority parties in Bulgaria and Romania since 2008.

Country / Election year	Extreme nationalist parties	Moderate nationalist parties	Minority parties
Romania (2008)	None	National Liberal Party	HDAR
Bulgaria (2009)	Attack	Order, Law and Justice; GERB	None
Romania (2012)	None	People's Party	HDAR
Bulgaria (2013)	Attack	GERB	MRF
Bulgaria (2014)	Bulgaria without Censorship; Patriotic Front; Alternative for Bulgarian Revival	GERB, BSP	MRF
Romania (2016)	None	Alliance of Liberals and Democrats; Save Romania Union; People's Movement Party;	HDAR
Bulgaria (2017)	United Patriots	GERB, BSP, Will	MRF

extreme right Attack won 9.4 and 7.3 percent of the seats, respectively. Three different nationalist parties accounted for 17.5 percent of the vote in 2014. The consolidated United Patriots (a coalition between Attack and the Patriotic Front) captured 9 percent of the vote again in 2017.

In Bulgaria, the post-accession period featured the obliteration of the moderate right, the solidifying of the nationalist political pole and a rise in political volatility. In 2009, the remnants of the anti-communist Union of Democratic Forces that engaged in the most pronounced structural reforms in the late 1990s, managed to gain only 6.8 percent of the vote. NDSV, which was in charge of finalising the EU accession process, did not win any seats in parliament. This election also marked the arrival of the centrist GERB, under the populist leadership of Boyko Borisov, the most important political leader in the country over the last decade. Borisov formed a minority government in 2009, but relied heavily and consistently on the parliamentary support of the nationalists from Ataka to pass legislation over the next four years.

The alliance between GERB and Ataka was hardly a coincidence. Speaking in front of the Bulgarian diaspora in Chicago in 2009, then-candidate Borisov suggested that the biggest challenge of Bulgaria is its low "human material" due to the 1 million Roma, 700,000 Turks and 2.5 million retirees (Telegraph 2009). Furthermore, the party's manifestos featured traditionalist views throughout the period and never mentioned protection of minorities or pluralism explicitly since 2009. This outlined a clear strategy for Borisov of appealing to the young members of the Bulgarian majority that felt alienated by the elite push for pluralism that the country had experienced. In spite of the turmoil in Bulgarian politics that saw three early elections being called between 2013 and 2017, Borisov was re-elected to be Bulgaria's Prime Minister three times. In addition, nationalist parties became a regular feature in Bulgarian politics. While Ataka gradually declined in popularity, three openly nationalist parties won about 16 percent of the vote in 2014.[1] The vote share of nationalist parties remained stable in 2017. In addition, for the first time since 1989, the Bulgarian Socialist Party (BSP), which won 27 percent of the vote in 2017, ran on a platform that featured explicit pro-nationalist language.

More recent debates in Bulgaria spilled over to other identity issues. In 2017 and 2018, the Council of Europe's initiative to get Bulgaria to ratify the 2011 Istanbul Convention on preventing and combating violence against women was met with protests from citizens that stood on both sides of the debate. This sparked a heated debate that revolved around issues of gender-based violence, as well as the definition and legal treatment of the term "gender". Following heated civil society debates, Prime Minister Borisov withdrew his ratification request on 7 March 2018, two months after notifying the Council of Europe that he would introduce it to parliament for final approval (Dimitrov 2018). Cabinet meeting notes revealed that eight out of the twenty government ministers were against it. Deputy Prime Minister Valeri Simeonov shared in an interview that all ministers with "normal sexual orientation" disapproved of the Convention's ratification (Panayotova 2018). Opposition came from the same parties that had embraced nationalist rhetoric since the EU accession and featured the United Patriots, but also the opposition Bulgarian Socialist Party and its leader Kornelia Ninova (Cheresheva 2018). The Bulgarian Orthodox Church also expressed vocal opposition to the Convention.

Romania had a much more stable political situation after the EU accession. The public debate focused more on issues of judicial independence and corruption and the nationalism-pluralism debate declined in salience. The Hungarian Democratic Alliance continued to enjoy small representation in the Chamber of Deputies and in the Senate but shifted its focus from pushing for cultural autonomy to channelling public and EU investment to bolster infrastructure and other investment projects. However, Romania continued to feature anti-minority parties: both the National Liberal Party in 2008 and the People's Party in 2012, took explicitly pro-majority positions in their manifestos, even if for opportunistic reason. (Gherghina and Chiru 2013)

Conclusion

This paper analysed Bulgaria and Romania through the lens of three criteria for democratic consolidation put forward by Robert Dahl: the absence of strong foreign influence hostile to democracy, weak subcultural pluralism, and the presence of democratic beliefs and political culture. It suggested that foreign influence that promotes pluralism and minority rights is indeed liberal. However, when external pressure is applied to a domestic context characterised by pro-majoritarian attitudes, it actually undermines the prospects for democracy, leading to popular backlash against both the domestic and European elites.

What the two countries exemplify is that what Dahl called "polyarchy" is a stable equilibrium. In other words, when the majority is not willing to embrace pluralism, imposing it from abroad will not work and can lead to the public seeing foreign actors and the domestic elites that support them as undemocratic themselves.

While both Romania and Bulgaria continue to not embrace their minorities fully, they experienced somewhat different trajectories since 1989. In Romania, where minorities represent a smaller fraction of the population, the multiculturalism-nationalism cleavage led to violent clashes early on. In Bulgaria, an initial period of trying to circumvent the issue of minority accommodation led to some quick fixes following EU conditionality. Nonetheless, currently a large number of parties are openly embracing majoritarian rhetoric and actively subverting efforts to reform legislation in a way that would make politics inclusive for marginalised groups that go beyond ethno-cultural identity.

The empirical analysis traces how the unique historical developments in the two countries and the configuration of domestic and EU elites throughout the process of EU accession might help us explain why, at this moment, the publics in Bulgaria and

Romania are more likely to both embrace majoritarian rule and view the EU as illegitimate and even undemocratic.

Minority-majority clashes immediately after the collapse of the communist regime highlighted the danger of minority exclusion in Romania, but also galvanised pro-majoritarian sentiment that led to the formation of anti-minority parties that won political representation. Throughout the 1990s, its legislature featured both parties that stood for majority domination and parties that promoted extending cultural autonomy to the minority regions. When pre-accession talks intensified in the late 1990s and early 2000s, Romania had already negotiated some concession for the minorities internally and had grappled with identity politics. It also happened to have a liberal majority government party that needed the support of the ethnic Hungarians to keep the more nationalistic opposition in check.

Bulgaria began its road to democracy by actively ignoring its more sizeable minority population. Early on, it found a way to allow the party that represented its Turkish minority in spite of a constitutional provision that banned ethnic parties. However, the overall spirit of the institutional framework did not create openings for multi-cultural accommodation. While this also kept the prominence of nationalist parties in check in the 1990s, it also left Bulgaria woefully unprepared for the demands of European integration. In the 2000s, the government had to make concessions to the EU, at least on paper, which created a powerful majoritarian backlash and brought a number of nationalist parties to political prominence, while pushing the parties that had guided Bulgaria to EU accession to oblivion. Deference to majority values has taken new forms in the most recent years, when the same parties that emphasised traditional Bulgarian values to marginalise ethnic minorities have stood against extending the egalitarian policy to women and LGBTQ citizens.

What the two cases highlight is that public acceptance of pluralism and equality is essential for a robust democracy that does not feature political competition along identity lines. Yet it also leaves a key unanswered question: If polyarchy is a sustainable arrangement and conditionality pushing for pluralism could backfire, how do we get weak subcultural pluralism to take root in newly competitive regimes that have a history of majority dominance? This is the question that future work on the region and beyond should seek to answer.

Note

1. The parties were the Alternative for Bulgarian Revival, Bulgaria without Censorship and the Patriotic Front.

Disclosure statement

No potential conflict of interest was reported by the author.

References

Bunce, Valerie. 2003. "Rethinking Recent Democratization: Lessons from the Postcommunist Experience." *World Politics* 55 (2): 167–192.

Bustikova, Lenka, and Petra Guasti. 2017. "The Illiberal Turn or Swerve in Central Europe?" *Politics and Governance* 5 (4): 166–176.

Cheresheva, Mariya. 2018. "Gender-Based Violence 'Widespread in Bulgaria' : Balkan Insight." *BIRN*. Accessed December 9, 2018. http://www.balkaninsight.com/en/article/gender-based-violence-in-bulgaria-widespread-underreported-experts-warn-09-27-2016.

Constantin, Sergiu. 2004. "Linguistic Policy and National Minorities in Romania." *Noves SL. Revista de Sociolingüística* 3. http://www6.gencat.net/llengcat/noves/hm04tardor/docs/constantin.pdf.

Dahl, Robert. 1998. *On Democracy*. New Haven, CT: Yale University Press.

Decaux, Emmanuel. 1992. *Sécurité et Coopération En Europe, Les Textes Officiels Du Processus de Helsinki*.

Dimitrov, Martin. 2018. "Bulgaria Scraps Plan to Ratify Women's Violence Convention : Balkan Insight." *BIRN*. Accessed December 9, 2018. http://www.balkaninsight.com/en/article/bulgarian-government-withdraws-plans-to-ratify-istanbul-convention-03-07-2018.

Dimitrova, Antoaneta L. 2018. "The Uncertain Road to Sustainable Democracy: Elite Coalitions, Citizen Protests and the Prospects of Democracy in Central and Eastern Europe." *East European Politics* 34 (3): 257–275.

Elster, Jon. 1997. "Ways of Constitution-Making." In *Democracy's Victory and Crisis*, edited by, Axel Hadenius, 123–143. Cambridge, UK: Cambridge University Press.

Escobar, A. 2000. "Collision and Collusion: The Strange Case of Western Aid to Eastern Europe 1989–1998." *American Ethnologist* 27 (1): 184–185.

Gherghina, Sergiu, and Mihail Chiru. 2013. "Taking the Short Route: Political Parties, Funding Regulations, and State Resources in Romania." *East European Politics and Societies: and Cultures* 27 (1): 108–128.

Hofmann, Rainer. 2008. "The Framework Convention for the Protection of National Minorities." In *Minority Rights in Central and Eastern Europe*.

Hughes, James, Gwendolyn Sasse, and Claire E Gordon. 2005. *Europeanization and Regionalization in the EU's Enlargement to Central and Eastern Europe Europeanization and Regionalization in the EU's Enlargement to Central and Eastern Europe*. New York: Palgrave Macmillan.

Ivanov, Andrey. 2015. "Roma Poverty in Bulgaria : How to Understand It and What to Do about It ?" 1. (December).

Jacoby, Wade, By Wade Jacoby, Judith Kelley, and Janine Wedel. 2006. "Randall Stone. Lending Credibility: The International Monetary Fund and the Post Communist Transition." *Review Article Inspiration* 58 (4). Accessed November 2, 2018. https://doi.org/10.1353/wp.2007.0010, https://muse.jhu.edu/article/212507.

Janos, Andrew C., Claus Offe, Jon Elster, and Ulrich Preuss. 1999. "Institutional Design in Post-Communist Societies: Rebuilding the Ship at Sea." *Slavic Review* 58 (1): 191.

Kelley, Judith. 2004. *Ethnic Politics in Europe. The Power of Norms and Incentives*. Princeton: Princeton University Press.

Kelley, Judith. 2008. "Assessing the Complex Evolution of Norms: The Rise of International Election Monitoring." *International Organization* 62 (2): 221–255.

Kiss, Tamás, and István Gergő Székely. 2016. "Shifting Linkages in Ethnic Mobilization: The Case of RMDSZ and the Hungarians in Transylvania." *Nationalities Papers* 44 (4): 591–610. https://www.

cambridge.org/core/article/shifting-linkages-in-ethnic-mobilization-the-case-of-rmdsz-and-the-hungarians-in-transylvania/2FEAE7FB1E42444F4F296B82BBF2C394.

Knaus, Gerald, and Felix Martin. 2003. "Lessons from Bosnia and Herzegovina: Travails of The European Raj." *Journal of Democracy* 14 (3): 60–74.

Lubbers, Marcel, and Marcel Coenders. 2017. "Nationalistic Attitudes and Voting for the Radical Right in Europe." *European Union Politics* 18 (1): 98–118.

Nancheva, Nevena. 2007. "What Are Norms Good for? Ethnic Minorities on Bulgaria's Way to Europe." *Journal of Communist Studies and Transition Politics* 23 (3): 371–395. doi:10.1080/13523270701507 048.

OECD. 1995. "Constitutions of Central and Eastern European Countries and the Baltic States." (2).

Pamporov, Aleksey. 2009. *Social Distances and Ethnic Stereotypes Towards Minorities in Bulgaria*. Sofia: Open Society Institute.

Panayotova, Dilyana. 2018. "8 Министри Гласували Против Истанбулската Конвенция, Разкри Симеонов - News.Bg." Accessed December 9, 2018. https://news.bg/politics/8-ministri-glasuvali-protiv-istanbulskata-konventsiya-razkri-simeonov.html.

Phinnemore, David. 2010. "And We'd Like to Thank … Romania's Integration into the European Union, 1989–2007." *Journal of European Integration* 32 (3): 291–308.

Rechel, Bernd. 2007. "State Control of Minorities in Bulgaria." *Journal of Communist Studies and Transition Politics* 23 (3): 352–370.

Reynolds, Andrew. 2005. "Constitutional Medicine." *Journal of Democracy* 16 (1): 54–68.

Salat, L. 2008. "Are Members of the Hungarian Minority in Romania Part of the Romanian Political Community?" *Studia Politica* VIII (2): 337–366.

Shcraad-Tischler, D., and C. Schiller. 2016. *Social Justice in the EU - Index Report* 2016.

Šisler, Filip. 2016. "Hungarian Dissent in Romania During the Ceausescu Era." *West Bohemian Historical Review* 2: 323–338.

Sobotka, Eva. 2009. "Bulgaria: Minority Rights 'Light.'" In *Minority Rights in Central and Eastern Europe*, edited by Bernd Rechel, 70–90. New York: Routledge.

Telegraph. 2009. "Mayor of Sofia Brands Roma, Turks and Retirees 'Bad Human Material.'" *The Telegraph*. https://www.telegraph.co.uk/news/worldnews/europe/bulgaria/4531391/Mayor-of-Sofia-brands-Roma-Turks-and-retirees-bad-human-material.html.

Tilly, Charley. 1995. "Democracy Is a Lake." In *The Social Construction of Democracy, 1870–1990*, edited by George Andrews and Herrick Chapman, 365–366. New York: New York University Press.

Tomova, Ilona. 1998. *Ethnic Dimensions of Poverty in Bulgaria*. Washington, DC: The World Bank.

Vogt, Manuel, Nils-Christian Bormann, Seraina Rüegger, Lars-Erik Cederman, Philipp Hunziker, and Luc Girardin. 2015. "Integrating Data on Ethnicity, Geography, and Conflict: The Ethnic Power Relations Data Set Family." *Journal of Conflict Resolution* 59 (7): 1327–1342.

Volkens, Andrea, Werner Krause, Pola Lehmann, Theres Matthieß, Nicolas Merz, Sven Regel, and Bernhard Weßels. 2018. *The Manifesto Data Collection*. Berlin: Wissenschaftszentrum Berlin für Sozialforschung (WZB).

Welzel, Christian. 2013. *Freedom Rising. Human Empowerment and the Quest for Emancipation*. Cambridge: Cambridge University Press.

Caesarean politics in Hungary and Poland

Robert Sata and Ireneusz Pawel Karolewski

ABSTRACT
We propose the new concept of Caesarean politics to explain democratic deconsolidation in Hungary and Poland. We argue the move towards illiberal democracy in both countries has been made possible by a shift towards Caesarean politics, in which radical changes are framed as "politics as usual", while in fact these challenge the essence of liberal democracy. Focusing on the three pillars of Caesarean politics: (1) patronal politics, (2) state capture, and (3) identity politics, we show how both countries become cases of Caesarean politics, where, using discourses of "friends" and "enemies", the leader coordinates vast patronal networks that capture the state.

Many were surprised by how fast the dissolution of democratic institutions took place in Hungary after Viktor Orbán and his Fidesz (Hungarian Civic Alliance) came back to power in 2010.[1] Poland has embarked on a similar project in 2015, when Jarosław Kaczyński and his PiS (Law and Justice) returned to power with the slogan to turn Warsaw into Budapest by the Vistula river. Both countries were once considered poster students of democratisation, pluralism and rule of law. Yet, the two countries present now the largest and sharpest drops in levels of democracy in CEE (Cianetti, Dawson, and Hanley 2018), dismantling the very institutions that made them models to emulate. Both Orbán and Kaczyński have abandoned liberal democracy, which they frame as a failure if not a treachery of the Hungarian and Polish people, although both were participants of the 1989 roundtable talks (Zgut et al. 2018). Both Fidesz and PiS claim that correcting the failed transition requires an urgent transformation of liberal democracy to give the power back to "the people" (Müller 2014). They have embarked on a conservative-nationalist project using a populist discourse, stripping away checks and balances, concentrating power to exert partisan control over public institutions. Notwithstanding these, both Fidesz and PiS have been able to secure high electoral support in national, municipal and European elections. We propose the new concept of Caesarean politics to explain the success of the authoritarian move in both countries. As a first step, we sketch out the conceptual contours of Caesarean politics, drawing on classic and modern literature on Caesarianism and adjacent research. We go beyond theories of strong men seeking power and we explore both the institutional and identity aspects of Caesarean politics proposing a new understanding of the term as a regime that rests on three pillars that systematically interact and reinforce each other: (1) patronalism and (2) state capture that are justified with (3) exclusionary identity politics. Next, we examine comparatively the mainstream parties' shift towards Caesarean politics in Hungary and Poland, exploring the three pillars of Caesarean politics in detail. Noting the differences between the two countries, we conclude how radical institutional changes are framed "politics as usual", while enacted changes in fact challenge the core of liberal democracy and thus represent a difference in kind rather than difference in degree: Caesarean regimes are different from previous post-transition regimes.

Caesarean politics

The notion of Caesarist politics or Caesarism has been used with reference to strong leadership (e.g. India under Indira Gandhi, Kaviraj 1986) or dictatorship-like rule (e.g. Kongo Kinshasa under Mobutu, Willame 1971). Past research on Caesarist politics is scant and mainly limited to historical studies of strong leaders seeking mass support. We move beyond this understanding and argue for a more contemporary notion of *Caesarean politics* (rather than Caesarist politics) that goes beyond both the Schumpeterian elitist conception of democracy (Ober 2017) and Bonapartist authoritarian rule based on plebiscitary acclamation (Steinmetz 2009, 464). Our understanding of Caesarean politics comes closest to what Max Weber described as "the plebiscitary character of elections, disdain for parliament, the non-toleration of autonomous powers within the government and a failure to attract or suffer independent political minds" (Casper 2007).

Caesarean politics affect both institutional and identity aspects of political rule. At the institutional level, Caesarean politics is a specific mode of political operation that favours the ruler and his (her) network(s) and goes hand in hand with state capture by particular interest to enable the individual leader who wins an election to govern the country as he or she sees fit. At the level of identity, Caesarean politics is related to discourses that tap into public xenophobia and frame collective identity in an exclusionary manner, applying the friend-enemy imagery (Karolewski 2012). While many identity discourses are exclusionary in nature, Caesarean politics pertains to political strategies constructing enemies and traitors to the *national cause* that is claimed to be represented by the government leader/party alone, thus questioning the legitimacy of pluralism. This way, Caesarean politics is executive rule legitimised through electoral success that uses patronalism, state capture and exclusionary identity politics to enact anti-pluralist regime change to help charismatic leader(s) become true Caesar(s).

We argue that the three elements of Caesarean politics – (1) patronalism, (2) state capture and (3) exclusionary identity politics – are interrelated elements, each being equally relevant and reinforcing each other in generating Caesarean politics. In this sense, the *triad* of Caesarean politics does not represent an additive concept but rather a relational one – a patterned matrix of relationships among political practices and discourses, both codified and informal, all pertaining to political power. The triad of Caesarean politics functions as "interaction order" (Goffman 1983), operating and operated by elites to coordinate and constrain social interactions and political competition.

The first key aspect of Caesarean politics is patronalism, a system, in which political authority centres on a single patron controlling an elaborate system of rewards and punishments. As Henry E. Hale (2014, 2017) argues, nationwide networks of loyal acquaintances profit politically and financially from the network of the patron. In these patron-client networks, informal understandings dominate over formal rules and personal connections are paramount. Since personal access to the patron is essential for political survival and enrichment (Hale 2017, 32), patronalism tends to political closure, which operates through subverting the political competition and amassing power. This is why control of the media plays a crucial role, as political success, in particular in political regimes allowing free elections, can depend on media coverage, outreach and impact. While post-soviet patronal networks cut across political parties, the "closed" political party remains relevant for power-hoarding in Hungary and Poland.

The second key aspect of Caesarean politics is state capture. State capture is not just widespread corruption but its essence lies in networks of corrupt actors that act collectively to pursue private interest at the expense of the public good (Fazekas and Tóth 2016). Abby Innes (2014, 88) argues that states in CEE cluster around two dominant modes of dominance over state institutions: the party state capture (political monopoly of a party taking control over key state institutions, including courts and enterprises) and corporate state capture where public power is exercised mainly for private gain. While the Czech Republic, Slovakia, Romania and Bulgaria are cases of corporate state capture (see also Kolev in this Special Issue), Hungary and Poland stand for party state capture, a re-monopolization of the political system in favour of one party (or a group of aligned parties). The difference between corporate and party state capture is crucial since while corporate capture aims to weaken or disable policies (i.e. state activity), party state capture strengthens policy implementation and responsiveness because party preferences are immediately turned into policies (e.g. the radical decommunization policies of PiS or the left-liberal elite purge of Fidesz). In contrast, a corporate (or cartel) state capture is less likely to be interested in changing the ideological core of policies but rather seek institutional and policy stability, reflecting static corporate demands (e.g. the "the state as a firm" ideology by Andrej Babiš in the Czech Republic).[2]

The third key aspect of Caesarean politics concerns exclusionary identity politics that are constructed to legitimize regime change. Since the primacy of the leader is the cornerstone of politics, identity discourses are employed to establish the leader/patron as the spearhead of the homogeneous community, surrounded by dangerous "others". The binary construction of "us" versus "them" leads to blaming and scapegoating strategies (Meeusen and Jacobs 2017). This "othering" serves promoting the proclivity of citizens to think of "others" in terms of "enemies" and mobilise them based on exclusionary practices (Schmitt [1932] 1996). The traditional target groups of exclusion are migrants and minorities (Walters 2002), but in CEE, liberals from opposition parties, in league with international organisations, or any critic of the regime can easily find themselves presented as internal and external enemies. Caesarean politics thus resemble to some extent what Pappas (2014) called "populist democracies", where society is split along a single cleavage, ostensibly dividing the good "people" from some evil "establishment". Feelings of insecurity, threat and resentment (Huysmans 2004, 2006) are perpetuated not only for legitimisation through fear, for instance, to increase chances of re-election, but also to tune the political system to limit political competition and dissent. As a consequence, Caesarean identity politics have the function of legitimising the expansion of the power of the ruler/party at the expense of both popular will (understood as something beyond simple majorities) and political opposition through self-serving reforms of state institutions, restrictive laws or denial of liberties and rights.

There is still limited understanding of what exactly determines shifts towards Caesarean politics. Almond (1956) claimed more than 60 years ago that fragmented political cultures and "immobilism" of the political system make democratic regimes less stable and increases the chances of "Caesaristic" breakthroughs:

> [...] these systems tend always to be threatened by, and sometimes to be swept away by, movements of charismatic nationalism which break through the boundaries of the political sub – cultures and overcome immobilism through coercive action and organization. In other words, these systems have a totalitarian potentiality in them. (Almond 1956, 408)

He ascribed "Caesaristic" potential mainly to "continental" democracies such as France or Italy, and argued that Anglo-Saxon countries show a much higher degree of stability and are immune to "Caesaristic" breakthroughs. Yet, today's political developments in the US and the UK would question Almond's belief in the merits of Anglo-Saxon political systems. Moreover, he failed to explain how exactly these "Caesaristic" breakthroughs come about and what form they assume, while there is difference between a Gaullist nationalism, a military junta or a fascist regime (for the critique of Almond's approach see Lijphart 1969).

We believe authoritarian political culture and polarised immobilist political systems are key for installing Caesarean politics. Even though dictatorial power and clientelism were the key features of the communist system and society, Caesarean politics as a concept has not been applied to CEE so far. We claim that our concept of Caesarean politics can explain post-transition political changes and the current retreat of liberal democracy in CEE, where authoritarianism and admiration for strong leaders persist in society (Todosijević and Enyedi 2008) and exclusionary identity politics find widespread support.

Swerving democracy in Hungary and Poland – a prelude to Caesarean politics

Although many have taken for granted that Hungary and Poland achieved democratic consolidation, the loyalty to democratic norms and values of both citizens and elites was weak way before Orbán and Kaczyński returned to power (see also Guasti and Bustikova in this Special Issue), paving the way for the Caesarean turn. Both countries show over the years decreasing attachment to democratic norms and values in different datasets of democratic consolidation. Declining levels of trust in public institutions and government make Hungary and Poland stand out as prime candidates for Caesarean seizure: unlike the rest of the CEE, both saw legislative trust decreased by more than half by 2000 from the levels of 1990. Similarly, trust in civil service dropped significantly only in these two countries of CEE (Catterberg and Moreno 2005). According to Eurobarometer, trust in government in Hungary declined steadily and by 2009 was as low as 14% – a figure reached by Poland in 2013, both Fidesz and PiS taking the helm of politics under identical circumstances, with society disillusioned with government and politics (Eurobarometer 2019).

The extreme polarisation between left-liberal and conservative-right parties not only led to a general distrust of society towards public institutions but parties on both side of the ideological spectrum engaged in mutual enemy construction, demonising each other, thus laying grounds for exclusionary identity politics. The bipolarization of politics has fatigued the majority of citizens and led to the emergence of demagogic and charismatic leaders with little focus on parliamentary politics and programmatic competition (for Hungary see Pappas 2014; Greskovits 2015). Polarisation also led to crystallization of patronal networks: in Poland already in the mid-1990s, social-democratic SLD (Alliance of the Democratic Left) established a "royal court" system of privileged businessmen, media moguls and clergy representatives. Similarly, Orbán's college roommate, László Simicska became Fidesz's financial mastermind running a vast business and media network that consolidated during the first Fidesz government in 1998–2002 (Magyar 2016, 84).

In addition to political apathy, economic turbulences left people disenchanted with politics in general. Many of the people felt they became "losers" of the democratic transition as the governments of the time were unable (and partly unwilling) to efficiently reform the labour market, strengthen the welfare systems and balance growing social inequality. The 2008 recession only fuelled economic fears of the people. Hungary was hit hard with one of CEE's highest levels of government debt and millions of homeowners threatened by non-performing mortgages (Körösényi 2018; Simon 2018). Although Poland's economy turned out to be highly resilient, the 2015 Swiss Franc crisis shook the feeling of economic security of many Poles (Hakim 2015; Holodny 2016). Left-liberal elites have discredited themselves allowing corruption to flourish while doing little to ease the social transition to liberal capitalism in growing globalisation (Greskovits 2015, also introduction to this Special Issue by Agarin). Furthermore, leaked secret recordings of ruling politicians in both countries seem to have played a role in ousting them from government, as these confirmed voters' suspicion that they are power-clinging cynics, only eroding state institutions serving public interest.[3]

This way, the grounds for Caesarean politics in both countries were laid prior to Fidesz and PiS taking power over. Nevertheless, it was only the 2010 Fidesz and 2015 PiS government that activated the "interactive order" of the triad of Caesarean politics that challenges the democratic "rules of the game", reflecting a difference in kind, rather than a difference in degree vis-à-vis prior regimes. Let us now examine how the elements of Caesarean politics work together in weakening liberal democracy.

Patronal politics

The primacy of the leader as the patron of all benefits and sanctions is the key element of Caesarean politics. Orbán and Kaczyński are uncontested party leaders, although Kaczyński chose to be a simple MP, not a PM like Orbán. Both Hungary and Poland have changed the law and adopted policies that enable personal rule by the book. In addition, a massive and deep elite purge at all levels of public administration was completed to widen the patronal network. New legislation ensured patronal interest in private sectors as well. This was coupled with the appropriation of the media, essential to guarantee patron/party-friendly coverage or straight-out propaganda to ensure public support for the new regime (Hale 2017, 33).

In Hungary, the period since 2010 has been marked by continuous efforts to establish a pro-Orbán elite at the expense of former elites. Orbán built an extensive hierarchical patronal network that stretches into all public sectors, justified with the need to get rid of the communist elite. State-run enterprises were filled with supporters, personnel at all levels of the public administration, even head teachers or hospital directors, were replaced with party loyalists without training or experience (Dimitrova 2018). Although largely ceremonial, the President's Office has been given to loyal party members, who in return, regularly abstain from exercising their constitutional veto rights over legislation. The independence of the Central Bank was taken away, its president became a close ally and former Fidesz economy minister, who actively supports party oligarchs. The number of ombudsmen was reduced from three to a single one, a position given to a former government commissioner, thus ensuring there is no oversight of government. In the same manner, the Prosecutor General, another long-time Orbán loyalist, regularly blocks corruption charges against Fidesz and state-coordinated corruption involving regime's favoured oligarchs remains uninvestigated by the police (Kostadinova and Kmetty 2018; Zgut et al. 2018, 9–11).

Many Orbán-inspired changes did take place in Poland, too. Large-scale personnel exchange took place in the public administration, state-owned enterprises and banks. The same justification for the complete personnel replacement was used as in Hungary: the necessity of purging the state of communists and liberals. The new staff consisted of PiS loyalists, oftentimes without proper professional experience. This appears to be a characteristic of patronal politics in both countries, yet there is an importance difference: the personal rule of Kaczyński is confronted with several networks that compete with each other, while Orbán is an uncontested patron. This way, Polish patronal politics resemble the *competing pyramid system*, rather than a *single pyramid system* (for the difference see Hale 2017, 32), where current PM Morawiecki's network competes with the rival network of Justice Minister Ziobro. The competition among networks might in fact weaken or limit the reach of patronalism. In contrast, in Hungary nobody can challenge Orbán, who singlehandedly decides who can succeed and who is to fail.[4]

The single pyramid patronal network is enabled and maintained by the authoritarian system that Orbán built to prevent fair elections. He overhauled Hungary's electoral system in repeated modifications to favour Fidesz and manipulated advertising and campaigning rules to benefit his party. New legislation adopted also encourages the creation of fake-parties to split the anti-Fidesz vote. The gerrymandering of the electoral districts secured two-third majority for Fidesz with only 45% of the popular vote in 2014 and just 50% of the vote in 2018. The State Audit Office, run by a former Fidesz politician, is used as a political weapon against the opposition as it levies fines and suspends state funds to opposition parties, whilst dismissing the same rules for Fidesz using public funds to run partisan campaigns (Zgut et al. 2018, 9–11). These changes and practices gradually disabled electoral competition as evidenced by international observers' reports that found already the 2014 elections gave Fidesz "an undue advantage" and the 2018 elections were "unfair" (Kelemen 2017; Bozóki and Hegedűs 2018).

PiS fell short of the Orbánesque changes of the electoral system, although it drafted a new electoral law in tune with the Hungarian reforms. Still, faced with numerous protests, Kaczyński did not to follow through with the law, especially with elections approaching in 2019. Following the election results that PiS considered disappointing despite winning, the reform might be back on the agenda. Yet, the PiS government is also not shy to use public institutions as weapons against the opposition to limit political competition (see also

Bochsler and Juon in this Special Issue). PiS controlled tax authorities or district attorneys harass opposition politicians. One example is the scandal surrounding the Financial Supervision Authority (KNF).[5] The PiS-appointed head of KNF, Chrzanowski has been arrested on corruption charges in November 2018. As a political retaliation, PiS Justice Minister Ziobro ordered the arrest of the former head of KNF, PO (Civic Platform) appointee Jakubiak in December 2018 (Omachel 2019) but had to release him for lack of evidence.

The control of the media has been in the centre of both Orbán's and Kaczyński's patronal politics. In Hungary, new media legislation was adopted "to correct leftist bias" (Dragomir 2017a) as Orbán blamed his earlier electoral defeats on the lack of right-wing, conservative media (supportive of him and his party). The Media Council, a body within the Media Authority, monitors and enforces the set of new media laws. The appointment system gives the government de facto control over the Media Council and Hungary's public service media outlets –national TVs, radio stations and the national news service (Brouillette and van Beek 2012). Despite large demonstrations against the new media laws (Jenne and Mudde 2012; Wilkin, Dencik, and Bognár 2015), the entire public media is now subordinated to Orbán's patronal network and it serves Fidesz's propaganda purposes (Bozóki and Hegedűs 2018). Since the Media Council can sanction journalists with penalties for content judged not "balanced, accurate, thorough, objective and responsible", it serves the patronal network perfectly – the fear of sanctions induces media self-censorship, thus limiting media freedom even further (Kelemen 2017).

A bulk of the changes initiated by PiS also aimed at replacing leading personnel in public radio and TV station outlets. Yet, since PiS had no constitutional majority to change institutions as Fidesz did, the party decided to sidestep these: in December 2015, the government passed controversial laws enabling the Minister of Treasury to directly appoint the heads of public TV and radio, thus circumventing the National Broadcasting Council – a constitutional institution to guarantee independent information in state-owned media. In 2016, PiS established the Council of National Media to appoint the head of the Polish Television, the Polish Radio and the Polish Press Agency. At the same time, the constitutional organ – the National Broadcasting Council – has been rendered powerless and eventually taken over entirely by PiS to pressure private media, exactly the case of the Hungarian Media Council. Since then, state-owned media became a platform for hate campaigns against politicians and journalists critical of the ruling party. In 2016, Kaczyński made Jacek Kurski, an important PiS politician and leading political campaigner for PiS, the head of the state-owned TVP, the largest and highly influential anchor. Kurski is infamous for organising smear campaigns against PiS competitors for which he was sentenced by Polish courts. Yet, this did not prevent him to become an MP for PiS in 2007 and a MEP in 2009. Kurski's position is symptomatic for the patronal system of rewards and punishments, as he fell out of Kaczyński's grace a number of times but could regain his position through effective work in favour of the network.

In Hungarian private media, non-transparent arbitrary licensing decisions benefited pro-government broadcasters (Dragomir 2017a). Only media outlets that supported Orbán's regime benefitted from public advertising funds following the logic of the patronal network. The few remaining critical outlets that publish on government corruption or scandals are thus disabled financially, with their future insecure. A 2014 law further raised barriers to Hungarian journalists' access to public interest information thus making it harder to scrutinise government actions. Moreover, restrictions of media freedom were coupled with a media take-over to assert total control. Private media owners were pressured to sell to oligarchs aligned with the party. Heinrich Pecina, a controversial Austrian investor close to the Fidesz, facilitated the transfer of a monopoly of regional dailies to Lőrinc Mészáros, Orbán's child-hood friend, turned media tycoon. Mészáros is also responsible for the infamous closing down upon acquisition of Hungary's largest daily newspaper, leftist *Népszabadság* (Nagy 2018, 207). Similarly, in 2015, Andy Vajna, film-maker and Orbán's close ally, purchased a national private TV (*TV2*) with credit from the state-owned Eximbank. By 2017, 90% of Hungarian media belonged either to the state or a Fidesz ally (Dragomir 2017b), confirming Orbán's incontestable patron position on the Hungarian media scene.

Similar to Fidesz, PiS has been trying to put pressure on Polish private media using its patronal network in control of the regulatory authorities. For instance, in 2017, one of the largest private broadcasters, TVN was fined by the PiS-occupied National Broadcasting Council for its allegedly one-sided reporting of the 2016 protests against the PiS reforms of the court system. The fine was criticised by the EU, the Helsinki Foundation for Human Rights and the US State Department as a violation of freedom of expression and intimidation of critical voices. In 2018, the Council withdrew its decision, mainly due to US pressure, as TVN was bought by the American Discovery Corporation in 2015 (Money.pl 2018). Other than Hungary, Polish private media are still free, consequently, reporting about scandals, enrichment and other misdeeds of the ruling class is quite frequent, although the PiS government limited access to officials, used advertising and subscriptions funds to influence news outlets and is threatening reporters with legal action.

In sum, although patronalism is not new for CEE governments, Hungary and Poland reached previously unseen levels of patronalism, incumbent parties and their charismatic leaders building vast networks reaching all segments of society. Patronal networks are extended using legislative power to deconstruct former institutions and regulation. Still, there are some differences between the regimes: PiS lacks the constitutional power to make wide and deep institutional changes and thus the opposition still has a voice. Furthermore, Poland seems to correspond to the competing pyramid system, in which several networks compete for their power position vis-à-vis the single patron, who prefers pulling the strings from behind, not taking an official position in government. In contrast, Hungary seems to correspond to the single pyramid system, where no one can challenge Orbán as the ultimate patron, with all powers concentrated in his hands.

Party state capture

As already mentioned, Hungary and Poland seem to follow the practices of party state capture, where the ruling party seeks total re-monopolization of the political system in its own favour. This is another feature of Caesarean politics, an essential instrument being the dismantling of the rule of law, since independent courts, in particular the Constitutional Court and the Supreme Court, are major hindrances to concentrating power and state capture. Claiming they were enacting the "will of the people", who felt betrayed by liberal democracy, both Fidesz and PiS embarked on reforming the legal system upon taking office. The systematic changes aimed mainly at the circumvention of democratic rule of law and the weakening of judiciary to the extent that one can speak of the introduction of rule by law, placing the ruler (and his party) above the law.

Citing his 2010 electoral win as a "ballot box revolution", Orbán set out to adopt a new constitution (called Fundamental Law) to signal the beginning of a new era for Hungary, breaking with the unsuccessful transition. In this spirit, the 2012 Fundamental Law was adopted as a reaction to Hungary's previous constitution. It gave up the egalitarian aims of the post-communist constitutional liberal democratic system and shifted towards an anti-egalitarian and ethnic concept of the nation, as a source of power, in sharp contrast to the inclusive value system of the previous constitution or the EU constitution (Lisbon Treaty) (Majtényi, Kopper, and Susánszky 2019, 4). This anti-egalitarian thrust is also signalled by the constitution writing process, where Fidesz has exercised exclusive control. The amendment of the old and the adoption of the new constitution were both done using the non-transparent expedited process, without any consultation with the opposition parties or the people (e.g. through referendum). Orbán's government also adopted a series of so-called Cardinal Laws that require two-thirds of votes in parliament to be adopted or amended (Kelemen 2017, 221–2), further entrenching Orbán's new system against possible challenge from the opposition.

Although the new Hungarian constitution left the parliamentary architecture essentially intact, Orbán substantially emptied this construction to cement his personal rule. Starting from 2010, he consciously diminished available options for political opposition or civic groups to take part in the legislative process. The earlier norms that the opposition could set up select committees in parliament (Enyedi 2015) are disregarded and the government no longer uses normal parliamentary procedures to submit bills to avoid legal obligations to initiate social consultation with civil society groups and opposition parties. Instead, the standard became that individual MPs submit bills, often through the fast-track procedure, because in such cases no consultations need to take place and there is no time to contest Fidesz proposals (Majtényi, Kopper, and Susánszky 2019). Since there is no transparency in the legislative process and the opposition cannot interfere, parliament lost its role and just rubberstamps Fidesz's proposals.

When PiS won both the presidential and parliamentary elections in 2015, it adopted the Hungarian roadmap of legal changes to remove checks and balances. PiS did not win any constitutional majority as Fidesz but was able to form a single party government, an unprecedented event in Poland after the 1989 regime change. Based on this, PiS claimed a broad legitimacy for radical political change, using the same ethno-nationalist rhetoric that Orbán employed. The PiS government of Beata Szydlo (largely Kaczyński's puppet) embarked on a series of reforms carried out in violation of parliamentary procedures, marginalising the opposition and pushing through laws at night and at a speed not allowing a sensible debate. In this sense, the Polish parliament stopped being a separate power representing the people and became a tool of executive power, pushing through controversial reforms (Sadurski 2018), similarly to the case in Hungary.

Both Fidesz and PiS aimed for not only uncontested legislative power but tried to disable the judicial checks and balances of executive power. Orbán dismantled the rule of law step-by-step, from top to bottom, strengthening political interference affecting judicial independence over the years (Dimitrova 2018). Upon taking office, the Fidesz government severely curbed the competencies of the strong and independent Constitutional Court and changed the procedure for appointing judges to allow for appointments without consulting the opposition. The Fidesz constitution expanded the membership of the Constitutional Court from 11 to 15 judges to make more space for Fidesz loyalists, turning the top judiciary into a party establishment within the patronal network. When the Court nevertheless found unconstitutional some newly adopted laws, the government in response amended yet again the constitution, granting constitutional status to laws that were previously declared unconstitutional, nullifying rule of law and installing rule by law instead (Kelemen 2017; Bozóki and Hegedűs 2018; Zgut et al. 2018).

To assert further control over the judiciary, the Fidesz government lowered the retirement age of judges from 70 to 62 years to purge government critics and fill it with Fidesz loyalists (Kelemen 2017; Körösényi 2018). All the EU could do is start discrimination charges and while Hungary eventually amended the law, most of the ousted judges never returned. The political appointment of a party affiliate as the head of Hungary's National Judicial Office further strengthened political control of the judiciary by the Fidesz patronal network. The party also plans to establish an Administrative High Court, allowing exclusively judges arriving from the state's public administration (loyal to Fidesz) to rule on cases involving elections, taxes and public procurement (Hungarian Helsinki Committee 2018). These Fidesz executed judicial reforms ensure no legal challenge can be voiced against the government and procedures that were originally designed to limit executive power are meaningless. Orbán shows no sign of compromise on the issue, not even since the EU started action against his government for undermining the bloc's democratic values and rule of law in 2018.

Very similar developments took place in Poland after 2015, although it was the liberal-conservative PO (Civic Platform) and PSL (Polish People's Party) that first interfered with the set-up of the Constitutional Court, fearing electoral loss to PiS. The PO-PSL parliamentary majority elected a number of "their" judges to the Constitutional Court months before the official retirement of the judges to be replaced. While it was a rather transparent attempt to rig the Constitutional Court in favour of PO and PSL, it also politicised the Court, weakened its legitimacy and prompted its eventual destruction by PiS, equipped with the argument that the Court is not impartial anymore. This way, the PO-PSL government opened the way for the "winner takes it all" practice, in which all institutions, including the courts, are "up for grabs", once a party wins election.

The new laws adopted by PiS changed the functioning of the Constitutional Court, demanding higher majorities between judges to come to valid decisions, a higher number of judges, as well as a chronological order of deciding on the constitutional complaints. The new law has been criticised both domestically and abroad as a de facto paralysis of the Court and in consequence, a suspension of the checks-and-balances principle (Sadurski 2018). In the stand-off, the Constitutional Court declared some of the PiS decisions unconstitutional, while the PiS government continued to reject rulings of the Court, arguing that the Court cannot decide on its own about its personnel. Eventually, the Constitutional Court has been functionally disabled as PiS was able to put party loyalists and enablers on the bench (Grzeszczak and Karolewski 2018). Since the European Commission started a probe into rule of law violations in Poland in 2016, the government responded by EU bashing, labelling the Commission as an "unelected" body that lacks legitimacy, exactly the way Orbán did when Hungary was criticised by the EU (see the introduction to this Special Issue by Agarin).

After the Polish Constitutional Tribunal has been turned into an appendix of PiS, the next step was to restructure the ordinary courts, the National Council of the Judiciary and the Supreme Court, which was undertaken all at once through a 2017 law and a number of amendments in 2018. Once again, Hungarian examples were closely followed: PiS decreased the mandatory retirement age for Supreme Court judges from 70 to 65 years (60 years for the female judges) to replace judges with PiS loyalists. As a result, although a 6-year tenure was guaranteed by the constitution, 27 of 72 judges of the Supreme Court have been forced to retire, including the First President of the Supreme Court, Malgorzata Gersdorf. The President of Poland was given the power to extend judges' tenure, although there was no such constitutional provision (Grzeszczak and Karolewski 2018). The Polish government partly retreated from the controversial reforms only after the 2018 ECJ preliminary judgment, establishing EU law violation and threatening financial punishment. Nonetheless, measures to ensure control over the judiciary were little affected and the EU does not seem to be capable of stopping these. For instance, the PiS introduced new disciplinary chamber of the Supreme Court has become one of the main instruments of Justice Minister Ziobro to intimidate dissident judges. In addition, the Ministry of Justice organises systematic harassment and smear campaigns against judges critical of the reforms in order to "break" them, using classified information, including details from ongoing trials and the judges' private sensitive data (Kubik 2019). The systematic influence of executive power over courts questions the respect for the rule of law, judicial authority, as well as court independence and judicial impartiality (Batory Foundation 2018).

All Hungarian reforms were justified by Orbán with the need to purge of the country from the "political other", following Ceasarean logic that aims at limiting competition and reducing pluralism. He claims there is a need to finish "decommunisation" (Palonen 2018, 8), a process incomplete for Orbán, who considers the present left opposition as direct continuation of the communist elite. Orbán used this anti-elite populist discourse (and the mass discontent with the left) to come to power, yet, his new constitution not only delegitimized communists but also, in fact, weakened mass participation in order to protect his personal rule from public dissent. The tool of referendum came to be a purely plebiscitary method in the hand of the executive government (Körösényi 2018) since Orbán claims to represent "the will of the people". At the same time, the European Court of Human Rights saw a dramatic 1177 percent increase in the applications filed by Hungarian citizens (Bozóki and Hegedűs 2019).

The radical reforms carried out by PiS after 2015 have been accompanied by a similar discourse on "lustration".[6] The main rationale for the PiS legal changes (e.g. the forced retirement of judges) was that post-communist cronies and liberal traitors of the Polish nation hijacked various branches of the Polish government, including the courts. Using the same populist rhetoric, allegedly, the post-transition democratic system served only the interest of "postcommunist elites" at the expense of ordinary Poles. This is even more striking as PiS itself seems to be a safe harbour for a number of former communist apparatchiks, including former prosecutors involved in political trials of the 1980s,[7] the "archenemies" of PiS supporters, who fancy themselves as victims of communism and the Third Republic.

These political changes Hungary and Poland show the extent party state capture goes hand in hand with the dismantling of the rule of law and the system of checks and balances. The party not only attempts to capture every corner of the state but aims at circumventing democratic institutions to limit political opposition and diminish the role of politics. Interference with the judiciary disables executive review, and installing rule by law assures no dissent can be voiced against the regime. In turn, undermining the separation of powers helps entrench and extend the patronal networks of the party leaders to an extent never seen before and ensures Caesar, who claims to serve the "will of the people" can rule the country as he wishes.

Exclusionary identity politics

The third key aspect of Caesarean politics relates to exclusionary identity politics going beyond nationalist and sovereigntist outlook of a given party. The discursive processes of "othering" serve the strengthening of the imagery of the homogeneous "true people", served by the Caesar against "dangerous others" in a continuous existential fight. Caesarean governments give the enemy a face and a name, using blame attribution to shield the system from criticism pertaining to consolidating power. The "others" can be minorities, refugees, international organisations such as the IMF or the EU but also the liberal-leftist opposition and/or critics accused of endangering the sovereignty of the community. In this sense, exclusionary identity politics does not have to be based on ethnic or religious cleavages, as the "other" can be anybody who opposes the Caesarean regime.

All constitutional changes in Hungary were justified using a populist discourse of friends and enemies of the nation that allowed Orbán to define the "enemy" as the liberals and the 1990-born system of liberal democracy (Pappas 2014), while the nation was rearticulated as the sole basis of legitimate politics (Palonen 2018). Orbán's populism is thus strategic politics of authority creation and elite transformation (Urbinati 2014), the constitutional changes weakening former power holders, promoting adversarial politics and favouring majoritarian norms at the expense of minorities, similarly to what Pappas (2014) described as "populist democracy". Orbán claims to be the sole representative of the people through a direct link of the so-called national consultations, regular questionnaires sent to the citizens. The questions are formulated in a way to appeal to identity fears of people, clearly signalling who (IMF, EU, migrants, civic actors, "Soros troops", etc.) are the enemies to be blamed for the different existential threats Hungary must defend against. Eight rounds of consultations took place between May 2010 and December 2018, but the outcome of the consultations has never been made public. This does not prevent Orbán to use this plebiscitary tool to sidestep both political opposition and citizens, shrinking politics instead empowering the people by claiming his public policy is the "will of the nation" (Enyedi 2015, 2016; Körösényi 2018).

Media control was crucial for the government propaganda perpetuating the populist image of Hungary in a Manichean world, surrounded by enemies, which in turn justified Orbán's concentration of power only to enable him fight the continuously re-created list of enemies and threats. Facing the economic crisis, the nationalisation of private pension funds allowed Orbán to kick the IMF out from the country and claim success against the EU and the IMF imposed austerity measures (Jenne and Mudde 2012). Pointing out the lack of democratic accountability in the EU and IMF, these became "enemies" of the people and Orbán declared already in 2012 that "Hungarians will not live as foreigners dictate" (Telek 2015), perpetuating sentiments of resentment and distrust of international organisations. Internal enemies of Orbán's system had a similar fate. For allegedly attacking Fidesz and Orbán on all possible forums, civic groups and philanthropist George Soros were identified as enemies of the nation in a conspiracy theory resembling very much the "deep state" narrative in the US, with Soros being "the puppet master allegedly pulling the strings of all the government's foes, including the NGOs, the critical media, the opposition parties, and the EU" (Krekó and Enyedi 2018, 45). Laws limiting the free operation and creation of NGOs were adopted (Dimitrova 2018) and the 2017 Hungarian Foreign Agent Act resembles Russia's infamous law that requires foreign-funded NGOs to register as foreign agents (Dragomir 2017b; Simon 2018).

The 2015 refugee crisis brought out the essence of Orbán's exclusionary identity politics, as he adopted a fierce anti-migration discourse and policy, making people think of the "others" exclusively in terms of "enemies", refugees being blamed for spreading crime and terrorism besides the Islamization of Europe. Taping into xenophobic public opinion, the refugee crisis presented this way became an existential threat, and anti-foreign sentiments rose to levels never seen before. Polls showed two-thirds of Hungarians supported Orbán in building a fence on the southern border to keep migrants out; and Hungarians were the most likely people in Europe to believe refugees increase the chances of terrorism (Lendvai 2018). Simultaneously, people in support of refugees were labelled "human traffickers", betraying the nation and selling out national interest, using the "deep state" narrative of foreign interest agents.

PiS has initiated similar discourses constructing internal and external enemies. One of the more salient ideologists of PiS, Andrzej Zybertowicz, said one of the major tasks for PiS should be the creation of the "Machine of Narrative Security", which would be a concerted system of "narrative" activities involving the Polish diplomacy, public administration and propaganda. Zybertowicz is also the author of the idea that the Polish state has been penetrated by "grey networks" of former communist security services and the public protests against PiS can be seen as a form of hybrid war Russia allegedly is leading against the new Polish government, identified with the "Polish nation" (Wilgocki 2018). This resembles the recurrent argument that protests against the PiS government might be initiated and even provoked by the Russian government with the goal of destabilisation of Poland.

The Polish government has backed Budapest in its anti-refugee politics since 2015. The migration crisis has become a central issue in Poland, too, even though the country was not located on the Balkan migration route. The PiS government discourse caused a similar dramatic drop in the readiness of Poles to accept refugees (Strzelecki 2017). Budapest and Warsaw have become adamant critics of the EU refugee relocation scheme, stressing its repressive nature and pointing out that migration policy is a prerogative of the member states. Moreover, the PiS discourse evoked physical threats posed by refugees, Kaczyński argued already in the 2015 campaign that "various parasites and protozoa in the bodies of those people [refugees], safe for them, can be dangerous to us" (Newsweek 2015). Kaczyński reiterated this construction of refugees as threatening "others" when he spoke of the danger of "radical lowering" of the living standards in Poland should refugees be accepted (Leszczynski 2017). By so doing, the PiS government played Caesarean politics, presenting itself as a cultural bulwark against the Islamization of Europe – exactly the same way that Orbán has argued Hungary is the gatekeeper of Europe in the face of migration.

Similar to Fidesz, the PiS government has been at pains to depict the EU (especially the European Commission) as a one-sided institution in league with the left political opposition, being a threatening "other". Former PiS foreign minister Waszczykowski criticised the alleged leftist leanings of the EU saying it opposed "what the majority of Poles represent – tradition, historical consciousness, patriotism, belief in God and a normal family between a man and a woman" (Bild 2016). This EU bashing went hand in hand with calling the parliamentary opposition traitors for siding with the EU (Lyman and Berendt 2015). At the same time, the PiS government was beguiling Orbán as its natural ally against the EU, playing a blame game against Brussels to mobilise their supporters at home and to support each other within the EU. In response to EU's criticism of undemocratic policies, Orbán and Kaczyński agreed that a "cultural counter-revolution" (Krekó and Enyedi 2018, 45) was needed to radically reform a post-Brexit EU, calling for more power to be devolved to national parliaments, which they see more legitimate (though both have been very active emptying these of democratic norms and practices).

Hungary and Poland show that discourses of identity fears outlining enemies, traitors and threats are central to justifying political changes in Caesarean politics. The discursive strategies employed in the two countries are strikingly similar, irrespective whether these have been employed to justify the exchange of the elite, the judicial purge, or the new legal and administrative setup that serve the patronal network and state capture. The same exclusionary identity policy and discourse is employed to rally support of the people and shield the regime from competition or criticism both domestically and internationally. The goal is to create the image of a Manichean world that justifies the power concentration in the hands of the ruler, portrayed as the bastion of the nation, while opponents can be deemed an enemy, labelled a traitor or defined as an external foe of the national cause. The traitors and threatening others can be found anywhere, not only among minorities or immigrants, political opponents but in the LGBT community or in international organisations, thus allowing for a rather flexible framing of exclusive identity. This way, Caesarean politics uses identity politics in a strategic way, readily changing and adapting to the needs of the ruler in identifying new enemies to be fought – be that cultural, religious, political or any other – to justify the latest changes in the regime.

Conclusions

We have argued that the application of our new theoretical tool comprised of the interactive triad of Caesarean politics – patronalism, party state capture and exclusionary identity politics – helps us better understand the nature of the new regimes in Hungary and Poland. Despite both Orbán and Kaczyński framing institutional and identity changes as "politics as usual", the deconstruction of liberal democracy in both countries went to the extent that the Caesarean regime represents a difference in kind, rather than a difference in degree from previous post-transition regimes. This is despite the fact that both countries witnessed weak entrenchment of and declining attachments to democratic norms, or that certain patronage and state capture practices were integral to domestic policies already under previous governments. Yet, Caesarean politics is unique in systematically denying political pluralism and dismantling the rule of law, using exclusionary discourses of enemies and traitors to deny opponents, amass power and limit competition, while vast patronal networks overtake the entire state.

We have noted how similar trajectories the two countries followed are and how these reflect the reinforcing interactive elements of Caesarean politics. Orbán and Kaczyński have made patronal networks the essential element of their political regime in Budapest and Warsaw. Unlike e.g. Russia, these patronal networks do not cut across parties, firms and NGOs but rather focus on the party of the patron itself, which becomes the main vehicle for power-hoarding and state capture. In turn, party state capture – unlike corporate state capture – ensures the rapid execution of identity policy preferences in the form of illiberal and authoritarian institutional and policy reforms. Political interference, radical elite exchange and far-reaching centralisation have led to questioning the separation of the different branches of government and ensure one party rule. The restrictions of media freedom, coupled with media control, make for a propaganda machinery at the disposal of Fidesz and PiS to maintain or increase societal support. This is where the third aspect of Caesarean politics comes into play: both Fidesz and PiS embarked on exclusionary identity policies centred on imageries of "friends" and "enemies" to substantiate threats that need to be fought, which in turn legitimate concentration of power and shutting off opponents (domestic or international). Groups portrayed as outsiders to the homogeneously constructed nation are labelled enemies and traitors – including not only multinational capital, refugees, liberal organisations, the EU but domestic groups such as the opposition, critical liberal activists or scholars – and have become the prime targets of discrimination and resentment. The different discursively created crises only contribute to generating more resentment against the various "others", while focusing on existential threats successfully diverts the attention of citizens from political deliberation or accountability of the executive that are circumvented by patronal networks and party state capture.

Still, there seem to be differences between the countries. The deconstruction of democracy has advanced to a higher degree in Hungary than in Poland. The extent of power-hoarding and pressure on critical voices is much greater in Hungary and the media is now under full control of Orbán. Poland followed this roadmap and used the legislative law machinery to same way to deconstruct the liberal democratic regime but has not (yet) succeeded with regard to a number of essential Caesarean steps such as electoral law reform or effective pressure on private media. This might be because Fidesz has been able to secure constitutional majority three times since 2010 and therefore has more means and legitimacy than PiS but this is one of the most crucial questions for any future analysis of Caesarean politics. Are the differences between the two countries due to Poland being a latecomer and PiS lacking constitutional means or are there other reasons for this "divergence in convergence"? One possible answer could refer to the different nature of patronal politics in the two countries. In Poland, we have a competing pyramid system, in which several networks compete for power. The system is less typical as Kaczyński does not have any official position in the government but is very effective in pulling the strings of power. In contrast, Orbán, a widely recognised, skilled and charismatic politician, heads Hungary's single pyramid system that ensures his total control.

Yet, some might claim that losing the 2019 local elections present a serious challenge for Orbán's Ceasarean rule and similarly the 2019 PiS general election results show that the Caesarean regime can be resisted. Yet, a closer inspection of the results show that Orbán's Fidesz did not lose votes but the opposition coordinated better its electoral strategy.

Similarly, PiS received the highest vote share by any party in Poland since the transition and did not obtain more seats because of the peculiarities of the electoral system. For both regimes, following the Caesarean logic of rule by law, the immediate response could be electoral law reform, as already intended by PiS and already once done by Fidesz. Another alternative for Orbán in response to the opposition success is to further diminish the power of local governments as already suggested by some Fidesz propositions (Nepszava 2019). The October 2019 parliamentary elections strengthened the PiS rule in Poland. Even though the PiS lost its majority in the Senate, the Senate can only postpone legislation, rather than block it. The decisive step will be the presidential election in 2020. We expect both Kaczyński and Orbán will concentrate on further entrenching their regime against any possible opposition as their success depends on being able to "stand for the people". The new (old) PiS government has been proceeding with its weakening of rule of law, mainly by establishing pressure on independent judges and putting further party loyalists on the bench of the Constitutional Court.

Notwithstanding the differences, the cases of Poland and Hungary show that highly polarised political systems with low levels of social trust in democratic institutions and prone to identity fears run the risk of Caesarean seizure. Hungary and Poland may be the forerunners but there are many others in CEE and in other parts of the world, who are/have imitated similar strategies of Caesarean politics to gain power and the danger of further democratic backsliding is real. Mobilising along the lines of "friends" and "enemies" enables leaders to strengthen their grip on power and exclude the opposition, portrayed as illegitimate and incapable of governing or traitor to the national cause. At the same time, plebiscitary tools can be used to sidestep both opposition and citizens, shrinking politics by claiming that public policy and discourse reflects the "will of the nation". Playing on identity fears, leaders divert public attention from party-controlled networks running the captured state that on turn disables any challenge of Caesarean leadership. Non-transparent procedures and the loss of liberties and rights make meaningless the democratic constraints of executive power or majority rule and everything becomes subordinated to conjured national interest – defined solely according to Caesar's taste. Caesar, the ruler-cum-patron, enjoys primacy over law, regulations, social norms, or the people – the very foundations of democratic rule of law.

Notes

1. Fidesz won in coalition with the Christian Democrats (KDNP), an insignificant political force in itself.
2. We would like to thank one of the anonymous reviewers for this point.
3. In Hungary, violent demonstrations followed a leaked admission of the Socialist PM that he lied for years to citizens to win elections in 2006. In 2014, secret tapes of leading PO politicians showed their arrogance and staggering distrust of the institutions of the Polish state they controlled (Chapman 2014).
4. This is well illustrated with the fate of Simicska, who was completely removed from the network in 2014 although he established Fidesz's financial base during the 1990s and 2000s and thus had great political influence due to surrogates in high positions in ministries and state-companies. He was replaced by Orbán's childhood friend, Lőrinc Mészáros, a gas pipe fitter who has become the second wealthiest man of the country, and Zsolt Nyerges, a family friend of Orbán, who took over the Simicska businesses (Petho and Szabo 2019).

5. The institution responsible for is responsible for the oversight of banking, capital markets and insurance institutions.
6. Political practices to purge the former employees and informants of the communist security services.
7. One of the more prominent examples is Stanislaw Piotrowicz, who played an active role in dismantling the Constitutional Court in 2016. Piotrowicz was a communist prosecutor during the Martial Law in Poland (1981-1983) and was actively involved in charging anti-communist dissidents.

Disclosure statement

No potential conflict of interest was reported by the authors.

ORCID

Robert Sata http://orcid.org/0000-0001-8945-2561
Ireneusz Pawel Karolewski http://orcid.org/0000-0002-7836-0001

References

Almond, Gabriel A. 1956. "Comparative Political Systems." *The Journal of Politics* 18 (3): 391–409.
Batory Foundation. 2018. "Report of the Stefan Batory Foundation Legal Expert Group on the Impact of the Judiciary Reform in Poland in 2015–2018." http://www.batory.org.pl/upload/files/Programy%20operacyjne/Odpowiedzialne%20Panstwo/Batory%20Foundation_Report%20on%20the%20judiciary%20reform%20in%20Poland.pdf.
Bild. 2016. "Polen-Minister verteidigt Mediengesetz." January 3. https://www.bild.de/bildlive/2016/14-polen-minister-44000764.bild.html.
Bozóki, András, and Dániel Hegedűs. 2018. "An Externally Constrained Hybrid Regime: Hungary in the European Union." *Democratization* 25 (7): 1173–1189. doi:10.1080/13510347.2018.1455664.
Bozóki, András, and Dániel Hegedűs. 2019. "Constraining or Enabling? Democratic Backsliding in Hungary and the Role of the EU." Denver, CO: European Studies Association (EUSA) Convention, May 9–11.
Brouillette, Amy, and Joost van Beek. 2012. "Hungarian Media Laws in Europe: An Assessment of the Consistency of Hungary's Media Laws with European Practices and Norms." Center for Media and Communication Studies. http://cmds.ceu.hu/article/2014-03-09/hungarian-media-laws-europe-assessment.
Casper, Gerhard. 2007. "Caesarism in Democratic Politics: Reflections on Max Weber." https://papers.ssrn.com/sol3/papers.cfm?abstract_id=1032647.

Catterberg G. and Moreno A. 2005. "The Individual Bases of Political Trust: Trends in New and Established Democracies." *International Journal of Public Opinion Research* 18 (1): 31–48.

Chapman, Annabelle. 2014. "Secret Tapes in Polish 'Waitergate' Scandal Could Cost Warsaw's Government a Key European Commission Post." *Newsweek*, July 15. https://www.newsweek.com/secret-tapes-polish-waitergate-scandal-could-cost-warsaws-government-key-258912.

Cianetti, Licia, James Dawson, and Seán Hanley. 2018. "Rethinking 'Democratic Backsliding' in Central and Eastern Europe – Looking Beyond Hungary and Poland." *East European Politics* 34 (3): 243–256. doi:10.1080/21599165.2018.1491401.

Dimitrova, Antoaneta L. 2018. "The Uncertain Road to Sustainable Democracy: Elite Coalitions, Citizen Protests and the Prospects of Democracy in Central and Eastern Europe." *East European Politics* 34 (3): 257–275. doi:10.1080/21599165.2018.1491840.

Dragomir, Marius. 2017a. "How the Hungarian Government Nationalized Criticism." *MediaLaws*, September 30. http://www.medialaws.eu/how-the-hungarian-government-nationalized-criticism/.

Dragomir, Marius. 2017b. "The State of Hungarian Media: Endgame." Media Policy Project. http://blogs.lse.ac.uk/mediapolicyproject/2017/08/29/the-state-of-hungarian-media-endgame/.

Enyedi, Zsolt. 2015. "Plebeians, Citoyens and Aristocrats or Where is the Bottom of Bottom-up? The Case of Hungary." In *European Populism in the Shadow of the Great Recession*, edited by Hanspeter Kriesi and Takis S. Pappas, 229–244. Colchester: ECPR Press.

Enyedi, Zsolt. 2016. "Paternalist Populism and Illiberal Elitism in Central Europe." *Journal of Political Ideologies* 21 (1): 9–25.

Eurobarometer. 2019. European Commission (1974–2019). https://ec.europa.eu/commfrontoffice/publicopinion/index.cfm.

Fazekas, Mihály, and István János Tóth. 2016. "From Corruption to State Capture: A New Analytical Framework with Empirical Applications from Hungary." *Political Research Quarterly* 69 (2): 320–334. doi:10.1177/1065912916639137.

Goffman, Erving. 1983. "The Interaction Order." *American Sociological Review* 48: 1–17.

Greskovits, Bela. 2015. "The Hollowing and Backsliding of Democracy in East Central Europe." *Global Policy* 6: 28–37. doi:10.1111/1758-5899.12225.

Grzeszczak, Robert, and Ireneusz Pawel Karolewski. 2018. "The Rule of Law Crisis in Poland: A New Chapter." *VerfBlog*, August 8. https://verfassungsblog.de/the-rule-of-law-crisis-in-poland-a-new-chapter/.

Hakim, Danny. 2015. "Homeowners in Poland Borrowed in Swiss Francs, and Now Pay Dearly." *New York Times*, January 28. https://www.nytimes.com/2015/01/29/business/international/polish-homeowners-feel-the-weight-of-a-heftier-swiss-franc.html.

Hale, Henry E. 2014. *Patronal Politics: Eurasian Regime Dynamics in Comparative Perspective*. Cambridge: Cambridge University Press.

Hale, Henry E. 2017. "Russian Patronal Politics beyond Putin." *Daedalus* 146 (2): 30–40.

Holodny, Elena. 2016. "There's Another Banking Crisis Brewing in Europe and Terrible Mortgages are to Blame." *Business Insider*, June 9. https://www.businessinsider.com/polish-mortgages-banking-crisis-swiss-franc-2016-6?IR=T.

Hungarian Helsinki Committee. 2018. "Attacking the Last Line of Defence. Judicial Independence in Hungary in Jeopardy." June 19. https://www.helsinki.hu/en/attacking-the-last-line-of-defence/.

Huysmans, Jef. 2004. "Minding Exceptions: The Politics of Insecurity and Liberal Democracy." *Contemporary Political Theory* 3: 321–341.

Huysmans, Jef. 2006. "International Politics of Insecurity: Normativity, Inwardness and the Exception." *Security Dialogue* 37 (1): 11–29.

Innes, Abby. 2014. "The Political Economy of State Capture in Central Europe." *JCMS: Journal of Common Market Studies* 52 (1): 88–104.

Jenne, Erin K., and Cas Mudde. 2012. "Can Outsiders Help?" *Journal of Democracy* 23 (3): 147–155. Project MUSE, doi:10.1353/jod.2012.0057.

Karolewski, Ireneusz Pawel. 2012. "Caesarean Citizenship and Its Anti-Civic Potential in the European Union." In *Civic Resources and the Future of the European Union*, edited by Ireneusz Pawel Karolewski and Viktoria Kaina, 196–2018. London: Routledge.

Kaviraj, Sudipta. 1986. "Indira Gandhi and Indian Politics." *Economic and Political Weekly* 21 (38/39): 1697–1708.

Kelemen, Daniel R. 2017. "Europe's Other Democratic Deficit: National Authoritarianism in Europe's Democratic Union." *Government and Opposition* 52 (2): 211–238. doi:10.1017/gov.2016.41.

Körösényi, András. 2018. "The Theory and Practice of Plebiscitary Leadership: Weber and the Orbán Regime." *East European Politics and Societies*. doi:10.1177/0888325418796929.

Kostadinova, Tatiana, and Zoltán Kmetty. 2018. "Corruption and Political Participation in Hungary: Testing Models of Civic Engagement." *East European Politics and Societies*. doi:10.1177/0888325418800556.

Krekó, Péter, and Zsolt Enyedi. 2018. "Orbán's Laboratory of Illiberalism." *Journal of Democracy* 29 (3): 39–51. Project MUSE, doi:10.1353/jod.2018.0043.

Kubik, Agnieszka. 2019. "Hejterka 'Emi' sypie 'Kastę' u Ziobry." *Wyborcza*, September 9. http://wyborcza.pl/7,75398,25171753,hejterka-emi-sypie-kaste-u-ziobry.html.

Lendvai, Paul. 2018. 'The Most Dangerous Man in the European Union' the Metamorphosis of Viktor Orbán." *The Atlantic*, April 7. https://www.theatlantic.com/international/archive/2018/04/viktor-Orbán-hungary/557246/.

Leszczynski, Adam. 2017. *Piętrowa bzdura Kaczyńskiego o uchodźcach i "cywilizacji opartej na chrześcijaństwie"*. OKOpress. https://oko.press/pietrowa-bzdura-Kaczyński ego-o-uchodzcach-cywilizacji-opartej-chrzescijanstwie/.

Lijphart, Arend. 1969. "Consociational Democracy." *World Politics* 21 (2): 207–225.

Lyman, Rick, and Joanna Berendt. 2015. "As Poland Lurches to Right, Many in Europe Look in Alarm." *New York Times*, December 14. https://www.nytimes.com/2015/12/15/world/europe/poland-law-and-justice-party-jaroslaw-Kaczyński.html.

Magyar, Bálint. 2016. *Post-Communist Mafia State: The Case of Hungary*. Budapest: Central European University Press. http://www.jstor.org/stable/10.7829/j.ctt19z391 g.

Majtényi, Balázs, Ákos Kopper, and Pál Susánszky. 2019. "Constitutional Othering, Ambiguity and Subjective Risks of Mobilization in Hungary: Examples from the Migration Crisis." *Democratization* 26 (2): 173–189. doi:10.1080/13510347.2018.1493051.

Meeusen, Cecil, and Laura Jacobs. 2017. "Television News Content of Minority Groups as an Intergroup Context Indicator of Differences between Target-Specific Prejudices." *Mass Communication and Society* 20 (2): 213–240.

Money.pl. 2018. "Gigantyczna kara dla TVN. KRRiT cofa decyzję z grudnia." January 10. https://www.money.pl/gospodarka/wiadomosci/artykul/kara-tvn-krrit,132,0,2396036.html.

Müller, Jan-Werner. 2014. "Eastern Europe Goes South. Disappearing Democracy in the EU's Newest Members." Foreign Affairs. February 12. https://www.foreignaffairs.com/articles/eastern-europe-caucasus/2014-02-12/eastern-europe-goes-south.

Nagy, Zsofia. 2018. "Mediation Opportunity Structures in Illiberal Democracies. Social Movement Responses to State Anti-refugee Propaganda in Hungary." In *Current Perspectives on Communication and Media Research*, edited by Laura Peja, et al., 203–216. Bremen: Edition Lumière.

Nepszava. 2019. "Orbán elkezdte a bosszút az önkormányzatok ellen." https://nepszava.us/orban-elkezdte-a-bosszut-az-onkormanyzatok-ellen/.

NewsweekPolska. 2015. "Kaczyński: Pasożyty i pierwotniaki w organizmach uchodźców groźne dla Polaków." October 13. https://www.newsweek.pl/polska/jaroslaw-Kaczyński-o-uchodzcach/89mwbx3.

Ober, Josiah. 2017. "Joseph Schumpeter's Caesarist Democracy." *Critical Review* 29 (4): 473–491.

Omachel, Radosław. 2019. "Zarzuty dla byłych szefów KNF Jakubiaka i Kwaśniaka okazały się wyssane z palca." *Newsweek Polska*, February 26. https://www.newsweek.pl/polska/polityka/zarzuty-dla-bylych-szefow-knf-jakubiaka-i-kwasniaka-okazaly-sie-wyssane-z-palca/p6nejbx.

Palonen, Emilia. 2018. "Performing the Nation: the Janus-faced Populist Foundations of Illiberalism in Hungary." *Journal of Contemporary European Studies* 26 (3): 308–321. doi:10.1080/14782804.2018.1498776.

Pappas, Takis. 2014. "Populist Democracies: Post-authoritarian Greece and Post-Communist Hungary." *Government and Opposition* 49 (1): 1–23. doi:10.1017/gov.2013.21.

Pethő, András, and András Szabó. 2019. "Inside the Fall of the Oligarch Who Turned Against Viktor Orbán." Direkt36.hu. https://www.direkt36.hu/en/feltarul-simicska-bukasanak-titkos-tortenete/.

Sadurski, Wojciech. 2018. "How Democracy Dies (in Poland): A Case Study of Anti-Constitutional Populist Backsliding." Sydney Law School Research Paper. https://papers.ssrn.com/sol3/papers.cfm?abstract_id=3103491.

Schmitt, Carl. [1932] 1996. *The Concept of the Political*. Chicago: University of Chicago Press.

Simon, Zoltan. 2018. "How Europe's Populist Ringleader Transformed Hungary: QuickTake." *Bloomberg*, May 16. https://www.bloomberg.com/news/articles/2018-05-16/how-europe-s-populist-ringleader-transformed-hungary-quicktake.

Steinmetz, George. 2009. "Caesarism and Parliamentarism." *Archives Européennes de Sociologie* 50 (3): 463–466.

Strzelecki, M. 2017. "Poles Value Denying Muslim Refugees Over Being in EU." *Bloomberg*. https://www.bloomberg.com/news/articles/2017-07-05/most-poles-prefer-banning-muslims-to-eu-membership-poll-shows.

Telek, Alphan. 2015. "Rise of the Far-Right Jobbik in Hungary." Political and Social Research Institute of Europe. http://ps-europe.org/rise-of-the-far-right-jobbik-in-hungary/.

Todosijević, Bojan, and Zsolt Enyedi. 2008. "Authoritarianism Without Dominant Ideology: Political Manifestations of Authoritarian Attitudes in Hungary." *Political Psychology* 29 (5): 767–787. http://www.jstor.org/stable/20447161.

Urbinati, Nadia. 2014. *Democracy Disfigured*. Cambridge, MA: Harvard University Press. http://www.jstor.org/stable/j.ctt6wpndf.

Walters, William. 2002. "Deportation, Expulsion, and the International Police of Aliens." *Citizenship Studies* 6 (3): 265–292.

Wilgocki, Michal. 2018. "Prof. Andrzej Zybertowicz patrzy na marsz KOD. I widzi wojnę hybrydową z Rosją." http://wyborcza.pl/1,75398,19699456,prof-andrzej-zybertowicz-patrzy-na-marsz-kod-i-widzi-wojne.html.

Wilkin, Peter, Lina Dencik, and Éva Bognár. 2015. "Digital Activism and Hungarian Media Reform: The Case of Milla." *European Journal of Communication* 30 (6): 682–697. doi:10.1177/0267323115595528.

Willame, Jean-Claude. 1971. "Politics and Power in Congo-Kinshasa." *Africa Report* 16 (1): 14–17.

Zgut, Edit, Vit Dostal, Lóránt Győri, Grigorij Meseznikov, and Wojciech Przybylski. 2018. "Illiberalism in the V4: Pressure Points and Bright Spots." Political Capital and FSE. June 5. http://www.politicalcapital.hu/pc-admin/source/documents/pc_fnf_v4illiberalism_pressurepoints_20180605.pdf.

In Europe's Closet: the rights of sexual minorities in the Czech Republic and Slovakia

Petra Guasti and Lenka Bustikova

ABSTRACT
This article explores the mechanisms of accommodation and backlash against a new identity group in the Czech Republic and Slovakia—LGBT. Minority demands spark political backlash because societal consensus lags behind the actual accommodation of sexual minorities. The legal framework of the European Union and international pressure groups further accelerate the process of accommodation and polarisation. Yesterday's accommodation in Western Europe is today's demand in Eastern Europe. The common European framework erodes the grip of domestic elites on minority rights and contributes to backlash by social conservative forces.

Introduction

In the summer of 2019, the backlash against the Lesbian, Gay, Bisexual, and Transgender (LGBT) rights escalated both in Poland and the Czech Republic.[1] The Archbishop of Prague adopted the term "rainbow plague", coined by the Cardinal of Cracow, and used it to criticise the Prague Magistrate's use of the rainbow flag:

> Still, to support the so-called "rainbow activities" by the capital [Prague] and others: I would expect at least the same support to multi-child families. They raise and care for their offspring, who will also be future taxpayers, without whom the future of the nation will not exist, and Europe will indeed be depopulated, as was the case with the plague.[2]

The universalism of sexual rights, the diffusion of LGBT accommodation in Europe, and EU legislation (e.g. a ban on workplace discrimination), the domestic demands of sexual minority groups have begun to make defenders of the status quo feel threatened (cf. Vasilev 2016). The current status quo excludes same-sex couples from legalised cohabitation, traditional marriage, and adoption rights, but is being contested. The proponents of expanding LGBT rights are emboldened to seek accommodation by looking "across the fence" to Western European countries, where policies such as marriage equality and full adoption rights have been successfully adopted. The opponents of accommodation are looking across the same fence with horror, realising that it may soon be no longer socially or legally acceptable to discriminate against citizens based on sexual orientation.

After thirty years of rebuilding democracy, minority grievances stemming from cultural and religious divisions, still haunt Central and Eastern Europe (CEE; Hroch 1993; Jasiewicz 2007; Hanley and Vachudova 2018; Bustikova 2019; Kolev 2020; Vachudova 2019). The transformation of the polity actually escalated identity politics when new democracies re-defined "the people" and accommodated the most vocal minorities (Pytlas 2016; Bustikova 2019). Simultaneously, emboldened political actors exploited identity politics (Appel and Gould 2000). The institutions of liberal democracy empowered minorities and facilitated the emergence of advocacy groups within a vibrant civil society.

Democratisation emboldened sexual minorities to seek an expansion of their rights (e.g. registered partnership, marriage, and adoption). With the help of the European Union (EU) anti-discrimination framework and LGBT advocacy groups, sexual minorities were empowered to seek channels of accommodation in the new democracies of Eastern Europe (Pavlik 2006; Guasti 2016, 2019; Vasilev 2016; O'Dwyer 2018a, 2018b).

This article explores new identity politics in Eastern Europe. The demands of sexual minorities – legal protection against discrimination, same-sex marriage, adoption of children – are universal and LGBT advocacy groups across Europe demand the same type of rights for the same type of actors. Whereas the demands of ethnic groups are diverse, the demands of sexual minorities are more or less uniform. In sum, the difference between the demands of ethnic and sexual minorities is the universalism of LGBT rights and the particularism of ethnic demands.

The European framework of anti-discrimination provided an excellent opportunity for LGBT groups to expand LGBT rights. Sexual minorities often seised these windows of opportunity. The result has been that issues related to gender and sexual conduct are increasingly politicised in Eastern Europe, and this new identity frontier has, in some countries, largely replaced the politics of ethnic accommodation (Brubaker 2013).

The existing literature on LGBT rights in Western Europe mostly approaches it "through the lens of transnational activism, and how the EU and other multilateral institutions have aided local LGBT activists in articulating human rights claims" (Kollman and Waites 2009). The research on the politicisation of LGBT rights in Central and Eastern Europe is comparatively limited (Mole 2011; Pelz 2014; Cunik 2015; Gould and Moe 2015; Gould 2016; O'Dwyer 2018a, 2018b; Weaver 2020), and mostly focuses on the role of the EU, the impact of Europeanization on domestic supporters of rights (Jacobsson and Saxonberg 2015) and the framing of the LGBT issues by advocacy groups (Cunik 2015).

Over the past 30 years, the LGBT advocates across the Central East European (CEE) region have achieved one demand – the introduction of registered partnership for same-sex couples in the Czech Republic and Slovenia (2006), Hungary (2009), Croatia (2014) and in Estonia (2016). The remaining CEE countries offer limited recognition of same-sex partnership.[3] Thus in most Eastern Europe, LGBT accommodation is slow and limited at best. At the same time, 16 of the 28 member states of the European Union have permitted marriage and adoption to same-sex couples.

Sexual minorities have shallow political backing and seek international allies. When doing so, they highlight the accommodation of demands and expansion of rights in Western Europe. Since the demands are novel to the CEE, it is easier to link the discomfort with the minority accommodation of new groups to an alien ruler: the European Union (Hechter 2013, on sovereignty, see: Siroky and Sigwart 2014). Newly politicised identity groups with "alien" demand trigger hostility and generate backlash.

Opposition to the expansion of LGBT rights is partially fuelled by the post-communism legacy and its conservative social values. For most post-communist citizens, the thought that sexual minorities should be allowed to adopt and raise children is unpopular (Takács, Szalma, and Bartus 2016). Quite often, LGBT demands have triggered a backlash similar to the backlash against the demands of the ethnic groups (cf. Bustikova 2019). To showcase these new sources of polarisation on identity politics, we focus on the LGBT minority. We focus on the politicisation of rights in the context of the transnational legal framework and diffusion of LGBT accommodation across the EU.

We explore the mechanisms of minority backlash against sexual minorities in former Czechoslovakia. The Czech Republic and Slovakia both experienced a backlash against the expansion of the rights of sexual minorities. Nevertheless, the Czech Republic and Slovakia represent two divergent approaches to LGBT accommodation in Eastern Europe; the former pursued legalisation of LGBT rights and the latter sought only limited accommodation. The Czech Republic (together with Slovenia) was the first Eastern European country to legalise registered partnerships. Conversely, Slovakia is a country where LGBT accommodation is limited more or less to the minimum required by EU law and the European Court of Justice (ECJ).

Since the Czech Republic and Slovakia belonged to the same federation until 1993 and shared the same legal framework, we can more readily identify the sources of policy divergence. To understand policy divergence after the breakup of Czechoslovakia, we focus on successful and failed institutional change – in the parliamentary arena (the Czech Republic, Slovakia) and a referendum (Slovakia). We investigate both pro- and anti-LGBT groups and their political allies. We pay particular attention to the role of the EU, given its importance in facilitating accommodation. Although the European Union generates a legal framework that protects the LGBT minority from discrimination, it is ultimately up to the domestic actors to push the framework forward or to push back against the expansion of minority rights to the extent legally allowed.

In short, this article traces the mechanisms of accommodation and backlash against LGBT. We find that although previous accommodation represents one path to backlash (Bustikova 2017, 2019), backlash can also ensue following "mere demands" for accommodation, without subsequent objective, policy-related accommodation. Whereas previous literature (Pirro 2014; Minkenberg 2015; Pytlas 2015; Bustikova 2019) explored the politicisation of ethnic group rights and its implication for political polarisation, this research focuses predominantly on traditional groups (Roma, Jews, various ethnic minorities) and domestic dynamics. We build on this literature by shifting the focus to a new groups as new sources of polarisation (Bustikova 2014, 2017, 2019; Bustikova et al. 2019). Furthermore, we incorporate the potential effects of the transnational legal framework in shaping the dynamics of domestic party competition (Guasti 2017, 2018, 2019; Guasti, Siroky, and Stockemer 2017). In doing so, the study advanced the state of the art and provide novel insights into the evolving politics of minority rights.

Theoretical and legislative framework

In order to account for the constraining effect of the European legislative and normative framework on domestic friends and foes of the rights of sexual minorities, we rely on the institutionalist approach (Hall and Thelen 2009; Mahoney and Thelen 2009; Thelen 2009).

We define institutions as "sets of regularized practices with a rule-like quality in the sense that the actors expect the practices to be observed; and which, in some but not all, cases are supported by formal sanctions" (Hall and Thelen 2009, 9). We focus on the domestic legal framework that grants same-sex couples the right to the registered partnership, marriage, and adoptions. The majority of EU member states currently provide their LGBT citizens with full rights (i.e. marriage and adoption available in 16 EU MSs as of 2019). Formal sanctions include anti-discrimination rulings by domestic Constitutional Courts and the European Court of Justice (ECJ). Furthermore, citizens might also seek redress at the European Court of Human Rights (ECtHR; Guasti 2017; Guasti, Siroky, and Stockemer 2017).

Institutional inertia leads to stability, since rational actors have an incentive to maintain the status quo as long as it "serves" the dominant actors (Hall 2005). For example, if public opinion regarding same-sex marriage is stable, and splits the population down the middle, mainstream catch-all parties will refrain from engaging in LGBT minority accommodation, since such an institutional change could polarise their electorate.

Nonetheless, institutions do evolve. The impetus for change comes from actors, such as friends and foes, in this case, of LGBT rights. Via their agency, actors can initiate a process of change (Hall and Thelen 2009, 15). The change in the institutional framework has essential spillover effects, and the expansion of LGBT rights around the significant world contributes to the impetus for accommodation. In this way, the diffusion of rights of sexual minorities in Europe significantly alters (narrows) the domestic opportunity structures.

Diffusion stems from the EU anti-discrimination legislation, which evolved from provisions to combat discrimination on the grounds of sexual orientation,[4] Citizens' Rights Directive, Employment Equality Framework Directive, and the European Court of Justice case law. Because there is freedom of movement, all EU member states must ensure that, where same-sex marriage is not possible, employees in a civil partnership must be granted the same benefits as their married colleagues and be treated equally.[5] Furthermore, EU member states have to recognise the same-sex marriage of EU citizens from other EU member-states for granting residency (Coman and Hamilton versus Romania, 2018).

When it comes to cohabitation, over the past decade, the case-law of the European Court of Human Rights (ECtHR) evolved from recognising the right of same-sex couples to family life. Yet it did not grant them entitlement to registered partnership or marriage (2010, Schalk and Kopf versus Austria). The ruling also banned the exclusion of same-sex couples from legal form of partnership, where those exist for opposite-sex couples (2013, Vallianatos and others v Greece). It set a precedent by establishing a legal obligation for states to provide legal recognition for same-sex couples (2015, Oliari and others v Italy), and confirmed that denial of marriage for same-sex couples does not violate the ECtHR (2016, Chapin and Charpentier versus France).

The sanction mechanisms to enforce the implementation of ECtHR judgments are significantly less potent than those following the failure to implement ECJ case law (Guasti, Siroky, and Stockemer 2017). However, most of the ECtHR judgments resulted in the expansion of LGBT rights. For example, as of 2019, Austria and France allow same-sex marriage, while both Greece and Italy provide same-sex couples the opportunity to enter into a registered partnership.

The EU legislation, the ECJ case law, and to a lesser degree, the ECtHR case-law represent important stimuli for institutional change in the EU and European Council (EC) member states. Transnational legislation constrains the legal options of domestic actors that oppose the expansion of LGBT rights. Domestic actors that oppose change to the status quo perceive this legislation as a clear threat to their autonomy.

The expansion of LGBT rights takes place because of key proponents (friends) of accommodation; the outcome depends on their ability to find political allies. The agency of a pro- and anti-LGBT advocacy groups is significantly affected by two factors– resources and political party strategies—since the expansion of LGBT rights requires coordination between pro-LGBT advocacy groups and liberal political parties. Political actors weight the cost of their action, and also consider other actors – political competitors and the agency of advocacy groups to sway public opinion. However, the introduction and evolution of transnational legislative framework and the EU anti-discrimination legislation shape the degree of accommodation and backlash.

Two strategies/processes are crucial in institutional change – defection and re-interpretation (Hall and Thelen 2009). Defection refers to a behavioural change among actors, such as a strategic shift among Czech and Slovak pro-LGBT advocacy groups to engage in public outreach to the general population. The focus turned from lobbying parliamentarians to shifting public opinion. Re-interpretation is a strategy in which "the actors associated with an institution gradually change the interpretation of its rules, and thus its practices, without defecting from or dismantling the formal institution itself" (Hall and Thelen 2009, 19). Re-interpretation is the shift of Czech pro-LGBT advocates to separate the issue of adoption, which resulted in a significant increase in support for adoption of partner's children – as opposed to adoption in general (cf. Streeck and Thelen 2005).

To summarise, we suggest that two factors are critical in explaining the process of accommodation. The first factor is exogenous - the EU anti-discrimination legislation, as well as ECJ and ECtHR case law. The second factor is endogenous - the agency of LGBT friends and foes. The expansion of rights depends on the agency of friends and foes – their ability to engage with the public to shift mass opinion and with political parties that can pass key legislation.

The role of the European Union in minority accommodation

Although domestic factors are crucial to understanding institutional change, Central Europe did not expand minority rights in a vacuum. EU accession was a strong incentive to modify, even to resolve the relationship between the majority and minority groups. EU pressure to adopt anti-discrimination legislation was crucial, for the commitment of domestic elites to minority rights was lackluster (Rechel 2009; Börzel, Soyaltin, and Yilmaz 2015; Agarin and Brosig 2016; Nancheva 2016). The European Union anchored the rule of law and civil liberties in the EU anti-discrimination framework (Vachudova 2005).

In seeking to address unresolved majority-minority issues, and entrench minority rights among the fundamental democratic rights, the EU pursued a controversial double standard for the member states and the accession countries (Börzel, Soyaltin, and Yilmaz 2015; Nancheva 2016). The Central European countries adopted all EU primary legislation on non-discrimination and established institutions dealing with minority issues. However, the CEE countries were more apt in establishing task forces and preparing action plans than actually implementing reforms addressing minority issues (Malova and Vilagi 2006; Rechel 2009).

EU conditionality influenced minorities indirectly by empowering domestic actors. This helped them to find allies, to overcome foes, and to implement reforms (Kelley 2004; Vachudova 2005; Sasse 2008). Notwithstanding the importance of changes in the legal and institutional framework, it is the agency of domestic actors, which accounts for differences in the scope of minority accommodation across countries (cf. Börzel, Soyaltin, and Yilmaz 2015). However, compared to the CEE countries, the EU and its (Western European) member states had significantly more progressive attitudes towards LGBT issues. This mismatch significantly increased the mobilisation potential of emerging minority groups and prepared the backlash against their accommodation.

After the accession, EU leverage decreased significantly, but the European Union continues to play an essential role in creating a legal framework of anti-discrimination. in 2000, the European Charter of Human Rights, gave constitutional status to the principle of minority non-discrimination (O'Dwyer 2018a, 900). While the EU prescribes non-discrimination, it does not provide guidelines for accommodation (Galbreath and McEvoy 2012). Minority accommodation is now entirely under the control of domestic actors – the courts (especially Constitutional Courts) and political actors. For example, the Czech Republic and Slovakia comply with the rulings of the European Court of Justice, but resist "soft" (non-legally binding) pressures of the European Commission and the European Parliament (Guasti 2017).

In contrast with the expansion of ethnic rights, the expansion of the rights of sexual minorities is universalistic and represents an even greater threat to the domestic status quo. For example, if Slovaks grant expansion of Hungarian language rights, or if Austria gives legal refugees access to public housing, the particularism of ethnic groups does not create a *general* threat (cf. Bustikova 2014, 2019). However, same-sex marriage in Germany (2017) and Austria (2019) is an identical demand that domestic LGBT groups are bringing to the table. The universalistic character of the demand and the increasingly comprehensive legal framework of the European Union threaten domestic foes of LGBT rights.

The European Union's assertive push for minority rights maps onto domestic divisions (cf. Malova and Vilagi 2006; Börzel, Soyaltin, and Yilmaz 2015). The politicisation of the European Union minority agenda is channelled through political entrepreneurs and is sustained through the dynamic of accommodation and backlash. This contentious dynamic of cooperation and conflict between friends and foes of minority accommodation is at the root of the politics of backlash against the liberal democratic principles of the European Union and the commitment of the new EU states to minority protection. We provide a systematic comparison of the strategic logic of backlash against LGBT minorities in the context of the European legislative framework in the next sections.

Comparing LGBT accommodation and backlash in the Czech Republic and Slovakia

In this section, we focus on the dynamics of LGBT accommodation and backlash in the Czech Republic and Slovakia. Radical right parties and prominent populist leaders in the Czech Republic (PM Babiš) and Slovakia (ex-PM Fico) all oppose accommodation of sexual minorities, but differ in the degree to which they emphasize sovereignty and to extent to which they fight institutional change. Whereas identity-based cleavages have been prominent in Slovak politics (Bustikova et al. 2019), the exclusionary approach to ethnic and social minorities has been much less important in the Czech Republic (Bustikova and Guasti 2018; Hanley and Vachudova 2018).

The Czech Republic

Czech *public opinion* is increasingly supportive of expanding LGBT rights, but political entrepreneurs have prevented shifts in public opinion from becoming policy by politicising the issue. Opponents have mobilised to defend the status quo. The former Presidents Václav Klaus and the current President Miloš Zeman both utilise the LGBT issue as a symbol of the conservative opposition, "discriminating the majority," and as the main challenge to the "traditional way of life". For the foes of LGBT rights, full equality represents a threat. In the last several years, the Czech Catholic Church, and especially Archbishop Dominik Duka, have emerged as crucial voices in the anti-LGBT camp. Duka's conservative rhetoric, inspired and often directly inspired by the Polish clergy, is extremely divisive, both within the Church and in the public domain.

While homophobia is present in today's Czech Republic (cf. O'Dwyer 2018a), there is broad public support for the expansion of LGBT rights that goes beyond the existing law, which allows for registered partnership between LGBT couples. In short, polarisation on LGBT accommodation is significantly stronger in the Czech parliament than among the Czech public (for more details, see Figure 2).

Passing the bill on registered partnership

Changes in the *legal framework* concerning the 2005–2006 Law on registered partnership illustrate the turbulent dynamic between friends and foes of accommodation. The bill on registered partnership was submitted to the Czech Parliament four times: in 1998, 1999, 2001 and 2005. After a cross-party group of MPs sponsored the bill, and as a result of intense advocacy by LGBT groups, it reached the floor in 2005. However, the political coalition of "friendscollapsed when the social democratic PM Paroubek claimed issue ownership just before the December 2005 parliamentary plenary debate". Immediately afterward, the coalition of friends unravelled when some opposition MPs withdrew their support for the bill.

What went wrong? The analysis of the 2005 roll-call data indicates that an ad hoc single-issue coalition of "friends" pushed the bill forward, but the Social Democrats, the ruling party at that time, were profoundly split on the issue. More than 30% of the social-democratic MPs abstained from the vote. Still, none of the Social Democratic MPs were willing to defy the party leadership by voting no, and instead opted for abstention as a way to balance party loyalty and their moral conscience.

Finally, in December 2005, the bill was adopted by a simple majority of 86 out of 200 votes (see Figure 1). The President vetoed the bill, however, and the subsequent vote in March 2006 was very dramatic. The bill needed a qualified majority (101 of 200 votes) to overrule the Presidential veto. To demonstrate his ability to get things done, PM Paroubek imposed party discipline. After considerable effort, the bill on registered partnership

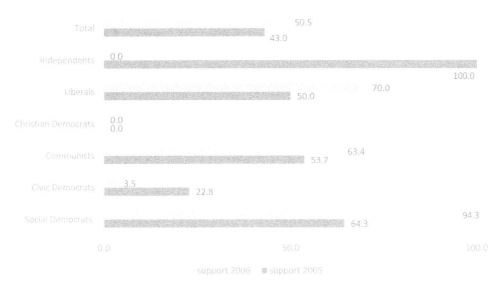

Figure 1. Roll-call voting on same-sex registered partnership in the parliament of the Czech Republic: 2005 and 2006. Source: Roll-call analysis by the authors.

was finally adopted in the Czech parliament (March 2006) by a coalition of social democrats, communists, and the liberal Freedom Union.[6]

Adoption

After this seminal victory for the LGBT advocates, the next demand of the LGBT community was to pass a law that would legally allow for adoption by gay and lesbian couples. This issue was debated in the parliament in 2016, prior to the summer recess and was not resumed. No vote took place before the end of the parliamentary term (2017), and even today registered same-sex couples still cannot legally adopt children in the Czech Republic.

LGBT advocates use "salami tactics" by creating different categories of children for adoption: children who already had an LGBT parent and children in institutional care. For example, the 2016 debate on "adoptions of children of partners" was an amendment to the 2006 law on registered partnership and excluded adoptions of children from institutional care.

The debate on adoptions cut across party lines more so than the 2005–2006 debate on registered partnership. The authors of the bill (a Social Democratic Minister and ANO MP) highlighted their personal experience and the difficulties encountered by "rainbow families." The foes attacked the bill and accused its authors of "making laws for their friends" and of "conceding their electorate at the expense of 'normal' families."

Christian Democrats and TOP 09, two conservative parties, opposed the bill.[7] Opposition to LGBT accommodation became the centre of the feud for issue ownership over the "who are the 'real' defenders of the traditional family?".[8] The foes claimed that the law represented interests of LGBT adults at the expense of the children. They rejected the further advancement of LGBT rights as legislative overreach.

The 2016 debate revealed deep divisions between the parties.[9] It also revealed the power of foes. Just as friends almost accomplished all their demands, the foes mobilised and successfully pushed back against further accommodation. Somewhat unanticipated was that several members of the radical right party, Úsvit (Dawn of Direct Democracy), not only supported the law but were members of the 25- member team that sponsored the bill. Unlike in the 2005–2006 debate, the Social Democrats were significantly less active in the plenary and were internally polarised on the issue. The bill on the adoption of children by same-sex couples never materialised.

Same-sex marriage

In the new parliamentary term (2017-today), LGBT advocates seek to move beyond registered partnerships to marriage. However, the 2018 parliamentary debate on the same-sex-marriage was highly polarised. Similar to the 2016 debate on adoption, it was inconclusive, interrupted without vote, and never resumed (as of December 2019).

Polarisation was a strategic choice by the foes of LGBT rights – combining the debates on same-sex marriage AND an amendment to the Bill of Rights on marriage being between a man and a woman, was a recipe for the perfect storm. Given the slight (2%) drop in support for same-sex marriage in the polls between 2017 and 2018 (from 52% to 50%), and futile efforts by ANO to court liberal voters, the governing ANO, which also controls the parliament, understood that same-sex marriage is no longer a winning issue in party competition and with the exception of three ANO MPs, disengaged.

The debate marked interesting shifts in positions (TOP 09 shifted from opposition to support); hedging (Christian democrats tried not to be associated with fellow opponents from the radical right); party unity (Pirates and Communist among proponents; Christian Democrats and SPD among the opponents) and party divisions (ANO and ODS). Both ANO and ODS dealt with rogue MPs – ANO with Karla Slechtova, a vocal proponent of the legislation, and ODS with Vaclav Klaus jr. an opponent willing to use the radical right rhetoric. Unlike in 2016, no single MP emerged as a key figure. As Social Democrats in 2016, ANO lost issue ownership due to internal divisions in 2018. The baton of LGBT friends has now passed to the Pirates. The parliamentary debate ended without outcome or vote, and LGBT couples have the legal option to register their partnership, but they still have no legal right to adopt children as a couple or to marry.

Backlash

The *foes* of LGBT rights mobilised and campaigned against LGBT rights. For example, in January 2019, President Miloš Zeman publicly announced his opposition to same-sex marriage and said he would veto any LGBT friendly legislation to protect the traditional family. He also voiced strong support for a Catholic priest Petr Pit'ha, who, in his September 2018 sermon in the St. Vitus Cathedral, summarised the opposition to the Czech Catholic church to the minority accommodation as follows:

> We are now supposed to succumb to the pressures of a powerful pressure group of gender activists and homosexuals and to make non-freedom law. Your families will be torn apart and destroyed.... Homosexuals will be proclaimed to be a superior ruling class. You will become a part of an inferior auxiliary class, and you will be forced to work according to the orders of powerful elites, which will be determining what can and what cannot be said in public.[10]

Public opinion on LGBT rights has shifted over time as a result of advocacy. In 2006, when the bill on registered partnership was passed, the public support for the LGBT rights was relatively high, but not uniform across policies: 61% Czechs supported the registered partnership, but only 38% Czechs supported same-sex marriage. Only 19% supported adoption rights for same-sex couples. Over time, as the issue became politicised and debated, support for LGBT rights grew significantly. By 2018, 74% of Czechs supported the registered partnership, and 50% supported same-sex marriage.

Attitudes towards adoptions shifted as well. By 2018, 64% of respondents supported the adoption of the child of the same-sex partner and 48% adoptions of children in institutional care. Figure 2 shows this continuous increase in support for LGBT rights over time, with a slight (2%) drop in 2018 on all categories. The public increasingly supports the adoption of the partner's child by the couple.

Although the European Union provides a unified framework of anti-discrimination, shifts in policies are driven by the agency and success of friends and foes who seek to secure political allies and to sway the public. Support for the rights of sexual minorities in the Czech Republic is a result of successful public advocacy by the proponents of LGBT rights and the increased media exposure to the everyday grievances facing "rainbow families", which positively resonated with both the public as well as with politicians.[11]

Between accommodation and backlash

The rights of sexual minorities in the Czech Republic now include registered partnership. In 2016, however, further demands to allow the adoption by same-sex couples triggered a

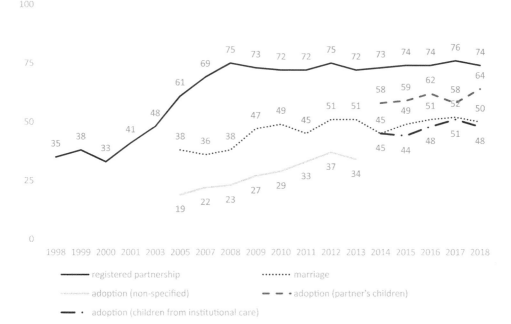

Figure 2. Support for LGBT rights in the Czech Republic over time (1998–2018). Source: Data compiled from the press releases of the Centre for Public Opinion Research by the authors.

backlash, and re-opened the debate about the extent to which LGBT minorities should be afforded the rights of heterosexual couples. In the 2005–2006 registered partnership debates, the competition took place between mainstream parties along the liberal/conservative cleavage. In 2013 and 2017, the Czech political landscape experienced significant fragmentation (see Bustikova and Guasti 2019) and two disruptions – the arrival of mainstream populists and the radical right (ANO and Dawn in 2013) and radical anti-establishment (Pirates in 2017). The strategies of both proponents and opponents of LGBT accommodation changed. Insurgents (ANO in 2016, SPD, and Pirates in 2018) challenged mainstream parties (Social Democrats in 2016 and ANO in 2018) and lost issue ownership of the LGBT issue.

Issue ownership aside, the presence of the radical right (Dawn in 2016, SPD, and emerging Tricolour in 2018) represented a challenge for mainstream parties and the right. For the mainstream parties adopting a catch-all strategy (ANO, ODS) presents the danger of losing voters both to the radical right (opponents of the expansion of LGBT rights) and to the liberal opposition (proponents of the expansion of the LGBT rights). In this situation, mainstream parties have little to gain and voters to lose. Stalling becomes the best strategy for cutting (potential) losses. For the mainstream right, radical right represents a twofold challenge – from within (ODS) and in framing (Christian Democrats). The challenge from within comes from radicalised elements within the party – which can lead to splinter groups (Václav Klaus jr. and his Tricolour established in 2019).

The challenge for the mainstream right is how to distinguish itself from the radical right when their issue position on the expansion of LGBT rights is identical. The answer is in framing – Christian democrats staunchly refuse to be anti-LGBT. They "just" want to be pro-family. Given the changing nature of public support and alliances, the Czech LGBT community is set on a path toward full equality, but LGBT foes are mobilising as well. Adoption and same-sex marriage constitute the last frontiers of LGBT rights in the Czech Republic. At a legislative level, however, the support of a mainstream party is essential for any legislative change.

Slovakia

While the Czech Republic has significantly expanded rights to sexual minorities, the position of the LGBT community in Slovakia is more precarious (Gould 2016) and the LGBT community does not have *public opinion* on its side. Slovakia is socially more conservative and religious than the Czech Republic. According to Froese, "Czechs emerged from communism as one of the most secularised countries in Eastern Europe." Only 6% of Czechs attended church every week compared to 33% of Slovaks, and 65% of Poles (Froese 2005, 269). The rights of sexual minorities politicised the Slovak Catholic church that supports a traditional view of marriage and sexual liaisons.

Both the friends and foes of sexual minorities understand that they need public opinion on their side. LGBT advocacy groups in Slovakia lobby both the general public and the state authorities. Since 2007, the umbrella organisation for LGBT rights *Otherness Initiative* (Iniciatíva Inakost')[12] has been organising a film festival and (since 2013) an annual Pride Parade in Bratislava. The main aim of the public advocacy is to convince the general public that LGBT people are "living the same lives as those of the majority, but facing issues based on their lack of recognition and equal status." In 2017, LGBT advocates launched a large-scale awareness campaign for trans-rights named: *"What you do not notice,"* for the first time with the direct government involvement (ILGA 2018).

However, the majority of Slovaks do not support same-sex registered partnerships and strongly oppose same-sex marriage. Figure 3 displays the evolution of public opinion on LGBT rights. Over one decade (2008–2018), support for registered partnership is lackluster and never exceeded fifty percent.[13]

Disproportional backlash

The lack of public enthusiasm for the plight of sexual minorities resulted in minimal expansion of LGBT rights beyond the EU anti-discrimination legislation. Slovakia adopted the antidiscrimination law in employment in 2004, the provision of goods and services in 2008, and the protection from hate speech in 2016. The adherence to the EU legislation, therefore, creates a paradox regarding same-sex marriage because it alerts to long-term incompatibilities with the (heteronormative) domestic legal environment. Although in general the public lacks the appetite for expanding rights, European legislature is undermining the power of national legislatures to regulate majority-minority relations. This alarms the foes.

Observing advocacy efforts in nearby countries (Germany, Austria, the Czech Republic), friends and foes accelerated their fight for Slovak hearts and minds. For example, on July 30, 2016, the capital city of Bratislava witnessed three simultaneous parades: a rainbow pride parade of 1,000 participants organised by LGBT advocates, a counter-parade of the far-right ĽSNS party of Marian Kotleba called "The Protest against the March of Perverts in Bratislava" and a counter-parade of a civic initiative "Proud of Family."[14] The parade of foes was supported by both catholic and protestant churches with traditional interpretations of families.[15]

The reactive logic of backlash against accommodation, driven by friend-foe dynamics, applies well to Kotleba's ĽSNS party, a significant adversary to the expansion of minority rights (Kissová 2018; Bustikova 2019; Harris 2019; Kazharski 2019). In 2015, Kotleba was one of the supporters of a failed referendum on same-sex marriage. Later, his party drafted several laws that would protect "traditional" families.[16] None of these laws were

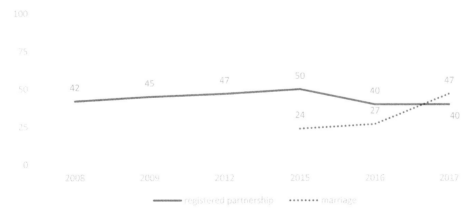

Figure 3. Support for LGBT rights in Slovakia over time (2008–2017). Source: Inakosť Initiative, Pew Research.

implemented. All were rhetorical posturing, but they mark the transition in Slovak politics away from the traditional Slovak-Hungarian cleavage towards new issues associated with sexual conduct. It also politicised the Slovak Catholic Church, since eighteen Catholic priests signed a petition to back the quest of L'SNS to restrict abortion (Topky 2018). Until then, the Catholic Church never so openly embraced such a deeply polarising, controversial issue in Slovak politics. These "new" identities have come to polarise Slovak politics.

An uphill battle for registered partnership

The expansion of LGBT rights cannot happen due to pressure from below unless the public opinion dramatically shifts. The agency of friends and foes determines the process of shifting and defending the status quo.[17] The LGBT community and their political allies, including political parties and civic advocates, have been working diligently to expand rights. Bills to recognise same-sex partnerships were introduced in the Slovak parliament four times: in 1997, 2000, 2012, and 2018. Regardless of these efforts, all of them were rejected.

A minor change was achieved in 2017. Since then, the unregistered cohabitation of couples is legally recognised and utilised by same-sex couples (although it is not explicitly designed for same-sex couples). Unlike in the Czech Republic, where some mainstream parties actively support the rights of the LGBT community, the major mainstream parties in Slovakia were reluctant to embrace the expansion of LGBT rights until 2012.

In 2012, the liberal and libertarian Freedom and Solidarity (SaS) party announced that it would submit a draft of the law on registered partnership to the Parliament. In August 2012, the draft was submitted to the parliament, only to be rejected by the ruling social democratic party SMER. The proponents of the bill, the Freedom and Solidarity party, argued that the state should recognise the commitment of LGBT citizens to their partners. The foes, mostly the Christian Democrats, argued that the law would "crash the entire legal system ... and change the face of the country." As a concession to the LGBT community and to save face, Prime Minister Fico (from SMER) established a committee to address the demands of the LGBT community as a forum for public debate in October 2012.[18] The committee drafted action plans with no real intention to enact them. This was an effort to window-dress a contentious issue and to placate the European Union. Similar smoke and mirrors strategies were well-rehearsed in the pre-accession period.

However, the issue did not go away. LGBT "friends" remained committed to their cause. The Freedom and Solidarity Party reiterated its commitment to the LGBT rights by resubmitting the registered partnership draft to the parliament in July 2018. In September 2018, the bill was defeated again. However, this time, the political coalition of "friends" was expanded. The Freedom and Solidarity MPs were joined by MPs from other smaller parties, including the Hungarian minority party, Most-Híd. The new political alliance supporting registered partnerships suggests a possibility that the advocacy coalition can be expanded even further in the future.[19]

Failed referendum against LGBT accommodation in 2015

As expected, the contestation of rights mobilised the opposition. The backlash against the attempt to expand LBGT rights peaked in 2014. The conservative group, Alliance for Family (Aliancia za rodinu) with the support of the Conference of Slovak Bishops, collected 400,000 signatures to support a law on banning same-sex marriage in 2014. The petition also opposed the adoption and raising of children by same-sex couples. It also advocated for the rights of parents to prevent their children from receiving sex education in schools. The Constitutional Court removed a fourth question, which proposed banning registered partnership, after President Andrej Kiska intervened.

In 2014, the Christian Democrats initiated an amendment to the Slovak Constitution banning same-sex marriage. Prime Minister Fico (SMER) offered to support the ban in exchange for support for his reform of the judicial system. The law was overwhelmingly passed in June 2014 (102 MPs voted for, 18 against). This significant change was approved as a part of a judicial reform package. The following change of the Slovak Constitution was approved: "Marriage is a unique union between a man and a woman. The Slovak Republic fully protects marriage as it aids its wellbeing." The proponents of the ban argued that "what is good for the family is good for the state" (quote: Jan Figel, the Chairman of the Christian Democratic Party). This was a significant victory for conservative forces in Slovakia.[20]

In 2014, the "friends" lost the battle in the parliament, but won a fight a year later in the public domain. The "friends" found a way to defeat the "foes" using a demobilisation strategy to lower participation in a referendum that would further curtail LGBT rights. The LGBT advocates campaigned for abstention in the referendum in order to lower turnout below the threshold for a binding outcome. This was a shrewd move. The abstention undermined the legal minimum 50% turnout for the referendum to be binding.

The referendum took place in February 2015. Conservatives mobilised their core supporters, but the turnout was not sufficient: only 945,000 citizens voted in the referendum. Although 94.5% of participants in the referendum supported the ban on same-sex marriage, 92.4% supported a ban on adoptions by a same-sex couple, and 90% supported a ban on sex education, the anti-LGBT groups failed to convince the public to participate and vote for the bans.[21] The referendum failed because only 21.4% of the adult population participated in it. The "foes" lost.

International allies and funding

Both the foes and friends mobilised international allies.[22] Conservative groups from Europe and the United States (such as the U.S. Evangelical donors and the Alliance Defending Freedom)[23] publicly supported the constitutional amendment. Among the most avid supporters of the law was Pope Francis, who blessed and praised the efforts of conservatives to "defend the family as a vital cell of the society." At the same time, the Pope wanted to avoid any conflicts and warned against the animosity towards the LGBT people.[24]

The friends of the LGBT groups were smaller and less organised than their conservative Christian counterparts, but were also supported from abroad, indirectly by the European LGBT advocacy groups. Despite having international backing themselves, the LGBT advocates criticised the involvement of foreign religious groups. At the domestic level, the "friends" also campaigned against the leading party SMER, and accused of it "pandering to the populist religious homophobia" as a distraction from economic issues.

Cracks in the legal system and a road to the expansion of rights

The defenders of the status quo are at a considerable long-term disadvantage due to the *legal framework* of the European Union. In June 2018, the façade of state sovereignty over same-sex couples' rights cracked due to the European Court of Justice (ECJ) ruling. It stipulated that the EU member states have to recognise a same-sex marriage from member-states that legalised same-sex marriage for a residency permit. Slovak authorities were forced to comply with the ECJ ruling.[25] This shift in the legal environment suggests that the demands of the LGBT minorities pose a serious long-term threat, for Slovakia might be forced to implement accommodation due to the European Union legislature and courts, despite lacking any political or a societal consensus to do so.

The friends and foes continue their struggle over LGBT rights in Slovakia. So far, the foes have prevented any expansion of LGBT rights for Slovak citizens. Unlike in the Czech Republic, the Slovak foes are strong. Conservative voices, supported by populists and the Catholic Church, dominate the political arena and block any attempts to accommodate sexual minorities. However, the abysmal turnout in the 2015 referendum and the 2019 election of the first female president, Zuzana Čaputová, signals that the ground has shifted.

Čaputová ran primarily on an anti-corruption platform, but she was also the only presidential candidate who openly embraced LGBT groups and same-sex adoptions. The democratic opposition united behind her, and she defeated her social conservative and populist contenders, winning the presidency in 2019. Čaputová has stated that she supports registered partnerships for same-sex couples, and educating the general public on LGBT relationships. In a discussion organised by SME Journal, she expressed her support for registered partnership and adoption for LGBT couples: "I prefer the child to have a biological mother and a biological father. If he were to grow up in institutional care, I think he'd be better off with two loving beings, even if they were of the same sex."[26] It is yet to be seen, however, if her presidency signals an erosion of the socially conservative status quo in Slovakia (cf. Kluknavska and Smolik 2016; Gyárfášová 2018; Gyárfášová and Henderson 2018).

Conclusion

Drawing on detailed evidence from the Czech Republic and Slovakia, the paper shows the dynamics of support and backlash against sexual minorities. The implementation of the EU anti-discrimination framework and current LGBT demands facilitates minority accommodation. It also threatens the status quo and has sparked opposition against minorities and their friends: the EU, advocacy groups, and civil society (cf. Cianetti, Dawson, and Hanley 2018; Kolev and Wang 2019; Agarin 2020; Bochsler and Juon 2020; Kolev 2020; Sata and Karolewski 2020). Domestic pro- and anti-LGBT advocacy groups have political allies, but the relationships are often instrumental. In both countries, pragmatic populists strategically align themselves with the winning side of the issue.

The mainstream political parties are rarely foes of minority accommodation. The extent to which they act as allies depends on their ideological orientation and political calculus. When the costs of minority accommodation are high, mainstream moderate parties shy away from pursuing a progressive agenda (Bustikova and Guasti 2017; cf. on CEE more broadly Pirro 2014).

In Slovakia, the mainstream party, SMER, traded support on the same-marriage ban for its proposed judicial reform. In the Czech Republic, Andrej Babiš's ANO used the LGBT issue to strategically appeal to the liberal voters. However, by 2018, ANO saw no reason to court liberal voters, and the marriage-equality legislation, sponsored initially by ANO, ended up caught in procedural delays. The aim of ANO is now to preserve the status quo, and to prevent the liberal and illiberal opposition from gaining more electoral support.

The European Union plays a role in the process of LGBT accommodation that is secondary to the domestic dynamics. However, from a long-term view, the EU threatens national sovereignty over LGBT rights. The European Union ensures anti-discrimination via legislation and the European Court of Justice judgments. Although Eastern European countries understood that minority protection was a core requirement to join the European Union, most citizens did not anticipate that the rights would be extended to sexual minorities any time soon. The public does not (yet) enthusiastically support same-sex marriage and same-sex couple adoption neither in Slovakia nor in the Czech Republic.[27]

While the European Union creates an essential legal framework that anchors minority accommodation, the contestation of minority issues is highly contingent on domestic configurations of friends and foes and their strategic considerations. Public opinion has been slowly shifting towards the expansion of LGBT rights in the past decade. However, the legal framework of the European Union might accelerate the process of the expansion of rights despite a limited domestic appetite to do so.

Eastern Europe has unexpectedly become a battleground for the social-conservative agenda and actors that support traditional families and limited access to abortion, oppose gender parity, same-sex marriage, and adoption of children by same-sex couples. It now attracts the attention of the Vatican, Russia, and Christian fundamentalists from the United States,[28] eager to assist domestic opponents of LGBT accommodation in defending the status quo. The friends were always transnational, and now the foes have "internationalized" as well. As a result, Eastern Europe is now caught in between two significant currents - global cleavages that pitch liberal and illiberal global forces against each other.

Notes

1. We thank Timofei Agarin, John Gould, Olga Gyarfášová, Darina Málová, Brian Mello, David Siroky, and two anonymous reviewers for constructive comments on the earlier version of the paper. The paper was presented at the 2019 European Union Studies Association conference in Denver and the 2019 Western Political Science Association in San Diego. We thank the Institute of Sociology, the Czech Academy of Sciences for institutional support, and to Simona Pátková for outstanding research assistance.
2. http://www.dominikduka.cz/vyjadreni/podpora-prohlaseni-o-svetonazorovem-totalitarismu/ last visited 18.10.2019
3. Most of these were adopted after the 2018 European Court of Justice ruling.
4. Article 10 and 19 of the Amsterdam Treaty, Article 21 of the Charter of Fundamental Rights, in effect since 2009,
5. Equal treatment, ECJ 2008 case Tadao Maruko v. Versorgungsanstalt der Deutschen Bühnen; and 2013 ECJ case Frédéric Hay v. Crédit Agricole mutual, (C-267/12)
6. Between 2006 and 2017, 2.818 couples entered into the registered partnership, 401 couples canceled their registration in the same period. Before the decision of the Czech Constitutional Court, which in 2016 enabled individuals living in registered partnerships to adopt children, men were significantly more likely to enter into the registered partnership. Since 2016 the number of women entering into registered partnership increased significantly.
7. Both parties are culturally conservative but differ on the economic dimension - Christian Democrats are more centrist and TOP 09 more liberal.

8. Their arguments were somewhat similar, as the two parties align on cultural issues (conservatives), but diverge on the economy (Christian Democrats are centrist, while TOP 09 right wing on the economic dimension of the LR cleavage).
9. The 2016 plenary debate was the first reading. In the vote after the first reading, the Parliament decided whether there will be a substantial debate both in the committees and subsequently in the plenary (second reading). Hence 2016 debate was more open (less bound by party positions).
10. Source: https://www.idnes.cz/zpravy/domaci/kazani-arcibiskupstvi-katedrala-svateho-vita-svaty-vaclav-petr-pitha-istanbulska-umluva.A181009_100435_domaci_lre Translation, the authors. The term "homosexuals" refers to the members of the LGBT community. The derogatory term "homosexualists" refers to the proponents of the expansion of LGBT rights.
11. The LGBT advocacy adopted an effective strategy - shifting the discourse from a debate about "adoption in general" to the differentiation between adoptions of partner's child/children from institutional care. The shift positively resonates with the Czech, public opinion.
12. Source: inakost.sk.
13. The public view of LGBT, of course, affects their day-to-day lives. In 2018, Inakost' (Otherness) surveyed more than 2.000 LGBT people. More than 80% of respondents considered prejudice as the most serious problem of their life. The Initiative Inakost' also reported that half of LGBT people experienced verbal or physical attacks (ILGA 2018).
14. Aliancia za rodinu (Alliance for Families) is a civic initiative founded in 2013. It supports traditional marriage and the traditional family. Source: www.alianciazarodinu.sk. The Slovak Catholic Church and churches of other denominations are supportive of the Alliance for Families initiative.
15. Source: Bratislavou sa prehnal dúhový pochod aj Kotlebovi fanúšikovia. 30.07.2016, SITA, TREND.sk. https://www.etrend.sk/ekonomika/bratislavou-sa-prehnal-duhovy-pochod-aj-kotlebovi-fanusikovia.html
16. In 2018, L'SNS proposed a law to restrict abortion, to extend maternity leave to three years and to increase child support conditional on "the desire of parents to work," which was aimed at restricting child allowances to Roma (L'S – Naše Slovensko 2018).
17. An important argument was put forward by Conor O'Dwyer (2018a, 2018b), who argues that attacks on LGBT rights, in fact, strengthen the LGBT movement who "benefit from the backlash." We do not dispute this argument but highlight that public support is not a sufficient condition for I change and accommodation.
18. This act was sharply criticized by the Christian Democrats and by the Slovak Conference of Bishops. Source: https://www.reuters.com/article/us-slovakia-gay/slovakia-parliament-rejects-gay-partnership-law-idUSBRE8A50V520121106.
19. Source: https://dennikn.sk/minuta/1234883/?ref=mpm.
20. Source: https://domov.sme.sk/c/7226301/chrania-manzelstvo-menia-justiciu-pozrite-si-kto-hlasoval-za-zmenu-ustavy.html
21. Source: https://archive.fo/20150208063828/http://volbysr.sk/en/tab01.html
22. On long-term negative implications of public support of conservative policies, see Grzymała-Busse 2015.
23. Among others, these organizations are active in Eastern Europe and meddle into referenda on same-sex marriage and abortion policies. They financially support the advocates of traditional families. The *Alliance for Freedom* has tripled its budget between the years 2012–2016. It has been very active in Romania, where they attempted to influence a referendum on same-sex marriage. Another organization, *The World Congress of Families*, has ties to Russia and the United States. It actively and publicly opposed gay pride parades in Prague and Belgrade. Source: Lotto Persio 2019. On Serbia, view: Gould and Moe 2015.
24. Source: https://www.advocate.com/politics/religion/2015/02/05/pope-has-kind-words-backers-anti-equality-measures-slovakia
25. The ruling stated that at least one partner must be an EU citizen, and the marriage must have taken place in the EU in order for Slovakia to recognize same-sex marriage for couples, in which one is not a Slovak citizen.

26. Source: https://domov.sme.sk/c/22045481/prezidentske-volby-2019-diskusia-caputova-vs-mistrik.html.
27. Although the level of support for both in the Czech Republic is closer to Western Europe than the CEE, including Slovakia.
28. The investigative journalists from *OpenDemocracy* found that 12 ultra-conservative Christian organizations from the United States have spent at least 51 million dollars on campaigns against LGBT and abortions in Europe. Source: Lotto Persio 2019.

Disclosure statement

No potential conflict of interest was reported by the authors.

Funding

The project has received funding from the Project "Changes in the Perception of the Role of Government after the Crisis. The Czech Republic in Comparative Perspective" (no. 16-04885S [2016 e 2018]) supported by the Czech Science Foundation.

References

Agarin, T. 2020. "Introduction to Special Issue. The (not so) Curious Rise of Identity Politics in Eastern Europe." *East European Politics* forthcoming.

Agarin, T., and M. Brosig, eds. 2016. *Trajectories of Minority Rights Issues in Europe: The Implementation Trap?* London – New York: Routledge.

Appel, H., and J. Gould. 2000. "Identity Politics and Economic Reform: Examining Industry-State Relations in the Czech and Slovak Republics." *Europe-Asia Studies* 52 (1): 111–131.

Bochsler, D., and A. Juon. 2020. "Authoritarian Footprints in Central and Eastern Europe." *East European Politics* forthcoming.

Börzel, T. A., D. Soyaltin, and G. Yilmaz. 2015. "Same Same or Different? Accession Europeanization in Central Eastern Europe and Turkey Compared." In *Europeanization of Turkey: Polity, Politics and Policies – A Scorecard*, edited by A. Güney, and A. Tekin, 217–234. London: Routledge.

Brubaker, R. 2013. "Language, Religion, and the Politics of Difference." *Nations and Nationalism* 19 (1): 1–20.
Bustikova, L. 2014. "Revenge of the Radical Right." *Comparative Political Studies* 47 (12): 1738–1765.
Bustikova, L. 2017. "The Radical Right in Eastern Europe." In *The Oxford Handbook of the Radical Right*, edited by Jens Rydgren, 565–581. Oxford: Oxford University Press.
Bustikova, L. 2019. *Extreme Reactions: Radical Right Mobilization in Eastern Europe*. Cambridge: Cambridge University Press.
Bustikova, L., and P. Guasti. 2017. "The Illiberal Turn or Swerve in Central Europe?" *Politics and Governance* 5 (4): 166–176.
Bustikova, L., D. Siroky, S. Alashri, and S. Alzahrani. 2019. "Predicting Partisan Responsiveness: A Probabilistic Text Mining Time-Series Approach." *Political Analysis*, 1–18. doi:10.1017/pan.2019.18, FirstView.
Buštíková, L., and P. Guasti. 2019. "The State as a Firm: Understanding the Autocratic Roots of Technocratic Populism." *East European Politics and Societies: and Cultures* 33 (2): 302–330.
Cianetti, L., J. Dawson, and S. Hanley. 2018. "Rethinking "Democratic Backsliding" in Central and Eastern Europe – Looking Beyond Hungary and Poland." *East European Politics* 34 (3): 243–256.
Cunik, M. 2015. Rights of LGBT couples in Central Eastern Europe: Complex paths towards equality.
Froese, P. 2005. "Secular Czechs and Devout Slovaks: Explaining Religious Differences." *Review of Religious Research* 46 (3): 269–283.
Galbreath, D. J., and J. McEvoy. 2012. *The European Minority Rights Regime: Towards a Theory of Regime Effectiveness*. Basingstoke: Palgrave.
Gould, J. A. 2016. "LGBTQ Politics in Post-communist Slovakia: The Intersections, Discourse and Politics of Marginalization." Working Paper, June.
Gould, J. A., and E. Moe. 2015. "Nationalism and the Struggle for LGBTQ Rights in Serbia, 1991–2014." *Problems of Post-Communism* 62 (5): 273–286.
Grzymała-Busse, A. 2015. *Nations Under God: How Churches Use Moral Authority to Influence Policy*. Princeton: Princeton University Press.
Guasti, P. 2016. "Development of Citizen Participation in Central and Eastern Europe After the EU Enlargement and Economic Crises." *Communist and Post-Communist Studies* 49 (3): 219–231.
Guasti, P. 2017. "The EU and Russia in the Pan-European Human Rights Regime." In *EU-Russia Relations in Crisis: Understanding Diverging Perceptions*, edited by T. Casier, and J. DeBardeleben, 178–198. London: Routledge.
Guasti, P. 2018. "Swerving Towards Deconsolidation?" In *Das Politische System Tschechiens*, edited by A. Lorenz, and H. Formankova, 39–62. Wiesbaden: Springer VS.
Guasti, P. 2019. The Effects of Insurgency: LGBT Accommodation in the Czech Republic. ECPR General Conference, P. 179 Internalising the Insurgency: Understanding the Interaction of Radical Anti-Establishment and Mainstream Parties, September 4-7, Wroclaw, Poland.
Guasti, P., D. S. Siroky, and D. Stockemer. 2017. "Judgment Without Justice: On the Efficacy of the European Human Rights Regime." *Democratization* 24 (2): 226–243.
Gyárfášová, O. 2018. "The Fourth Generation: From Anti-Establishment to Anti-System Parties in Slovakia. New Perspectives." *Interdisciplinary Journal of Central & East European Politics and International Relations* 26 (1): 109–133.
Gyárfášová, O., and K. Henderson. 2018. "Slovakia and the Turnout Conundrum." *East European Politics* 34 (1): 77–96.
Hall, P. A. 2005. "Institutional Complementarity: Causes and Effects." *Socio-Economic Review* 3 (2): 373–378.
Hall, P. A., and K. Thelen. 2009. "Institutional Change in Varieties of Capitalism." *Socio-economic Review* 7 (1): 7–34.
Hanley, S., and M. A. Vachudova. 2018. "Understanding the Illiberal Turn: Democratic Backsliding in the Czech Republic." *East European Politics* 34 (3): 276–296.
Harris, E. 2019. "Nation Before Democracy. Placing the Rise of the Slovak Extreme Right Into Context." *East European Politics* forthcoming.
Hechter, M. 2013. *Alien Rule*. Cambridge: Cambridge University Press.

Hroch, M. 1993. "From National Movement to the Fully-Formed Nation." *New Left Review I* 198 (March–April): 80.
ILGA. 2018. Annual Review of the Human Rights Situation of Lesbian, Gay, Bisexual, Trans and Intersex People in Europe. Brussels. https://www.ilga-europe.org/sites/default/files/Attachments/annual_review_final2018_web.pdf.
Jacobsson, K., and S. Saxonberg, eds. 2015. *Social Movements in Post-Communist Europe and Russia*. London: Routledge.
Jasiewicz, K. 2007. "Is East-Central Europe Backsliding? The Political-Party Landscape." *Journal of Democracy* 18 (4): 26–33.
Kazharski, A. 2019. "Frontiers of Hatred? A Study of Right-Wing Populist Strategies in Slovakia." *European Politics and Society* forthcoming.
Kelley, J. G. 2004. *Ethnic Politics in Europe: The Power of Norms and Incentives*. Princeton, NJ: Princeton University Press.
Kissová, L. 2018. "The Production of (Un) Deserving and (Un) Acceptable: Shifting Representations of Migrants Within Political Discourse in Slovakia." *East European Politics and Societies* 32 (4): 743–766.
Kluknavska, A., and J. Smolik. 2016. "We Hate Them All? Issue Adaptation of Extreme Right Parties in Slovakia 1993–2016." *Communist and Post-Communist Studies* 49 (4): 335–344.
Kolev, K. 2020. "Weak Pluralism and Shallow Democracy: The Rise of Identity Politics in Bulgaria and Romania." *East European Politics*. Pages TBD, forthcoming in the Symposium.
Kolev, K., and Y. Wang. 2019. "Ethnic Group Inequality, Partisan Networks, and Political Clientelism." *Political Research Quarterly* 72 (2): 329–341.
Kollman, K., and M. Waites. 2009. "The Global Politics of Lesbian, Gay, Bisexual and Transgender Human Rights: An Introduction." *Contemporary Politics* 15 (1): 1–17.
Lotto Persio, S. 2019. US Christian groups 'donated millions to anti-LGBT causes in Europe'. PinkNews. March 28, 2019. Source: https://www.pinknews.co.uk/2019/03/28/us-christian-groups-anti-lgbt-europe/?%20fbclid=IwAR0o1UN66qQWzDMprZz8TVm_pXFBP1XoHzRLp6lsyCydMLaOP41CVGwrftQ.
Mahoney, J., and K. Thelen, eds. 2009. *Explaining Institutional Change: Ambiguity, Agency, and Power*. Cambridge: Cambridge University Press.
Malova, D., and A. Vilagi. 2006. "European Integration and Ethnic Minorities: A Case Study." *Sociológia* 38 (6): 507–532.
Minkenberg, M. 2015. *Transforming the Transformation? The East European Radical Right in the Political Process*. Milton Park and New York: Routledge.
Mole, R. 2011. "Nationality and Sexuality: Homophobic Discourse and the 'National Threat' in Contemporary Latvia." *Nations and Nationalism* 17 (3): 540–560.
Nancheva, N. 2016. "Imagining Policies: European Integration and the European Minority Rights Regime." *Journal of Contemporary European Studies* 24 (1): 132–148.
O'Dwyer, C. 2018a. "The Benefits of Backlash: EU Accession and the Organization of LGBT Activism in Postcommunist Poland and the Czech Republic." *East European Politics and Societies: and Cultures* 32 (4): 892–923.
O'Dwyer, C. 2018b. *Coming Out of Communism: The Emergence of LGBT Activism in Eastern Europe*. New York: New York University Press.
Pavlik, P., ed. 2006. *Shadow Report on Equal Treatment and Equal Opportunities for Women and Men*. Prague: Gender Studies.
Pelz, M. 2014. Europeanization, Party Systems, and LGBT Rights: The Cases of Estonia, Latvia, Montenegro, and Serbia. In IPSA World Congress, Montreal, QC, July (Vol. 21, p. 266).
Pirro, A. 2014. "Digging Into the Breeding Ground: Insights Into the Electoral Performance of Populist Radical Right Parties in Central and Eastern Europe." *East European Politics* 30 (2): 246–270.
Pytlas, B. 2015. *Radical Right Parties in Central and Eastern Europe: Mainstream Party Competition and Electoral Fortune*. Milton Park and New York: Routledge.
Pytlas, B. 2016. 'We – the People'? The Breakthrough of Participative Populist Narrative in Poland. Paper presented at the ECPR Joint Sessions of Workshops, Pisa 24-28 April.
Rechel, B., ed. 2009. *Minority Rights in Central and Eastern Europe*. London: Routledge.
Sasse, G. 2008. "The Politics of EU Conditionality: the Norm of Minority Protection During and Beyond EU Accession." *Journal of European Public Policy* 15 (6): 842–860.

Sata, R., and P. I. Karolewski. 2020. "Caesarean Politics in Hungary and Poland." *East European Politics*. Pages TBD, forthcoming in the Symposium.

Siroky, D. S., and H. J. Sigwart. 2014. "Principle and Prudence: Rousseau on Private Property and Inequality." *Polity* 46 (3): 381–406.

Streeck, W., and K. A. Thelen, eds. 2005. *Beyond Continuity: Institutional Change in Advanced Political Economies*. Oxford: Oxford University Press.

Thelen, K. 2009. "Institutional Change in Advanced Political Economies." *British Journal of Industrial Relations* 47 (3): 471–498.

Takács, J., I. Szalma, and T. Bartus. 2016. "Social Attitudes Toward Adoption by Same-sex Couples in Europe." *Archives of Sexual Behavior* 45 (7): 1787–1798.

Topky, 2018. Katolícki kňazi podporujú Kotlebu! Vo výzve zverejnili dôvody, je medzi nimi aj kontroverzný Kuffa. www.topky.sk/cl/100535/1711385/Katolicki-knazi-podporuju-Kotlebu–Vo-vyzve-zverejnili-dovody--je-medzi-nimi-aj-kontroverzny-Kuffa.

Vachudova, M. A. 2005. *Europe Undivided: Democracy, Leverage, and Integration After Communism*. Oxford: Oxford University Press.

Vachudova, M. A. 2019. "From Competition to Polarization in Central Europe: How Populists Change Party Systems and the European Union." *Polity* 51 (4): 689–706.

Vasilev, G. 2016. "LGBT Recognition in EU Accession States: How Identification with Europe Enhances the Transformative Power of Discourse." *Review of International Studies* 42 (4): 748–772.

Weaver, C. 2020. "I'm Gay, but I'm Not Like Those Perverts": Perceptions of Self, the LGBT Community, and LGBT Activists Among Gay and Bisexual Russian Men. In *LGBTQ+ Activism in Central and Eastern Europe*, edited by R. Buyantueva, and M. Shevtsova, 101–124. Cham: Palgrave Macmillan.

Nation before democracy? Placing the rise of the Slovak extreme right into context

Erika Harris

ABSTRACT
Focusing on the People's Party Our Slovakia (ĽSNS), the article systematically explores the political environment in Slovakia in order to best explain the parliamentary breakthrough of this extreme right party that is hostile to representative democracy and is ideologically rooted in wartime authoritarianism. It is argued that the success of the ĽSNS ought to be viewed from the perspective of persistent ethno-nationalist trend in Slovak politics which runs through Slovakia's national development from precommunist times to the present. While migration crisis was an additional catalyst, ethno-centricism and illiberalism have a longer tradition in post-1989 Slovakia than the ĽSNS.

Introduction

When compared to other Visegrád (V4) countries, particularly Poland and Hungary and to a lesser degree the Czech Republic, Slovakia is considered a functioning democracy and does not take up a prominent place in literature on "democratic backsliding".[1] Yet, the 2016 general election delivered a surprise to the political establishment, public and observers: the extreme right Kotleba – People's Party Our Slovakia (Ľudová Strana Naše Slovensko, henceforth ĽSNS) entered the 150 member Slovak parliament with 14 seats after winning 8.04% of the vote. Its electoral victory demonstrated that the cautiously declared success of Slovakia's post-communist transition to consolidated democracy remains fragile.

With its slogan "One God, One Nation" (Za Boha, za národ), the party identifies with the Nazi-sponsored wartime clerico-fascist Slovak State (Slovenský štát, 1939–1945) which established its own form of Christian National Socialism. It discriminated against all non-Catholic and non-Slovak citizens, and deported its Jewish co-citizens to concentration camps (Henderson 2002, 11–15; Kamenec 1992; Nedelsky 2001). While the wartime Slovak State remains a controversial period in Slovak history (Harris 2002, 93; Nedelsky 2001, 218), evocative of this regime, the ĽSNS official website (http://www.naseslovensko.net/o-nas/) declares the party's three founding principles to be: national, Christian and social (národný, kresťanský a sociálny). The ĽSNS openly denies the value of representative democracy (Kazharski 2017, 3) and in its 10-point Manifesto, it promises to protect the fatherland and expel all immigrants who were enforced on Slovakia by the

EU, to "protect the public from the growing gypsy terror" and to ensure that Slovakia leaves the EU and NATO (http://www.naseslovensko.net/wp-content/uploads/2015/01/Volebný-program-2016.pdf).

This article focuses on the ĽSNS and a wider political environment in Slovakia and its neighbourhood with one overarching aim: to increase our understanding of the rise of this extreme-right party. Within this overall aim, while contributing to a rather sparse literature on extremism in Slovakia (Kluknavská and Smolík 2016), the article examines similarities and differences between Slovakia and her neighbours and draws out the wider questions about the rising illiberalism across the region.

In the recent literature Slovakia is often subsumed within Central Europe, whether it comes to "democratic backsliding" (Cianetti, Dawson, and Hanley 2018), rising illiberalism (Kazharski 2017; Rupnik 2016; Krastev 2016) or the radical right (Pirro 2014; Mareš and Havlík 2016). When focusing solely on Slovakia, scholarly attention has been given to explanations of voters' behaviour (Gyárfášová, Bahna, and Slosiarik 2017) and the "stable instability" of the party system (Haughton 2014). Haughton on the pages of this journal, argues that the Slovak case highlights the "importance of the past", but less the communist past and more the pre-communist past, as well as "politics of independence" (Haughton 2014, 211), but does not go into detail about the dynamics of this process. Both the past and independence are inherently linked to appeals to the nation, perception about its identity and ultimately nationalism which is the perspective explored in this article.

Following Minkenberg (2013) who argued that "future studies of right-wing extremism will have to pay more attention to the whole political context of this political movement, instead of being preoccupied with traditional party and electoral studies", (9) and Pirro (2019) who also stresses the "idiosyncrasies of the context", this article is not focusing on party politics. The contribution of this article rests on the exploration of the socio-political context within which the public became receptive to extremist nationalist appeals of the ĽSNS in the 2016 elections.

According to the current research into extremism in Slovakia (Bútorová and Mesežnikov 2017) at both public and political party levels shows that the majority of Slovakia's public are concerned about extremism and hold a very negative image of its supporters. At the same time, the survey shows benevolence toward activities and organisations which underlie extremism and spread its message. Noteworthy is the overall rise of xenophobia and social distance toward practically all minority groups when compared to 2008, particularly Muslims by 41%, immigrants from less developed countries by 38% and Jews 20% (Bútorová and Mesežnikov 2017, 17).

These trends can be explained, but only partially, by the migration crisis of 2015–2016. The Slovak mainstream politicians, just as in the neighbouring Hungary, Poland and the Czech Republic, all responded by playing the national card and engaging in anti-immigrant rhetoric and incitement of fear of terrorism – all supposedly in the name of protecting the culture and safety of the population. It included, but was not limited, to the leading *Smer* party under the leadership of the then Prime Minister Robert Fico who even changed the party's main campaign slogan from "We work for the people" to "We will defend Slovakia" (Haughton, Malova, and Deegan-Krause 2016; Marušiak 2019).

The ĽSNS entered the political scene before the migration crisis, already in 2013 when Mr. Kotleba became the chairman of the Banská Bystrica regional self-government in Central Slovakia (*Banskobystrický kraj*). He and his party suffered a major defeat in the elections to the bodies of self-governing regions in November 2017 by winning only two out of 416 seats (http://volby.statistics.sk/osk/osk2017/en/data03.html). Nevertheless, the continuing support for the ĽSNS averaging around 10%, according to the *Teraz* website publishing regular results of voters' preferences by different polling agencies (http://preferencie.teraz.sk/) and the 10% support for Mr. Kotleba's candidature in the first round of presidential elections March 16, 2019,[2] necessitates the present analysis. The question I am seeking to answer consists of two parts: how this party gained success in the first place and what were the contributing factors to its breakthrough as a legitimate parliamentary party.

After drawing out the specificities of the party family to which the ĽSNS belongs, I place it within the accepted typologies in the literature on *the far right which incorporates both radical and extreme right* in Eastern and Central Europe. All authors concur that the important distinction between radical and extreme actors rest not only on their relationship with liberal democracy, but also on the extent to which these ethnocentric and racist parties are inspired by the right-wing authoritarianism, or fascism of the interwar years. I adopt the same framework here. While the extreme right in Slovakia is a part of a wider European far right trend (Pirro 2015, 2019), it is also embedded in a broader regional context the exploration of which then follows. I seek to demonstrate that despite Slovakia's democracy comparing rather well with its neighbours, it struggles to deflect the rise of anti-establishment or even anti-system extremist forces (Mesežnikov and Gyárfášová 2018, 83). Based on literature, primary and secondary sources and interviews, the article continues with analysis of the political environment in Slovakia. I argue that: (a) the success of a party such as ĽSNS ought to be viewed from the perspective of ethno-nationalism, the origins of which go back to pre-communist times and are augmented by communist and post-communist legacies, and only then intensified by the current discontents with liberal values sweeping the whole of the EU; (b) there is a persistent ethno-nationalist trend in Slovak politics to which the migration crisis served as an additional catalyst and that illiberal trends have a longer tradition in post-1989 Slovakia than the ĽSNS (Androvičová 2016; Mesežnikov and Gyárfášová 2018; Kazharski 2017, 15; Kluknavská and Smolík 2016).

Categorising People's Party Our Slovakia

The leader of the ĽSNS Marian Kotleba was primarily known as a leader of a neo-Nazi political movement Slovak Togetherness (*Slovenská Pospolitosť, SP*). He and his supporters styled themselves and their uniforms on the Hlinka Guard (*Hlinková Garda*), the paramilitary organisation that assisted the leading party of the wartime Slovak state under the name Hlinka's Slovak People's Party (*Hlinková Slovenská ľudová Strana*, HSĽS). The SP was a part of a whole grouping of movements, associations, paramilitary units, etc. who subscribed to the *Memorandum of the first post-November generation of the Slovak Youth* (post-November refers to November 1989, the fall of the communist regime in Czechoslovakia).

This movement did not constitute a homogeneous unit (Mesežnikov and Gyárfášová 2016, 18), but they presented a united position at the huge manifestation "For the future of our children" in Nové Zámky which coincided with anti-Roma violence organised by SP in the east of the country. The ideological basis of the *Memorandum* was marked by: rejection of liberal-democracy, undermining of fundamental principles of market economy, historical revisionism (which extended to Holocaust denial), anti-minority stance, anti-Semitism, anti-Americanism, pan-Slavism, anti-Roma racism, and strong support for Christian values.

The movement was outlawed by the state prosecutor in 2006 and its manifesto deemed a breach of the Slovak Constitution which prevented this movement to ever register as a political party. This did not stop Mr. Kotleba and his sympathisers in their political ambitions. In order to circumvent the law on the formation of political parties and registration of required signatures, they legally acquired an already registered "Friends of vine" party.[3] After a number of changes to the name of this defunct party, in 2010, they registered it under its current name *Ľudová Strana Naše Slovensko* with Kotleba as its chairman (since 2015 known as Kotleba – *Ľudová Strana Naše Slovensko*). According to Pirro (2019), the ĽSNS is an example of a "far-right movement party" (788) which draws on prior activities of the *Slovenská Pospolitosť* movement and maintains ideological link with it, thus merging political protest (rallies, street demonstrations, riots) with electoral mobilisation (788). Discarding their paramilitary image and adapting their nationalistic and xenophobic rhetoric to active criticism of the Roma, immigrants, the establishment, the EU and NATO, the ĽSNS mobilised enough support to make a breakthrough as a legitimate, if extreme political party (Kluknavská and Smolík 2016, 336; Kazharski 2017).

The ĽSNS belongs to an ever growing family of political parties placed at the far right wing of the political spectrum which encompasses both radical and extreme right parties. In this article, as in Slovakia,[4] the ĽSNS is described as an extreme right party. This categorisation is not without controversy and requires some justification. According to Mudde's well established work on radical right parties in Europe (2007) and Pirro's work on Central and Eastern Europe (2015), the primary differentiation between the radical and extreme right rests on their relationship to (liberal) democracy which shifts in ascending order from hostility to rejection. While extreme right is anti-democratic (Mudde 2007, 23), radical right is merely hostile to some "principles of democratic constitutional order" (Pirro 2015, 3); in other words, extremists, such as the ĽSNS are opposed to the existing democratic system.

In the context of this article, there is a further and rather meaningful distinction. Minkenberg (2017) in an effort to provide conceptual clarification of the post-communist East European radical right, situates the debate between alternate concepts such as fascism, populism, and extremism (5). In the table (4.3, 74), mapping the major radical right actors in Eastern Europe after 2010, he places Kotleba's party among extremist right described as fascist-autocratic right, often including racism or xenophobia. Tellingly, the Slovak National Party (*Slovenská Národná Strana*, SNS) appears in the same table as ethnocentrist right with additional explanation as racist or xenophobic right, but excluding fascism. The distinction between the ĽSNS and the SNS is important on two levels. It illustrates the difference between the well-established SNS which while subscribing to the usual far-right notions of exclusionary right-wing politics has been and currently is a member of the government coalition and the extremist anti-systemic ĽSNS, drawing inspiration from the interwar authoritarianism. Secondly, to Minkenberg and the present author, the far right is a spectrum along which parties with a similar ideological profile shift from radicalism to more or less extremism according to the context within which they seek to mobilise voters' support.

Similarly, Mareš and Havlík (2016) characterise extreme right parties by "intolerant nationalism, nativism and hard law and order approaches to homeland security" (324). They make a distinction between "traditional" extreme right parties that utilise a history of fascist or authoritarian regimes from the interwar period, reject liberal values and often employ paramilitary or vigilante organisations. According to them "modern" extreme right parties, are not grounded in historical context, are not against liberal democracy *per se*, but focus "primarily on the Roma minority, immigrants and Muslims and emphasise homeland security within a state structure rather than non-state vigilantism" (324).

Slovakia's ĽSNS combines all "traditional" and "modern" aspects of extreme right. While it shifted from the paramilitary image connected to the wartime fascist state to a more modern politics of extreme right, they have not given up on vigilantism. The party organises vigilante "security patrols" (Bútorová and Mesežnikov 2017, 8; Mesežnikov and Gyárfášová 2018, 86) wearing green t-shirts with the party logo who patrol regional trains. They claim on their website under the category "our work" (*naša práca*) to "protect decent citizens" against "anti-social criminal elements" (http://www.naseslovensko.net/kategoria/nasa-praca/hliadky-vo-vlakoch/).

All far right parties respond to social changes by "radicalising inclusionary and exclusionary criteria of belonging" (Minkenberg 2013, 1), whereby the nation serves as the primary "we" group. In Eastern and Central Europe, the major social changes took place in 1989 which marked not only political and economic transformation but also a wholesale re-writing of national histories. Mareš and Havlík (2016), Minkenberg (2013) and Zaslove (2011, 21) all suggest that the main distinction between various forms of today's extremism is the extent to which the post-communist far right is inspired by right-wing authoritarianism or fascism of the interwar years. In many Central and Eastern European countries there is a history of fascism (Slovakia, Croatia, Hungary, Romania), strongly connected to the ideas of Christian nationalism, national independence and historical injustice (Mihaylova 2015; Nedelsky 2001; Pastor 2012, 5; Mihálik and Jankoľa 2016).

The official policy of all post-independence governments in Slovakia has been to distance today's Slovakia from its first independent state with its grim history of Jewish deportations[5] and discrimination of all non-Catholics and the Romany. Nevertheless, there have been attempts to rehabilitate the first Slovak State. Its president Dr. Jozef Tiso was a Roman Catholic priest who was executed for crimes against humanity. Some revisionist historians[6] during the early years of post-communist state-building argued that the Catholic Church tried to save many Jews and blamed his execution on a post-1945 communist propaganda (Kocúr 2016; Harris 2002, 81–82).

Mr. Kotleba, in his pre-ĽSNS days spoke about the Jewish question and its handling by the Slovak State. In his speech which is available on You Tube he said that "we are of Slovak nationality, not Jewish nationality and therefore the Jewish question as such is of no interest to us" (https://www.youtube.com/watch?v=02dAWAfuDww). The clothes may have changed, but the party's ideological link to the wartime Slovak State remains. In 2017, it celebrated 14 March 1939 when the Slovak State was declared as the "day of Slovak stateness" with a sermon for Jozef Tiso, referred to as "so far the only real president of Slovakia" and the gala dinner for 400 invited guests, as was reported on the blog of *DennikN* newspaper (March 20, 2017 https://dennikn.sk/blog/709155/kotleba-ludova-strana-nase-slovensko-1488/).

Despite different levels of intensity, all far-right parties share the same characteristics: nativism, authoritarianism and populism (Pirro 2014, 601; Pirro 2015, 2; Mudde 2007, 26). Nativism is a particularly virulent form of ethnic nationalism which holds that the state belongs to or should be inhabited exclusively by a native group, a particular and exclusive nation expressed in ethnic terms (Harris 2012, 339; Androvičová 2016, 339; Kazharski 2017, 15). It does not only divide the people into "in" and "out" group, but it present the "out" group as dangerous or harmful to the values, safety and identity of the native people (Mudde 2007, 19).

Authoritarianism stands for a strictly ordered society in which the individual freedoms and democratic principles are subordinate to the state. Radical right populism is related to both nativism and authoritarianism with the core element of its rhetoric being "the people" (Brubaker 2017, 362). The widely used definition of populism is a vision of society as divided between the good "pure" people and the "corrupt" elites (Pirro 2014, 601; Brubaker 2017). The "pure" stands for hard-working, ordinary and decent people who are struggling against "the elite", inhabiting a different world of privilege with little regard for ordinary people and their values. But, the "populist anger" (Brubaker 2017, 363) is not directed only at elites. It is also directed toward those labelled as parasites and scroungers – people who don't deserve state benefits or respect of good people – and also at outsiders who do not belong to the culturally and ethnically bound nation.

For example, the ĽSNS which combines all above mentioned components of far-right extremism calls on its official website for: "bravery against the system" and claims that it is

> the only alternative and opposition to the corrupted and criminal "democratic" system and the current parliamentary parties, which all have been more or less participating in stealing the treasures of our country and in betraying and selling out our nation. (http://www.naseslovensko.net/en/about-us/)

In its "10 Commandments" programme it claims to "prevent foreigners from buying land in Slovakia" and "strengthen the control of illegal employment of foreigners, immigration and visa policy". Moreover, to "put a stop to the preferential treatment of all social parasites, including gypsy parasites" (http://www.naseslovensko.net/en/our-program/).

I am suggesting that the migration crisis provided nativists with the ideal "out" group. This could explain the anti-immigrant rhetoric, except that there are no large numbers of immigrants in Slovakia, even if there is a (manufactured) fear of them. Slovakia was the last EU member state to adopt migration policy in 2014 and its integration policies "raise major doubt about their effectiveness" (http://visegradrevue.eu/slovak-migration-policy-poisoned-by-hypocrisy/). Slovakia's mainstream and extreme political parties exploited anxiety about immigrants with some 70% of the population believing that it leads to the rise of criminality and terrorism (Mesežnikov and Gyárfášová 2016, 40–41).

Pirro (2014) noted the different context of the far right in Central and Eastern Europe when compared to Western Europe. He argues that while the most prominent hypothesis about the emergence of the populist radical right in the West rests on unemployment and xenophobia, this is an inadequate lens through which to analyse the far right in Eastern Europe and that the more appropriate is the lens of historical legacies and idiosyncrasies

Slovakia in the context of Central Europe

Today's Slovakia was established 1 January 1993, after the break-up of post-communist Czechoslovakia. The first independent Slovakia was a short-lived wartime Slovak state which emerged after the Munich Agreement (1938) and Hitler's subsequent declaration of the "Protectorate of Bohemia and Moravia" (1939), thus breaking up the first Czechoslovakia (1918–1938). Though it owed its existence to Hitler's favour, the Slovak state is the only experience of Slovak people with political independence, prior to 1993 (Nedelsky 2001, 215). Perhaps inevitably, its existence and its legacy influenced the early years of post-1993 independence with some political parties, mainly the Slovak National Party (*Slovenská Národná Strana,* SNS) and Christian Democratic Movement (*Kresťanskodemokratické hnutie*, KDH), showing a degree of ambivalence toward the first Slovak state. However, it is important to emphasise once more that while many Slovak politicians, past and present, employ nationalist rhetoric as a matter of political discourse (Walter 2017, 175), it can't be argued that contemporary Slovakia has ever viewed itself as a successor state of its wartime predecessor.

With its party politics being shaped by national identity, post-communist legacies, Europeanisation and corruption, Slovakia resembles "postcommunist Europe in miniature" (Haughton 2014, 211) and it is therefore a constructive case for the exploration of Central European political space, also known as the Visegrád group (V4). This regional arrangement between Slovakia, the Czech Republic, Hungary and Poland was formed in 1991, originally for the purpose of the preservation of a distinct Central European regional identity and gaining EU membership which was successfully accomplished in 2004. But, Slovakia differs from Hungary, Poland and the Czech Republic on a number of levels.

First, Slovakia is a newly independent state; its history is less well-known than that of its V4 neighbours. As elaborated elsewhere (Harris 2002, chapter 4; Henderson 2002), its political legitimacy is tightly connected to nationalism and its past which is still being constructed and formalised within an ongoing nation-and state-building process. Second, democracy was slower in coming to Slovakia than to its neighbours. In 1997, Slovakia was initially excluded from the leading group of post-communist countries to negotiate EU membership, because it did not "fulfil in a satisfying manner the political conditions set out by the European Council" (EU Commission report, cited in Harris 2002, 197). After the 1998 elections, dynamics in the country changed from the ambivalent attitude to liberal democracy, combined with strong nationalist leanings and hostility to minorities (Henderson 2002, 72) to the restoration of democratic transition which was synchronised with the "Europeanisation" (Harris and Henderson, forthcoming). Slovakia did join the EU in 2004 together with the rest of the V4 and these days, it appears to be the least problematic among them (Mesežnikov and Gyárfášová 2018, 78).

As of January 7, 2019, the *Nations in Transit 2018* gives Slovakia the unchanged score of 2.61/7 (whereby 1 is the most democratic and 7 is the least democratic) for the third year running (https://freedomhouse.org/report/nations-transit/2018). While Poland with considerable decline in the category of democratic governance remains within the cluster of consolidated democracies at 2.89, the highest cumulative decline at 3.71 shifts

Hungary to a semi-consolidated democracy. In both Hungary and Poland their leading parties (*Fidesz* and *PiS* [*Prawo i Sprawiedliwość*] respectively) frame their "nationalistic, socially conservative appeals in populist terms" (Cianetti, Dawson, and Hanley 2018, 245). From one-time democratic frontrunners, both Hungary and Poland are now largely viewed as paradigmatic cases of "democratic backsliding" (Cianetti, Dawson, and Hanley 2018). The Czech Republic's score has been dropping year on year and stands at 2, 29.

The Czech Prime Minister Andrej Babiš, who is facing unresolved criminal charges for EU subsidy fraud is, ironically, using anti-corruption platform to win and maintain power (Hanley and Vachudova 2018, 277). The notable distinction between the Czech Republic and the rest of the V4 is that Babiš appeals to voters with a more technocratic than nationalist agenda, but Hanley and Vachudova (2018) argue that his partnership with the notoriously xenophobic and Eurosceptic President Miloš Zeman is nevertheless taking the Czech Republic down a new and less democratic path.

Economically, Slovakia is said to be one of the fastest growing economies in Europe (https://tradingeconomics.com/slovakia/gdp-growth) and achieved a higher standard of living than Hungary and even Poland which with a higher GDP growth rate (1.02) has lower GDP per capita. According to the *Trading Economics* website (https://tradingeconomics.com/), the GDP growth rate in Slovakia averaged 0.98 percent from 1995 to 2019; in the same period the Czech Republic averaged 0.59 percent and Hungary 0.62 percent.

Notwithstanding its democratic credentials and robust economy, a hugely polarising issue in Slovak politics remains corruption which enrages civil society (Kazharski 2017, 23; Harris and Henderson, 2019). Corruption is the lowest category (3.75 unchanged since 2013 and never below 3.25 since 2009) of all democratic criteria by which Slovakia's democracy is being assessed (https://freedomhouse.org/report/nations-transit/2018/slovakia). The low score for corruption is comparable to the Czech Republic (3.5) and Poland (3.5), but not to Hungary which has dropped to 4.75. Nevertheless, it is Slovakia that in February 2018 experienced the murder of a journalist Ján Kuciak (and his fiancée). Kuciak was investigating links between organised crime, business groups and the state bureaucracy. His murder triggered massive demonstrations, under the banner "Movement for decent Slovakia", demanding resignations of the then prime minister Robert Fico and Interior Minister Robert Kaliňák who if not directly implicated in corruption, were blamed for their inability to prevent it. Both eventually resigned under the pressure of protesters and the new prime minister became Fico's deputy Peter Pellegrini.

In connection to many corruption scandals in Slovakia which public perceives to affect all mainstream parties – left and right – noteworthy are two issues. First, Kotleba's extreme right ĽSNS which claims to be an alternative to all mainstream parties "combines its anti-EU and anti-migration narratives with anti-corruption" (Kazharski 2017, 23) in what turned out to be a successful strategy to make a political breakthrough. Second, the victory of a liberal lawyer Zuzana Čaputová as the first female President of Slovakia against the leading *Smer* party candidate Maroš Šefčovič ought to be seen within the context of public discontent with corruption. Given the steady rise of illiberal politics across Central Europe, her victory was celebrated in western press as "ray of hope", a victory of "liberalism in a populist age" (https://www.ft.com/content/f0902de6-5255-11e9-9c76-bf4a0ce37d49) and a "rebuke to nationalism" (https://www.bloomberg.com/nNotews/articles/2019-03-30/anti-graft-activist-set-to-be-slovakia-s-first-woman-president). Not wishing to diminish the significance of liberal forces in Slovakia it is too premature and oversimplifies the issue of post-communist politics as the rest of this article will show and as has been argued by Michael Rossi in LSE blog (https://blogs.lse.ac.uk/europpblog/2019/06/14/slovakias-progressive-turn-is-a-rejection-of-corruption-not-a-stand-against-populism/).

This regional assessment in levels of democracy has its drawbacks, particularly if democratic regression in Slovakia is viewed through the prism of Hungary and Poland. Slovakia is not seeking to build an "illiberal state" as Orbán claims to do (*Financial Times*, August 29, 2016). Nor has the EU launched proceedings against Slovakia as it has against Poland for its attempts to impose controls over the media, the election of civil servants and judiciary, as reported by the *European press roundup*, December 21, 2018 (https://www.eurotopics.net/en/191524/eu-commission-launches-proceedings-against-poland). At this stage, it is unlikely that the ĽSNS would win a parliamentary majority. On the other hand, there is value in probing issues of regional convergence and divergence in order to interpret political dynamics in Slovakia.

Slovakia's accession to the European Union has been a political and economic success. The opinion survey commissioned by the Globsec Policy Institute (November 2017) shows 69% support for the membership of the EU (https://www.globsec.org/wp-content/uploads/2018/02/Analyza-prieskumu-verejnej-mienky.pdf) with some 85% of the population rejecting Brexit.[7] As the only Eurozone state within the V4, Slovakia is economically more (inter)dependent on the EU than its neighbours, but its relationship with Brussels remains complex. Its desire to belong to the core of the EU is based on fear of exclusion and economic interests rather than a desire for greater integration which is then at odds with the hostility towards the immigrants, but in tune with the rest of the V4. Robert Fico has filed a breach of EU rules case against migrant quotas at the European Court of Justice, but then accepted 16 refugees as a part of the quota system. The promise to take more was enough to avoid the infringement procedures that the ECJ began against the Czech Republic, Hungary, and Poland in December 2017 (www.netky.sk/clanok/komisia-spustila-pravne-konanie-voci-cesku-madarsku-a-polsku-kvoli-odmietaniu-utecencov).

While some political analysts claim that Hungary (and Poland) "with their aggressive anti-EU rhetoric have ceased to be partners to Slovakia's future within the EU",[8] Hungary's Prime Minister Viktor Orbán's aggressive anti-Muslim, anti- immigrant rhetoric resonates well with a strong anti-Islam rhetoric by the now departed Prime Minister Fico. Ahead of his third time election victory in 2016, he vowed that he would not accept "a single Muslim", and that "Islam has no place" in Slovakia (*Independent*, May 27, 2016; Haughton, Malova, and Deegan-Krause 2016).

The governing *Smer* party statement (which I received during my visit to party's headquarters in April 2016 from the then party's spokeswoman Katarína Vidovičová) explains that the resistance to migration quota reflects the concern about the integration of people "from very different cultures, with different values and traditions", into historically a relatively culturally homogeneous Slovakia. It argues that in the context of the migration crisis, the Christian refugees from the Middle East appear to represent a group with "the greatest integration potential" because they have at least something in common with "our environment". On my second visit in the spring of 2017, Syrian Christian refugees were not accepted either. No amount of inducements would convince local communities to accept refugees; they "expressed deep sorrow about their situation, wished them well, but they did not want them in their midst".[9] We can only infer that a common faith does not constitute enough integration potential and that the resistance to refugees lies in a fact that they are foreign.

Are the observers who claim "the unravelling of the post-1989 order" (Krastev 2016, 69) and the "normative rupture between the East and the West" (Kazharski 2017, 2) overly alarmist? The "compassion deficit" (Krastev 2015) in handling the migration crisis was disturbing and the success of illiberal political parties is concerning. On the other hand, illiberalism nourished by xenophobia is "surging everywhere", not just "in the East" (Kazharski 2017, 2; Brubaker 2017).

The point I am making is that the situation in Slovakia, despite a relative health of its democracy, is not different to that of their neighbours. The threat to democracy does not come from extremists only, but from the accumulation of factors that undermine its embeddedness in society. As I have already shown, since 1989 to this day Slovakia's political scene has been marked by an ongoing confrontation between liberal-democratic and national-populist forces which have a tendency toward more authoritarianism. The latter includes the two most powerful forces in Slovak politics: the HZDS (Movement for a Democratic Slovakia- *Hnutie za Demokratické Slovensko/*) and *Smer* – SD (*Direction*- Social Democracy). The HZDS under the leadership of Vladimír Mečiar and three-time prime minister dominated post-1989 Slovakia. He presided over Slovakia's split from Czechoslovakia and came to symbolise the difficult transition of Slovakia.

Robert Fico formed *Smer* – *SD* while in opposition (1999). Benefitting from both a vacuum on the left and his ability to win nationalist voters from Mečiar's HZDS, he became the longest serving prime minister in independent Slovakia to date (2006, 2010, 2012 and 2016). These two parties created coalition governments in 1992, 1994, 2006, 2010, 2012 and 2016 (Mesežnikov and Gyárfášová 2018, 81; Haughton 2014; Harris and Henderson, forthcoming). Noteworthy is the presence of the previously mentioned (radical) nationalist SNS in both Mečiar governments (1992 and 1994) and in *Smer*-led governments since 2006, with the exception of 2012–2016 when *Smer* formed a single-party government.

While neither party managed to significantly subvert the liberal-democratic system as is currently happening in Hungary and Poland, their confrontational style of politics, inclination toward cronyism and nationalism have created an environment in which liberal-democratic values appear to be negotiable and relative to the political aims of the moment.

Mihálik and Jankoľa (2016) demonstrate that at the peak of migration crisis (May–October 2015) the most negative response to migrants in the Media came from the governing party *Smer,* followed by the parliamentary SNS and the at that time still non-parliamentary ĽSNS (13–17). Slovakia is in tune with its neighbours in ethnic interpretation of the nation and increased preference for national sovereignty, despite the fact that there was no direct threat to its sovereignty, negligible number of immigrants and a very low risk of terrorism.

The breakthrough of the ĽSNS into a legitimate parliamentary party ought to be seen within this political environment – the persistence of ethno-nationalist interpretation of national identity by nearly all parties since 1990 and the radicalisation of this rhetoric by the mainstream in recent years (Kazharski 2017, 21; Mihálik and Jankoľa 2016;

Mesežnikov and Gyárfášová 2018, 84; Walter 2017). There are deep-rooted underlying factors why that is the case and why riding that particular wave is electorally advantageous.

"The people" in Eastern and Central Europe

One way or another, right-wing radicalism is connected to nationalist politics. In an effort to explain the persistence of nationalism in post-communism, Harris (2012) defended the notion of "eastern nationalism", on the basis of a different historical sequence between the emergence of Eastern and Western European nations. Almost all of Eastern Europe was subsumed within the Habsburg, Romanov and Ottoman empires where the only possible political mobilisation of nationalities against the existing order was an ethnic principle (Harris 2012, 341; Minkenberg 2015, 38).

This is contrary to the majority of Western European nations which developed within or alongside states. Hence, the dichotomy between eastern ethnic conception of nationhood and western civic conception of nationhood (the former tending toward illiberalism, the latter toward democracy). Notwithstanding the well-justified criticism of this geographically inspired dichotomy (Harris 2012; Juttila 2009; Kuzio 2002), it bears relevance to the present discussion. My point is that not geography, but historical contingency and socio-political conditions are responsible for nationalism and its character. Therefore, there are a number of region's specific factors which explain the prevalence of, if not "predisposition to ethnic nationalism" in post-communist Europe (Harris 2002, 2012; Brubaker 1996; Kazharski 2017, 14).

The national question in Eastern and Central Europe goes back to the collapse of empires and the imposition of nation-states in regions where people's national aspirations were time after time suppressed by the hostile empires or deprived of territories they considered their homelands. This fed the interwar nationalism which in some cases led to the wartime disintegration of post-1918 multinational states, such as Czechoslovakia (and Yugoslavia), the annexation of territories and the establishment of authoritarian regimes across the whole region.

The post-1945 communist regimes manipulated historical memory and people's political allegiances and made the national question an enemy of the prevailing communist ideology. But, the story of the ethnic nation did not disappear during the communist period. On the contrary, it was institutionalised through nationality policies which distinguished between state citizenship and ethnonational groups, either as federal units within multinational communist federations or as minorities (Brubaker 1996, 26–29; Harris 2012, 342). While communist centralised authoritarian states sought to remove any social and political differentiation, they maintained folk festivals, ethnic cultural organisations and generally exploited, exalted and victimised ethnicity at the same time (Harris 2012, 343; Verdery 1996, 86).

The understanding of the eastern nation has thus been formed through all too frequent changes of regimes and borders during the pre-communist and communist era, each time adding another layer of ethnic nationalism to the existing one. This was the nationalism that overwhelmed post-communist transitions and became an answer to democratisation when the "national" question would be answered once and for all.

The post-1989 disintegration of communist multinational states was typically, once more, accompanied by the rise of the nation-state whose national elites promote the core (ethnic) self-determining national group in whose name and on behalf of which the state came into existence. This is not because people in the eastern part of the European continent are anachronistic, but because democracy requires a legitimate political unit for "the people" to exercise it. Historically, in Eastern and Central Europe, the answer to "which people" and "whose state" is answered by ethnicity (Harris 2016, 244) which to this day holds political significance.

The establishment of the new states changes regional interethnic dynamics and ads even more significance to ethnicity. The promotion of language, culture, demographic position and political hegemony of the state-forming ethno-cultural group tends to alienate minorities. Their resistance galvanises their kin-state across the border into protecting their co-ethnics in the newly nationalising state, so that there are three different mutually interacting nationalisms around the border of nearly all new states (such as Slovakia). This "triadic" condition maintains ethnicity (Brubaker 1996; Minkenberg 2013, 16) at the centre of political life due to historically motivated mistrust between neighbouring states and ethnic groups. Where the nation-building elites perceive "the nation" to have been divided by state boundaries, as for example in Hungary, it exacerbates attempts at irredentism or the other side of the same coin – the fear thereof as in Slovakia. While in western countries, minorities are rarely viewed in terms of territorial integrity of the state, in post-communist Europe, they are often understood in terms of loyalty to their kin-state that in the past was historically and politically more powerful if not hostile to the current majority nation (Androvičová 2016, 341; Henderson 2002).

The Slovak-Hungarian relationship in the early 1990s was an example of such mistrust between Slovakia, its Hungarian minority and Hungary. It impacted on the post-independence Slovak political party system, it fed the rhetoric of the SNS and the HZDS and slowed down its democratic consolidation. Any political demand by the Hungarian minority was seen as a threat to the Slovak nation and its new state. While this is no longer the case and the Hungarian minority parties have been and currently are in the governing coalition, Hungary's own role as a kin-state bearing "responsibility for the fate of Hungarians living beyond its borders" is constitutionally endorsed in the Article D of the Fundamental Law of Hungary (Harris 2012, 348).

The sensitivity of this issue can be seen in the "Amendment to the Act on Slovak state citizenship" (§9.16). In response to the new post-2010 Hungarian dual citizenship applicable since 2011 for all ethnic Hungarians living in the "lost" territories, the Slovak government presented it as a threat to Slovak territorial integrity and passed a law by which "a citizen of the Slovak Republic will lose Slovak citizenship on the day he/she voluntarily obtains citizenship of a foreign country" as is explained by the Legal Monitoring & Partners (www.futej.sk/data/enu/Legal%20Information%20and%20Analysis/Memorandum-Extensive-amendment-to-the-act-on-Slovak-state-citizenship.pdf). Thus, ethnic Hungarians in Slovakia can obtain Hungarian citizenship only if they are willing to be stripped of their Slovak citizenship which given that the majority of them have lived in Czechoslovakia at least since 1918 did not attract many takers.

This historically conditioned ethnic interpretation of national identity impacts on political rhetoric in a number of interrelated ways. In post-communist Europe "the socio-cultural division remains central to political party competition, and not socio-economic division as is the tendency in Western Europe" (Kazharski 2017, 14–15) which accounts for the continuing politicisation of ethnicity. Nationalism is not confined to the far right, but constitutes the mainstream itself (Minkenberg 2015, 39; Kazharski 2017) which explains why in Slovakia, a socio-economically left-leaning leading governing party *Smer* engages in the right-wing nationalist rhetoric (Mihálik and Jankoľa 2016, 10).

Relatedly, due to "a relatively short period of political plurality" (Gyárfášová, Bahna, and Slosiarik 2017, 4), post-communist political parties did not develop along established societal cleavages, but were formed mostly by political elites for the purpose of their own electoral advantage. In the absence of long-term loyalty of their voters, they tend to fill the loyalty gap and supplement ideologically shallow roots by pervasive narratives about "the nation", its identity and national survival. The result is that in post-communist countries, unlike in Western Europe, radical and extreme right are not operating within a system where there is a clear *cordon sanitaire* between the mainstream and the far right (Minkenberg 2015, 50). I am arguing that in order to appeal to voters disillusioned with the mainstream, parties such as ĽSNS employ more extreme rhetoric which has been thus legitimised by the mainstream.

Nation before democracy? Nationalist persistence in Slovak politics

So far, I have argued that ethno-nationalism and identity politics are a part of political competition in post-communist countries generally, but even more so in a newly independent state such as Slovakia. The frequency of the rise and fall of states, regimes and borders, loss of territories, real or perceived threats and compromised sovereignty impact hugely on the understanding of "the nation" and its relationship to the state. My argument is in line with Hiers, Soehl and Wimmer (2017) who question the mainstream literature on immigration with its focus on competition for jobs. Instead, they place "long-accumulated threats to the territorial integrity and political sovereignty of the nation" (Hiers, Soehl and Wimmer 2017, 383) at the centre of their analysis. While migration is behind the rise of the radical and extreme right and populism everywhere, the alarming rhetoric from Central European political leadership, including Slovakia, relied on certain pre-conditions which made this discourse familiar and therefore acceptable to public.

First, is the direct link between migrants and the security of the country which relied on a long-standing experience of electoral success in the securitisation of minorities as was discussed earlier. Second, is the absence of any previous experience with discussions around migration (Androvičová 2016, 359), the claims by politicians were not refuted because the public had no experience of migration and there were no norms or parameters for this discussion established before. Third, a little regard for international obligation to accept migrants. Slovakia's Interior Ministry's statistics on asylum and migration show that in 2017 out of 166 applications for asylum, only 29 were awarded and 16 refugees were given protection; in 2018 only 3 out of 168 applications for asylum were awarded and 22 refugees accepted (http://www.minv.sk/?statistiky-20).

Nový Čas, January 20, 2018 reported Fico at a meeting of V4 leaders saying that:

> I reject the formation of Muslim communities in Slovakia. Slovakia is a safe country, I want a safe country and I don't see any reason for bringing in thousands of Muslims from around the

world, as Brussel or perhaps other states are asking us to do. This is my politics, the politics of safe Slovakia. (https://www.cas.sk/clanok/649151/najdrsnejsie-vyjadrenie-fica-o-moslimoch-na-slovensku-kym-bude-robo-premierom-toto-sa-nikdy-nestane/)

By emphasising the safety of the country, is he really expressing a fear of a small nation (Henderson 2002) whose entrance into history is too short as not to be threatened by the influx of foreigners, however small their numbers may be? What are the reasons for a "deeply rooted mistrust of the cosmopolitan mindset" (Krastev 2016, 93) in post-communist Europe?

The first reason may be the lack of trust in internationalism which after all was a catchphrase of communism from which they have liberated themselves only recently. The second reason could be that having achieved the possession of the state by the majority and having secured economic survival of it through European integration when liberal democracy was the only option, the continuing ownership of the state by its "rightful" owners is considered a legitimate political strategy. In Hungary and Poland, nationalist populism is a strategy to curb media independence and ignore the fundamental democratic principle of separation of powers. Yet, their populations, having shaken off political authoritarianism seem less concerned by new illiberalism when it is presented as the "restoration of popular sovereignty" (Rupnik 2016, 79).

The same must be said about Slovakia. The persistence of ethnic understanding of the nation as the rightful people in charge of their political destiny is blurring the boundary between democracy and nationalism. For example, opinion polls show that 40% of the population prefers social order and social "justice" at the cost of curbing other democratic freedoms (Mesežnikov and Gyárfášová 2016, 41).

The long-existing polarisation between the proponents of liberal democratic values and pro-Western foreign policy orientation and those more indifferent to democratic values and sceptical about the results of transition and European integration is now as intense as it was in the early 1990s. The mainstream politicians who were well versed in nationalist and anti-minority rhetoric with its emphasis on the state-forming nation have taken advantage of the migration crisis. They remobilised the slowly subsiding ethno-centrism that animated the post-independence state-building era of Slovak politics (Haughton 2014, 219), Whether as a result of their efforts, or the increasingly more racist online media and propaganda of far right parties, the recent polls show that only 18 percent of the Slovak public accepts the idea of refugees settling in their country (Mesežnikkov and Gyárfašová 2018, 86).

Exclusionary ethno-centrism is a competitive rhetorical field though. Fico's vehemently anti-immigrant election campaign in 2016 contributed to his third election victory (Haughton, Malova, and Deegan-Krause 2016; Mesežnikov and Gyárfášová 2018, 86). His socio-economic left-populist variant was competing with the right-wing conservative version of his coalition partner, the Slovak National Party. But, both were rhetorically outdone by the ĽSNS to which I am now returning in order to convey the specific conditions which made its extremism attractive to Slovak voters.

The ĽSNS which in Slovakia (and in this article) is referred to as the extreme right, as opposed to other "ultra nationalist" parties with certain similarities has participated in 3 general elections since its formation in 2010. As Table 1 shows, "ultra nationalist" parties were negligible in terms of electoral results and eventually disappeared from the political

Table 1. Results of ultranationalist and extreme right parties in parliamentary elections 1992–2016 (in %).

Parties	1992	1994	1998	2002	2006	2010	2012	2016
Ultra nationalists								
Slovenská ľudová strana (SĽS, Slovak people's party)	0.30	–	0.27	–	0.16	–	–	–
Slovenská národná jednota (SNJ, Slovak national unity)	–	–	0.13	0.15	–	–	–	–
Hnutie za oslobodenie Slovenska (HzOS, Movement for the liberation of Slovakia)	0.32	–	–	–	–	–	–	–
Extreme Right								
Ľudová strana Naše Slovensko (ĽSNS)						1.33	1.58	8.04

Source: Compiled using the information from the Slovakia's Office of Statistics (Štatistický úrad SR 1992–2016) http://volby.statistics.sk/.

scene altogether. This concurs with Mareš and Havlík (2016, 323) who argue that the surprising success of the Hungarian *Jobbik* in 2014 20.2% owes much to the fact that "in Hungary the extreme right draws on a long tradition" and that "only Slovakia has a similar situation" (332).

Haughton, Malová and Deegan-Krause argued in the *Washington Post* article "Slovakia's newly elected parliament is dramatically different and pretty much the same" on March 9, 2016, that the election results "show that Slovakia is everywhere". They point to the frustration and disillusion of voters with politicians, corruption and poor governance and stress that these challenges are faced by all modern democracies. In that sense, the ĽSNS, offered extreme solutions – rejection not just of foreigners, but the rejection of the whole system in which "the nation" is no longer in charge. In other words: the nation comes before democracy.

Besides historical and political environment which I have been exploring, *other factors contributed to the success of the ĽSNS*. First of all, Mr. Kotleba's political role of a regional governor (2013) gained him personal legitimacy. This despite his past involvement in violence against police and participation in anti-Roma violence which however in his case were not followed by a criminal record, unlike with other members of his party. Second, not ever having governmental responsibility, the vote for him was not necessarily for this party, but the rejection of other parties and politicians frequently embroiled in corruption scandals. The 2016 election results show rising radicalisation of society and a significantly increased public dissatisfaction with established political parties, including Fico's *Smer* (Gyárfášová, Bahna, and Slosiarik 2017, 19; Haughton, Malova, and Deegan-Krause 2016). Thirdly, as already suggested, radical rhetoric has been legitimised by the mainstream parties. Besides *Smer's* anti-immigration rhetoric and anti-Hungarian and anti-Roma rhetoric by the *SNS* in the past, there was also a ferocious anti-EU rhetoric by Richard Sulík, the leader of the parliamentary party *SaS* (Freedom and Solidarity[*Sloboda and Solidarity*]) who were a part of the government 2010–2012. Kotleba, more than any other party contesting the 2016 elections, stole nationalist thunder from the SNS (Pirro 2019, 788) and the mainstream anti-immigrant rhetoric made his ferocity at all things foreign appear less extreme.

Fourthly, returning to this party's ideological links to wartime authoritarianism, its current legitimacy is impacted by education, if indirectly. The school curricula do not deal with the history of the Second World War in Slovakia which means that young people are not aware of crimes committed by the Slovak State during its reign 1939–1945. This history was not a part of the communist education either, because the regime underplayed the Holocaust and subsumed it under crimes of the German Nazism against communists and others. This official political stance had for many years not only inhibited debates about the Holocaust at both official and personal levels (Salner 2017, 87), but conspired in nearly removing the collaboration of Slovak citizens in the deportation of their Jewish co-citizens to concentration camps from Slovakia's history. While Slovak politicians have recently been attending and financing Holocaust memorials (http://newsnow.tasr.sk/featured/president-and-premier-open-holocaust-museum-in-sered/) they have not curbed hostile rhetoric against the Roma, Muslims and other minorities which allows for anti-Semitism to continue within radical circles.

Finally, there appears to be a little if any teaching about the character of totalitarian regimes and ideologies, liberal-democratic values or human rights. Equally, there is little said about the danger of ethno-nationalism and racism or religious intolerance. All leads to the relativisation of certain historical events and to numbing of critical understanding of themes propagated by the ĽSNS.[10]

The most alarming aspect of the 2016 success of ĽSNS is that 22% of its vote was young people or people who have never voted before (Mesežnikov and Gyárfášová 2016, 37–38). It is clear that this party has an appeal among voters which previously remained untapped by other parties. After the 2016 elections, the ĽSNS was politically isolated and until recently it was assumed that it has no coalition potential. Fico claimed that his party will be a "barrier against extremism". However, recent developments suggest that the barrier is slowly crumbling.

Smer (together with the populist *Sme Rodina* party and the Slovak National Party) has recently sought the support of the ĽSNS to halt the ratification of a European Treaty designed to combat violence against women (https://www.socialeurope.eu/zuzana-caputovas-victory-slovakia). The ĽSNS voted with *Smer* (the SNS and *Sme Rodina*) in passing the age pension ceiling bill and Fico thanked them for their support (https://ekonomika.sme.sk/c/22086018/poslanci-schvalili-zastropovanie-dochodkoveho-veku.html). With the campaign for 2020 general elections having kicked off, it should not be assumed that its coalition potential will remain weak and therefore the parliamentary breakthrough of the ĽSNS poses a considerable challenge to Slovakia's democratic future.

Conclusion

My aim here was to explore the recent political dynamics in Slovakia in order to make sense of the electoral breakthrough of the extreme right People's Party Our Slovakia (ĽSNS) to a parliamentary party. I pursued this aim not through the analysis of party politics, but by exploring the socio-political context within which public became receptive to extremist appeals of the ĽSNS. I demonstrated its ideological links to the wartime fascist Slovak State (including vigilantism), the rejection of liberal democratic values and all things non-Slovak, immigrants and the Roma. Its xenophobic exaltation of the Slovak nation is then augmented by the populist condemnation of the political system and its elites. This is consistent with the academic literature on the extreme right in Eastern and Central Europe which I analysed in some detail.

Situating Slovakia within its Central European context, we can't get away from the fact that the region is in democratic difficulties. Slovakia, while currently achieving higher democratic credentials than its neighbours has failed to deflect the rise of the far-right extremism. I argue that this failure is connected to deeply rooted ethno-nationalism which runs throughout Slovakia's historical, political and national development, from pre-communist times to the present. Post-communist transition to democracy and European integration also failed to diminish the very narrow ethnic conception of the Slovak nation among many people. This condition was then exacerbated by the radical rhetoric of the mainstream political parties which was emboldened by the migration crisis, as well as compounded by the specificities of Slovakia's educational system which has consistently ignored the darker side of Slovakia's past during the interwar period.

I have also argued that the current tide of illiberalism in Central Europe and its expression in the radicalisation of the mainstream parties, as well as the presence of the extremist ĽSNS in the Slovak parliament rises within societies where socio-cultural divisions eclipse socio-economic divisions. It is not necessarily the competition for jobs and resources that drove the hostile response of Central European political establishment to the migration crisis of 2015–2016. It is the accumulation of threats connected to their dramatic and insecure national histories which have shaped their perceptions about sovereignty, democracy and European integration. In times of a heightened sense of threat – real or manufactured – democratic norms and principles come secondary to the nation, its identity and its sovereignty.

The relativisation of liberal-democratic values and xenophobia are contributing to the overall rise of populism across the EU. From that perspective there may not be a normative rupture between the East and the West as has been claimed in the view of ever declining democracy in Poland and Hungary. There is however a gap between historical, political, cultural and economic developments in the East and the West. This gap was obscured or perhaps willingly ignored by elites during post-communist transitions which were happening too fast to significantly change perceptions and alleviate national insecurities; certainly too shallow to withstand the current "populist moment" (Brubaker 2017, 357) and illiberal trend facing both Eastern and Western democracies. The case of Slovakia shows that the concern should be with historical legacies and the political context within which extremism rises – anywhere.

Notes

1. Special issue. 2018. "Rethinking 'democratic backsliding' in Central and Eastern Europe" *East European Politics* 34(3); *Journal of Democracy* 29(3), 2018, particularly articles by Jacques Rupnik, Péter Krekó, Wojciech Przybylski, Jiri Pehe and Grigorij Mesežnikov and Oľga Gyárfášová.
2. The run-off presidential election on March 30th was won by Zuzana Čaputová, a female liberal lawyer. Her victory, according to an article by Erika Harris in *Social Europe* should be seen within the continued battle for Slovakia's political future – moving towards more autocratic populist governments, or sustaining the premise of liberal-democratic institutions and values (https://www.socialeurope.eu/zuzana-caputovas-victory-slovakia)
3. Interview with Tomas Nagy, Senior Researcher at Globsec, Bratislava March 31, 2017.
4. In Slovakia, the radical right usually refers to the parliamentary Slovak National Party (SNS) known for its explicitly nationalist agenda. The ĽSNS is referred to as extreme in the press and by political analysts.
5. The majority of 130,000 Slovak Jews (90,000) remained in the Slovak State and 40,000 were living in the territory which was annexed by Hungary and came under its jurisdiction. Approximately, 12,000 returned from the concentration camps (Jurová and Šalamon 1994).

6. For example, the book *Zamlčaná Pravda o Slovensku* (Partizánske: Garmond 1996), consists of contributions of a number of revisionist historians, under the collective name "Friends of President Tiso in Slovakia and abroad", defending the Church and its role in deportations of Jews.
7. Interview with Vladimír Bilčík, senior researcher at the Slovak Foreign Policy Association (SFPA) March 31, 2017 in Bratislava.
8. Interview with Tomáš Stražay, senior researcher at the SFPA, April 6, 2017.
9. Interview with Tomas Nagy, senior researcher at the think-tank Globsec, March 31, 2017.
10. Interview with Oľga Gyárfášová, analyst at IVO (*Inštitút pre verejné otázky*) April 7, 2017.

Disclosure statement

No potential conflict of interest was reported by the author.

ORCID

Erika Harris http://orcid.org/0000-0001-9284-0215

References

Androvičová, Jarmila. 2016. "Immigration and Refugee Crisis in Political Discourse in Slovakia." *Current Politics and Economics of Europe* 27 (3–4): 342–373. https://web-b-ebscohost-com.liverpool.idm.oclc.org/ehost/pdfviewer/pdfviewer?vid=2&sid=ae536db6-c662-4111-883e-47a9a050a90b%40pdc-v-sessmgr06.
Brubaker, Rogers. 1996. *Nationalism Reframed: Nationhood and the National Question in the New Europe*. Cambridge: Cambridge University Press.
Brubaker, Rogers. 2017. "Why Populism." *Theory and Society* 46 (5): 357–385. doi:10.1007/s11186-017-9301-7.
Bútorová, Zora, and Grogorij Mesežnikov. 2017. *Zaostrené na Extremizmus* [Extremism in Focus]. Bratislava: Inštitút pre verejné otázky. http://www.ivo.sk/8226/sk/aktuality/zaostrene-na-extremizmus-vyskumna-studia.
Cianetti, Licia, James Dawson, and Seán Hanley. 2018. "Rethinking 'Democratic Backsliding' in Central and Eastern Europe – Looking Beyond Hungary and Poland." *East European Politics* 34 (3): 243–256. doi:10.1080/21599165.2018.1491401.
Gyárfášová, Oľga, Miloslav Bahna, and Martin Slosiarik. 2017. "Sila Nestálosti: Volatilita Voličov na Slovensku vo Voľbách 2016." [The Strength of Instability: Voter Volatitlity in the Slovak General Elections 2016]." *Středoevropské Politické Studie* XIX (1): 1–24.
Hanley, Seán, and Milada Vachudova. 2018. "Understanding the Illiberal Turn: Democratic Backsliding in the Czech Republic." *East European Politics* 34 (3): 276–296. doi:10.1080/21599165.2018.149357.
Harris, Erika. 2002. *Nationalism and Democratisation: Politics of Slovakia and Slovenia*. Aldershot: Ashgate.
Harris, Erika. 2012. "What Is New About "Eastern Nationalism" and What Are the Implications for Studies of Ethnicity Today?" *Nationalism and Ethnic Politics* 18 (3): 337–357. doi:10.1080/13537113.2012.707500.

Harris, Erika. 2016. "Why Has Nationalism Not Run Its Course?" *Nations and Nationalism* 22 (2): 243–247. doi:10.1111/nana.12185.
Harris, Erika, and Karen Henderson, forthcoming. "Slovakia Since 1989." In *Central and Southeast European Politics Since 1989*, edited by Sabrina Ramet and Christine Hassenstab, 2nd ed, 191–220. Cambridge: Cambridge University Press.
Haughton, Tim. 2014. "Exit, Choice and Legacy: Explaining the Patterns of Party Politics in Post-communist Slovakia." *East European Politics* 30 (2): 210–229. doi:10.1080/21599165.2013.867255.
Haughton, Tim, Darina Malova, and Kevin Deegan-Krause. 2016. "Slovakia's Newly Elected Parliament Is Dramatically Different and Pretty Much the Same. Here Is How." *The Washington Post*, March 9. https://www.washingtonpost.com/news/monkey-cage/wp/2016/03/09/slovakias-newly-elected-parliament-is-dramatically-different-and-pretty-much-the-same-heres-how/?utm_term=.6cb93c3ce2c.
Henderson, Karen. 2002. *Slovakia: The Escape from Invisibility*. London: Routledge.
Hiers, Wesley, Thomas Soehl, and Andreas Wimmer. 2017. "National Trauma and the Fear of Foreigners: How Past Geopolitical Threat Heightens Anti-immigration Sentiment Today." *Social Forces* 96 (1): 361–388. doi:10.1093/sf/sox045.
Jurová, Anna, and Pavol Šalamon. 1994. *Košice a Deportácie Židov v Roku*. Košice: SAV.
Juttila, Matti. 2009. "Taming Eastern Nationalism: Tracing the Ideational Background of Double Standards of Post-cold War Minority Protection." *European Journal of International Relations* 15 (4): 627–651. doi:10.1177/1354066109345054.
Kamenec, Ivan. 1992. *Slovenskỳ štát (1939–1945)*. Anomal: Prague.
Kazharski, Aliaksei. 2017. "The End of 'Central Europe'? The Rise of the Radical Right and the Contestation of Identities in Slovakia and the Visegrad Four" *Geopolitics*, Advance online publication. doi:10.1080/14650045.2017.1389720.
Kluknavská, Alena, and Josef Smolík. 2016. "We Hate Them all? Issue Adaptation of Extreme Right Parties in Slovakia 1993–2016." *Communist and Post-Communist Studies* 49 (4): 335–344.
Kocúr, Miroslav. 2016. *Tiso's Ghost in 2016 Slovakia*. Bratislava: Institute for Public Affairs Bratislava. http://www.ivo.sk/7974/sk/aktuality/tiso-s-ghost-in-2016-slovakia.
Krastev, Ivan. 2015. "Eastern Europe's Compassion Deficit." *The New York Times*, September 8. https://nyti.ms/1K57YQf.
Krastev, Ivan. 2016. "The Unraveling of the Post-1989 Order." *Journal of Democracy* 27 (4): 88–98. doi:10.1353/jod.2016.0065.
Kuzio, Taras. 2002. "The Myth of the Civic State: A Critical Survey of Hans Kohn's Framework for Understanding Nationalism." *Ethnic and Racial Studies* 25 (1): 20–39. doi:10.1080/01419870120112049.
Mareš, Miroslav, and Vratislav Havlík. 2016. "Jobbik's Successes. An Analysis of Its Success in the Comparative Context of the V4 Countries." *Communist and Post-Communist Studies* 49 (4): 323–333. doi:10.1016/j.postcomstud.2016.08.003.
Marušiak, Juraj. 2019. "Change of Political Landscape in Central Europe Since 2010." In *Diskurs i Politika*, edited by Dejana Vukasovi and Peter Matić, 237–249. Belgrade: Institute for Political Science.
Mesežnikov, Grigorij, and Oľga Gyárfášová. 2016. *Súčasnỳ Pravicovỳ Extrémizmus a Ultranacionalizmus na Slovensku*. Bratislava: Inštitút pre verejné otázky.
Mesežnikov, Grigorij, and Oľga Gyárfášová. 2018. "Slovakia's Conflicting Camps." *Journal of Democracy* 29 (3): 78–90. doi:10.1353/jod.2018.0046.
Mihaylova, Aneta. 2015. "The Negotiated Past: The Memory of the Second World War in Post-communist Romania." *Bulgarian Historical Review* 43 (1–2): 64–75. https://www.ceeol.com/search/article-detail?id=497474.
Mihálik, Jaroslav, and Matúš Jankoľa. 2016. "European Migration Crisis: Positions, Polarization and Conflict Management of Slovak Political Parties." *Baltic Journal of Law & Politics* 9 (1): 1–25. doi:10.1515/bjlp-2016-000.
Ministerstvo vnútra Slovenskej Republiky. 2018. "Azyl a migrácia/ Štatistiky." Accessed October 27, 2018. http://www.minv.sk/?statistiky-20.
Minkenberg, Michael. 2013. "The European Radical Right and Xenophobia in West and East: Trends, Patterns and Challenges." In *Right Wing Extremism in Europe. Country Analyses, Counter Strategies*

and Labour Market Orientated Strategies, edited by Ralf Melzer and Sebastian Sarafin, 9–34. Berlin: Friedrich Ebert Stiftung.

Minkenberg, Michael. 2015. *Transforming the Transformation? The East European Radical Right in the Political Process*. London: Routledge.

Minkenberg, Michael. 2017. *The Radical Right in Eastern Europe*. New York: Palgrave Pivot.

Mudde, Cas. 2007. *Populist Radical Right Parties in Europe*. Cambridge: Cambridge University Press.

Nedelsky, Nadya. 2001. "The Wartime Slovak State: A Case Study in the Relationship Between Ethnic Nationalism and Authoritarian Patterns of Governance." *Nations and Nationalism* 7 (2): 215–234. doi:10.1111/1469-8219.00013.

Pastor, Peter. 2012. "Inventing Historical Myths. Review of Hungary in World War II. Caught in the Cauldron by Cornelius Deborah S." *AHEA: E-Journal of the American Hungarian Educators Association.*" *Volume 5*: 1–29. http://ahea.pitt.edu/ojs/index.php/ahea/issue/view/6.

Pirro, Andrea. 2014. "Populist Radical Right Parties in Central and Eastern Europe: The Different Context and Issues of the Prophets of the Patria." *Government and Opposition* 49 (4): 599–628..

Pirro, Andrea. 2015. *The Populist Radical Right in Central and Eastern Europe*. London: Routledge.

Pirro, Andrea. 2019. "Ballots and Barricades Enhanced: Far-Right 'Movement Parties' and Movement – electoral Interactions." *Nations and Nationalism* 25 (3): 782–802. doi:10.1111/nana.12483.

Rupnik, Jacques. 2016. "Surging Illiberalism in the East." *Journal of Democracy* 27 (4): 77–87. doi:10.1353/jod.2016.0064.

Salner, Peter. 2017. "Mlčať? Hovoriť? [Be Silent? Talk?]." In *book Rozprávanie a Mlčanie: Medzigeneračná Komunikácia v Rodine* [Keeping Silent and Talking: Intergenerational Communication in the Family], edited by Monika Vrzgulová, Ľubica Voľanská, and Peter Salner, 86–109. Bratislava: Veda.

Štatistický úrad Slovenskej Republiky (Office of Statistics of the Slovak Republic). http://volby.statistics.sk/.

Verdery, Katherine. 1996. *What Was Socialism and What Comes Next?* Princeton: Princeton University Press.

Walter, Aaron T. 2017. "The Good, Bad, and Ugly of Populism: A Comparative Analysis of the U.S. and Slovakia." *Slovak Journal of Political Sciences* 17 (2): 166–183. doi:10.1515/sjps-2017-0007.

Zaslove, Andrej. 2011. "Radical Right Populism as a Party Family: Contextualizing the 'Third Wave'." In *The Re-invention of the European Radical Right*, edited by Andrej Zaslove, 19–45. Toronto: MQUP. https://ebookcentral.proquest.com/lib/liverpool/reader.action?docID=3332232&query=Zaslove%2C+Andrej.

Latgale and Latvia's post-Soviet democracy: the territorial dimension of regime consolidation

Geoffrey Pridham

ABSTRACT
The state of centre-periphery relations reflects on the "depth" of democratic consolidation. This is tested by applying the territorial dimension of democratisation, a neglected theme in regime change studies, utilising the "partial regimes" approach, one especially justified with regard to regions disaffected with regime change. This approach is applied to the Latvian region of Latgale with a four-point analysis, looking in turn at the structural/institutional, intermediary actors, the socio-political and the external. Contrary to received opinion, it is found that, despite a pattern of socio-economic deprivation and continuing resentment towards Riga, systemic loyalty and societal stability there are fairly strong, that centre-periphery relations are essentially centripetal and that counter pressures from neighbouring Russia have had a limited effect.

Introduction: Latvia's post-Soviet democracy

A new democracy's consolidation may be broadly defined as the stabilisation, institutionalisation and legitimation of patterns of democratic behaviour producing the dissemination of liberal democratic values through the internalisation of the new rules and procedures. It embraces therefore both the strengthening of elite commitment to a new democracy and top-down effects from this but also – more crucially than in democratic transition – bottom-up developments that support if not promote democratic consolidation.

The entire democratic consolidation process normally takes a couple of decades, ranging between two and three, given deeper changes are necessary such as sufficient remaking of political culture. The actual time span required depends of course on the country in question and the extent of its historical legacy and transition problems. But several decades have certainly been necessary for the rather difficult democratisations in Central & Eastern Europe (CEE) that succeeded Communist regimes from 1989.

Latvia's liberal democracy has continued to be marked by both positive and negative aspects. In 2005, more than halfway through this post-Soviet period, a democracy audit by the University of Latvia concluded with the warning: "Democracy is not just democratic institutions and procedures; democracy cannot function effectively if it is not rooted in public confidence" (*How Democratic is Latvia* 2005, 14–15). According to a further democracy audit in 2014, membership of the EU and NATO during the decade in-between had been decisive in Latvia's democratisation but this influence had related to procedural and institutional aspects of democracy. There was still much to do to transform societal attitudes and value orientation in order to adhere to Western standards, a process much slower and more complicated. On specifics, the institutional framework, the judicial system and the rule of law had been strengthened but alienation between the holders of power and the general public still existed and relations between the major ethno-linguistic groups in Latvia had still not been settled *(How Democratic is Latvia?* 2015, 16–18).

In short, the structural tasks of democratic consolidation have largely been achieved but those in the attitudinal and behavioural spheres have remained incomplete. In particular, a vibrant political culture underpinning the newly established system and strengthening political pluralism is rather lacking while there is still a need for a stronger modern political elite free of oligarchical influence (Pridham 2017, 202). The external environment has certainly looked less threatening compared with the interwar period, when Latvia found itself located between Nazi Germany and the Soviet Union. However, this now has to be qualified in the light of Russia's aggressive behaviour since the Crimea annexation of 2014 (Pridham 2017, 200–201). Altogether, Latvia has made significant and in some respects considerable progress towards achieving democratic consolidation; but this process has been incomplete making Latvia's liberal democracy still vulnerable to serious adverse circumstances whether political, socio-economic or international. In short, the deficiencies mentioned above have pointed to a lack of depth in the country's progress towards a consolidated liberal democracy.

One relevant and fresh way of addressing this problem is to take a more in-depth approach to democratic consolidation by viewing the political system's operation subnationally, especially for any area of a country which may be seriously disaffected which might call into question the prospects for democratic consolidation. This approach may be termed the territorial dimension of democratisation. It has hardly been explored in the generally well-developed field of democratisation studies.[1] In applying this approach a region may be revealed as reinforcing new system loyalty or detracting from it. Do, for instance, centre-periphery relations operate centripetally or centrifugally; and, do socio-political conditions in the region serve to underpin or undermine democratic consolidation? Are external links relevant and if so do they confirm or conflict with the consolidation process? It may also take into account whether historical factors mark out the region as significantly divergent or not from the national pattern.

In Latvia's case, the eastern region of Latgale has historically been burdened by severe socio-economic deprivation as a source of political disaffection and this has not essentially changed in the post-Soviet period. The region's identity has been marked by some cultural differences from the rest of Latvia, notably its Roman Catholicism and having its own language of Latgalian. It furthermore has a strong minority population, especially Russian, proportionally greater than the national average; and, being a frontier region, Latgale is particularly vulnerable to influences and pressures from the Russian neighbour.

This article utilises elite interviews conducted in Riga in 2015, 2016 and 2017 and in Latgale in 2016 and 2017, with national and local officials as well as NGO leaders and some journalists and academics. Interviews were semi-structured using a questionnaire with questions grouped under the political, socio-economic and external dimensions; and they were tape-recorded. This project on Latgale has also drawn on relevant books and journal articles, official reports, some opinion surveys and regular news reports of

LETA (the national news agency), of the Riga Human Rights Centre and of Latvian newspapers.[2]

The territorial dimension of democratic consolidation

There has for long been a pronounced national-level focus in published work on post-authoritarian/totalitarian regime change to liberal democracy. This has understandably reflected a general tendency in comparative politics – in which field most transitologists have been located – and it has reflected the fact that transitions to democracy have invariably commenced in national capitals for obvious reasons. The dominant theoretical approach to democratic transitions, sometimes called genetic, was driven by an emphasis on agency, namely the important role exercised at this point by national actors, particularly in comparative work on Latin America and Southern Europe (O'Donnell, Schmitter, and Whitehead 1986). This is of course a rather elitist approach though with some justification for in the early stage of democratisation key elite figures usually play a decisive part. But it nevertheless runs the risk of underrating public developments outside the capital that might nevertheless have some influence on the course of events, a point noteworthy in some East European examples.[3]

The territorial dimension of democratisation comes really into play once regime change has shifted from the transition to the consolidation of a new democracy. It encompasses the role of regions or significant areas in the emergence, establishment and persistence of new democracies. Standing theories on democratic transition and democratic consolidation have hardly at all addressed the territorial dimension. A new interest in sub-national authoritarianism drew attention to the fact "we know little about how democratisation struggles are fought across territory" (Gibson 2005, 105), this lack of attention due to the general neglect of stateness issues in the literature on democratisation (Linz and Stepan 1996, chapter 2). It remained for the widespread regime changes following the end of Communist rule to introduce general issues like the role and structure of the state in new democracies simply because many new sovereign states were created at this time. State- and nation-building became recognised as the third transformation in post-Communist regime change along with the political and the economic.

Looking back at earlier work on democratisation, there is one device that should easily accommodate the territorial dimension. Schmitter proposed focussing on "partial regimes" in that process referring especially to the central institutions of representative government and the party system but also to areas like interest associations and civil society (Gunther, Diamandouros, and Puhle 1995, 410–412). Looking at different components of the political system as a whole, it is quite possible that democratic consolidation may be uneven between them; but in the end how they interact becomes decisive. In this schema, introducing the territorial dimension is viable as one extra partial regime although that was not considered by Schmitter and others who have utilised this useful and actually realistic approach.

There are a number of key reasons for including the territorial dimension in democratisation studies, some of which are fairly straightforward. It applies obviously to new democracies which are structured along federal or decentralised lines. Moreover, these sub-national levels may contribute towards democratic consolidation by bringing policy-making closer to the public. Of course, there is a special argument for this in the case of multi-ethnic societies where minorities may be present in significant numbers in certain regions but not in others. Clearly, there is bound to be quite some cross-national variation in applying the territorial dimension of democratisation given the wide variety of political systems in Europe at least.

Whatever the particular sub-national structure of the political system, a healthy state of centre-periphery relations may be considered as vital evidence of democratic consolidation. This is all the more so given the tendency since the 1970s in Western Europe for regional empowerment thus increasing the weight of regional actors in national politics. EU membership has furthermore reinforced the role and powers of sub-national authorities through the development of its regional policies and structural funds, the subsidiarity principle and treaty provisions recognising the participation of regions in EU institutions. This EU-inspired change has also affected the new member states from Central & Eastern Europe.

The territorial dimension thus provides a "deeper" insight into the democratic consolidation process. It may be applied both generally and in particular with regard to problem areas. In general, it embraces several features that reflect on the functioning of and support for a new democracy such as effective performance by sub-national authorities and the role of political parties at the regional and even local level in integrating political activity there into the whole political system thereby influencing the state of centre-periphery relations.

It is not unusual for support for a new democracy to vary across a country undergoing post-authoritarian regime change. While institutional structures may be uniform across the country, the "infrastructure" of democratic society is not so easily or readily created. Normally, post-authoritarian civil societies emerge first of all in urban environments, especially in national capitals, as they are most conducive to new political energy and perhaps more open to outside influences and so become the focus of modernising trends; while rural areas are more likely to be conservative or traditionalist (with exceptions usually due to local political traditions or sub-cultures). The latter may include, more worryingly, areas which remain strongholds of authoritarian attitudes which are resistant to regime change. Whether that becomes a serious problem often depends on how much such attitudes are activated, such as through anti-system parties. In the course of time, the dynamics of democratisation may carry over into such problem areas especially if this process is successful elsewhere in the country. If that change does not occur, then such areas may allow infractions of the rule of law and so the limits to civil society acting as a democratising agent become apparent. The basic lesson here is that regime change invariably occasions systemic uncertainties; and these may become focussed on centre-periphery relations, especially if there is a legacy problem of unresolved tensions between certain regions and the state.

The territorial dimension may become particularly difficult if combined with the problem of frontier regions. Frontier regions (and not all regions actually border on international frontiers) are those based on "an area adjacent to an international boundary, whose population is affected in various ways by the proximity of that boundary" (Anderson 1982, 1). Political difficulties which particularly relate to frontier regions are usually boundary disputes, subversive activities across the international boundary, the problems of peripheral location within the state and the interpenetration of activities with neighbouring regions in other states (Anderson 1982, 1). In short, the stability and also the effectiveness of international boundaries is the underlying problem and this must have consequences for the chances of successful democratisation.

Danger points may particularly come from interference in a dissident region by outside powers notably those which border on the region in question and are hostile to liberal democracy. One special and fairly recent problem for post-Communist democratisations – and also for other European democracies – has been Putin's Russia acting as the pole for the authoritarian alternative to liberal democracy. A key factor here in Moscow's eyes has been the presence of strong Russian minorities in former Soviet republics feeling aggrieved at national citizenship policies. This has highlighted the Baltic States in particular because two of them have the greatest proportion among ex-USSR republics of Russian minorities within their populations, with Latvia having the highest.

In applying the concept of democratic consolidation to the territorial dimension, the above discussion points to a four-point analysis including: the structural/institutional; intermediary actors; and, the socio-political. Structural consolidation tasks will be tested with respect to centre-periphery relations especially with a difficult regional case. Intermediary actors, notably political parties and political elites, play an important role in integrating the regional and the national; while the socio-political clearly refers to conditions within the region in question. Added to this are external links in considering frontier regions.

In this analysis the key question must be how far the region's actions and development in this period contribute towards or detract from the consolidation process. In line with the "partial regimes" approach, note must be taken of the overall national political system in this process, namely whether consolidation progress in other "partial regimes" counters regional problems or not. If not, then an onus is placed on the region in question. As emphasised by the democracy audits, the attitudinal and behavioural spheres of consolidation have in Latvia remained incomplete making the country vulnerable to adverse circumstances. In the past decade, there have in fact two major crises – the economic crisis from 2008 and the crisis with Russia's much more assertive foreign and defence policy which intensified over Ukraine after 2014. Furthermore, the timing of this analysis falls exactly between two and three decades since post-Soviet democratisation commenced. Hence, it a very apt moment to assess the state of the country's democratic consolidation in this respect. First of all, however, brief attention is given to the case study and historical legacy problems.

The case of Latgale and historical legacy problems

How much did Latgale's somewhat different historical trajectory influence its role in Latvia's post-Soviet liberal democracy and did this affect the consolidation of that system? The answer should focus on matters of change and continuity as well as problems of historical memory; but the key concern must be the importance of different legacies within the parliamentary democracy that succeeded the end of the USSR.

Latgale presents many of the typical problems relating to frontier regions. It is the country's eastern region having a 276km long border with Russia while most of the rest of its eastern border is with Belarus, Russia's strategic ally. Latgale is therefore strategically vulnerable given Russia's vast military superiority over Latvia's forces. Latgale furthermore illustrates several of Anderson's political difficulties relating to frontier regions. While there are no longer boundary disputes following a 2007 treaty with Russia, Latgale has suffered from a peripheral location within the state, it shows interpenetration of activities with neighbouring cross-national regions and there have been patterns of subversive activities across the international boundary. Of course, these frontier problems have particularly marked Latvia's independent status as distinct from when the country was incorporated under Russian rule whether during the Tsarist Empire or the Soviet Union.

Latgale's strong minorities, Russian and also Polish, point to its being a classic example of a border region that has played a part in several different national historiographies resulting from multiple geopolitical border changes over the centuries. The region was historically part of Poland-Lithuania from 1569 to 1772, when Roman Catholicism was embedded in the region; of the Russian Empire from 1772 to 1918; of the interwar Republic of Latvia from 1918 to 1940; of the Third Reich through Nazi occupation (which attempted to separate Latgale from Latvia) from 1941 to 1944; and, of the Soviet Union from 1940 to 1941 and from 1944 to 1991 before becoming part of the restored Republic of Latvia from 1991 (Gibsone 2014, 13).

Latgale has had a much higher Russian population than any other part of the country: 40.1% compared with the national average of 28.8% in 2004, the other regions having 10.6% (Vidzeme), 15.9% (Kurzeme) and 19.2% (Zemgale) and 35.4% in the case of Riga. Latgale also had a higher proportion of Poles (7.2% cf. 2.5% nationally) and Belarussians (5.8% cf. 3.9% nationally). Russians are particularly concentrated in the two main towns of Daugavpils (where they are a majority) and Rezekne with Latvians more prominent in smaller towns and rural areas. Altogether, this meant that Latvians have been in a minority in the region (43.6% cf. 58.6% nationally) (UNDP 2005, 33). Latgale's multi-ethnic society therefore marks its distinctiveness in an area of importance for democratic consolidation.

Latgale must be seen as the territorial weak point in Latvia's post-Soviet liberal democracy. It is the one area of the country where at times separatist ideas have circulated albeit as a minority concern (among some Russian circles there and on the part of various cultural figures) and in which neighbouring Russia has shown a rather too close interest for political comfort. Clearly, its severe and long-lasting socio-economic backwardness has remained a continuing source for political disaffection placing a strain on state loyalty. There have remained some patterns of Soviet nostalgia and ways of thinking that might influence political behaviour. Latgale's historical past, lack of modernisation and geographical proximity to Russia as well as the strong Russian population would suggest a more powerful attachment to Soviet memories than elsewhere in Latvia. A recent survey of opinion in Latgale showed strong support for the view that life was better during the Soviet period than it was now, with only 22% thinking that living conditions had improved in Latvia and Latgale after the fall of the USSR. This was fairly clear evidence that the region's backwardness tended to buttress Soviet nostalgia. Also, the highest feeling of belonging to the former USSR was observed in Latgale (34.6%) compared with other regions. However, it should also be pointed out that attachment to Latvia was considerably high (though slightly less than elsewhere) as well as to Europe in this survey (National Defence Academy of Latvia 2016, 26–27). In other words, the region revealed multiple identities taking account also of identification with Latgale.

Noticeable in Latgale are the persistent effects of the Soviet period right up to the present day, at least in the sense of people attributing developmental problems to these. One NGO organiser involved in socio-economic project work in the region pointed to a "post-Soviet cultural problem" in promoting enterprise there. This was evident in automatic expectations of state help in place of taking initiatives and people not being ready to promote transparency in business. In Rezekne, the head of the district council commented in 2016 in reference to promoting electoral involvement: "We should increase society's activity, starting in rural areas, up to the political level and get rid of post-Soviet thinking, namely others telling one what to do".[4] What we have in these local cases is a micro-illustration of historical influences acting as a "confining condition" within a process of political change (Pridham 2000, chapter 2.3).

Democratic transition usually witnesses some mixture of change and continuity. The former is most evident in the replacement of one political regime by another; while the continuity is most likely in socio-economic and political-cultural areas if only because at this deeper level change moves more slowly. It is here that democratic consolidation becomes relevant. The national and also international context for Latgale's role within Latvia's political system changed markedly after the end of the USSR; but set against this were powerful elements of continuity that weighed heavily and seemed to act as a constraint on moving forward to different times. At the same time, location as a border region threatened to have a fatalistic effect on Latgale's chances for such development.

The structural/institutional

With independence Latvia opted for restoring the 1922 Constitution in favour of a centralised state with conventional decentralisation in the form of local governments. Regional structures were not seriously considered and there was no question of Latgale being selected for any special status within the state. However, the Regional Development Law of 2002 created five planning regions in the country, one of these being for Latgale, established in 2006. These had narrowly defined competences and so they lacked the characteristics of genuine autonomous regional administrations and their representative bodies are not directly elected (Vilka 2015). In other words, although Latgale has a greater sense of regional identity than any of the other regions in Latvia,[5] this distinctiveness is not represented within the state structure.

Nevertheless, local governments have tended to enjoy a relatively high standing or rather a higher rating than national institutions, suggesting a certain "closeness" to the public. In February 2017, a poll showed that people in Latgale and the western region of Kurzeme were the most satisfied with the performance of their local governments, more than in the other regions, with as many as 57% there saying they were on the whole satisfied with the work of their current local governments (LETA, Latvian News Agency, 26 February 2017). Back in 2003, a report from the Latvian Naturalisation Board concluded that trust in and support for municipalities was substantially greater in Latgale than elsewhere in the country. It observed this was significantly true of non-citizens (predominantly Russians), for the percentage of these not taking part in local events and not showing interest in what happens in the municipality was lowest in Latgale compared with other regions in the country (Naturalisation Board of Latvia 2003, 101, 109). This positive aspect should be taken into account when assessing public dissatisfaction there with the performance of the Latvian state. All the same, local government leaders have suffered over the years from financial restraints and have regularly mentioned the lack of sufficient funding as a greater obstacle to their performance than inadequate policy scope within the system

(Vilka 2015, 235). This is bound to add to tensions in centre-periphery relations because of their financial dependence on Riga.

Resentment towards Riga in Latgale has drawn not only on long-standing socio-economic deprivation but also on expectations of state help, such as over social benefits, fostered by the experience of the USSR.[6] Households in Latgale depend more on income from pensions and benefits than people in the rest of the country (*The Baltic Times*, 29 June-13 July 2017). These expectations were more pronounced among Russians than Latvians in the region.[7] In the past decade and more, a new source of resentment has appeared over the distribution of EU funding since Latvia joined the EU in 2004 (when Latgale was acknowledged as being the poorest region in the whole EU), whereby Latgale despite its greater socio-economic needs than elsewhere in the country did not receive special treatment due to party-political patronage on the part of the government which favoured other, richer, regions. The Riga region received the lion's share of EU funding showing that the economically stronger regions were favoured over the weaker ones, thus contradicting the EU goal of balanced regional development (UNDP 2009, 115).

Media commentators in Latgale tended to play up this resentment towards Riga, no doubt because it made for dramatic news. In doing so, they nevertheless reflected feelings among some sectors of the regional population sensing that decision-makers in Riga were not seriously interested in the region, a feeling encouraged by the under-reporting of Latgale's affairs in the national, Riga-based, press. In 2005 the then prime minister Aigars Kalvitis admitted in a press interview he was struck by complaints during a visit to Daugavpils that "Riga ignores us" and that "Riga doesn't pay attention to us", although he became evasive when pressed about giving Latgale special assistance (*The Baltic Times*, 24 February–2 March 2005). Such negative feelings in Latgale were voiced not so much in favour of self-determination and therefore of restructuring state policy-making power but rather on demanding effective policy responses to Latgale's special needs. These pressures have increased in recent years. The question therefore is how far the state has accommodated such demands and whether its response has prevented disaffection from becoming systemically problematic. This outlook of neglect, seemingly taking Latgale for granted, changed mainly as a result of the Crimea crisis of 2014 which produced a severe shock effect in Latvia.

Already, following the country's economic crisis from 2008 and with the assistance of some EU funding, the national government had started to lend special attention to Latgale's developmental needs. What initially provoked this concern from Riga was the marked emigration from Latgale to EU countries in the decade following Latvia's EU membership (which commenced in 2004) under the rules of free movement of labour across national boundaries. This population decline has continued with Latgale suffering most among the regions of 2.3% in 2016 according to the Central Statistics Bureau (*The Baltic Times*, 29 June-13 July 2017). Eventually, the growing fear of Russia's intentions with regard to Latgale and new suspicions about separatism prompted Riga's rather belated attention to Latgale's crying needs. The strong vote there in the 2012 referendum on recognising the Russian language gave a decided push to policy makers in Riga.[8] A national ministry official commented in the summer of 2015 that "we keep in mind the geopolitical side" when dealing with Latgale matters,[9] an attitude already apparent before the Ukraine crisis but much strengthened since then. The document outlining the 2015 plan for regional growth in Latgale referred to "the present geopolitical context – events in Ukraine in the year 2014 – means that it is indispensable to further the development of Latgale's planning region which is especially important and urgent taking account also of external political risks" (Cabinet of Ministers 2015, 2).

There have been two successive special development programmes for Latgale using funding from the European Regional and Development Fund, the first one introduced in 2012 for three years, covering investments, the establishment of a Latgale enterprise centre, road renovation, projects to improve the business environment and films for popularising Latgale (*The Baltic Times*, 14 April 2015). Three years later a second development programme for Latgale was introduced. This applied some lessons from the first programme, in particular the need for more precise result indicators, a greater strictness in the distribution of investment and more attention to indirect impacts of policy projects.[10] This new programme for 2015–17, with most of its 52.24m Euros coming from the ERDF, had the aim of boosting economic activity in Latgale by establishing new companies and expanding existing ones resulting in the creation of new jobs and by revitalising degraded land. Political aims were present with the intention to strengthen NGOs in the region as well as developing public participation and initiatives and furthering inter-cultural dialogue (Cabinet of Ministers 2015, 3). Changing "the negative tendency" of emigration and the national security aspect with regard to Russia were again indicated as policy motives (Cabinet of Ministers 2015, 5, 7–8).

But there remained huge problems in turning the region around economically. Latgale's socio-economic backwardness was so deeply rooted that this was not easily solved by three-year programmes. The enterprise centre's limited success had also shown there were cultural difficulties contrasting with a similar project in western Latvia where young people had proved to be more individualistic than in Latgale.[11] A national deputy from Zilupe, a district right up against the Russian border with an unemployment rate of nearly 30%, summarised many general attitudes by saying that the government's latest development programme for Latgale for 2015–17 was "not strong enough to change the situation, it was only a first step towards that".[12]

Some administrative efforts have been made to improve regular centre-periphery relations. One head of a *novads* (district) in north-east Latgale noted with appreciation that each ministry in Riga had staff looking at ways of helping Latgale such as by creating jobs and infrastructure. He quoted this as explaining reduced local resentment towards the national capital.[13] At the Riga end, a high official in one of the relevant ministries pointed out that he spoke every week with local authorities from Latgale and that there was "intense coordination" with the Latgale Planning Region. He claimed that this made complaints about "Riga's neglect of Latgale" somewhat outdated.[14]

The key question is whether Riga's late and rather defensive concern for Latgale's special needs, driven by two serious crises, will serve to contain serious problems in centre-periphery relations. Meanwhile, it may be concluded that, whereas Latvia's post-Soviet democracy has generally been structurally consolidated, in Latgale's case relations with Riga were still somewhat fragile and open to institutional tension.

Intermediary actors

Intermediary actors play a crucial role in the operation of centre-periphery relations through performing at both national and sub-national levels and thus may act as integrative agents within the political system. Do they strengthen centripetal or alternatively centrifugal tendencies in that system and if the latter does the region in question provide an outlet for anti-system activity which may be problematic in a democracy not yet fully consolidated? Attention is given mainly to political parties with some reference to the development of NGOs as an indicator of the state of civil society.

Latgale is known for its proliferation of local parties, many of these being active in just one area. This is even true of the region's capital, Daugavpils, making it difficult there for the Russophile Harmony Centre which should normally be dominant given the strong Russian ethnic presence. Most of these local parties in the city tend to present interesting and attractive personalities with a local appeal and they, according to a local historian, are inclined to be ideologically centrist, meaning moderate but also Latvian.[15] This general situation made for party-political fragmentation. However, that was modified by local politics in the region being characterised by a strong pragmatism prompted by the need to deal with real concrete problems which are very pressing. It is not unusual for ideological differences to appear much less intrusive at the municipal level compared with national politics. One district council leader commented that, whereas cooperation with the Russophile Harmony Centre in national government was impossible, it was acceptable locally "where issues are common to all parties and there is a sense of community".[16] Many interviews, both in Riga and in Latgale, noted that personalities counted for a great deal in Latgale's local politics and were even regarded as more important than parties. As the head of Rezekne district council remarked, "parties determine which personalities – which are trustful – but personalities actually are the more important".[17] A national deputy from Latgale quoted the example in his own area of the mayor of Zilupe (a town right near the border with Russia), who used to represent Harmony Centre but switched parties to Latgale's Party and still remained popular and electable despite this change.[18] This localistic pragmatism tends therefore to mitigate the kind of political conflict encountered in Riga both at the national level and also in city politics there.

The practice in national elections is for some local parties to form alliances with national parties in order to secure possible representation in the Saeima (the national parliament) in Riga – a clear case of centripetalism. In summer 2012 there was formed Latgale's Party with ambitions to create a region-wide presence and with the support of many local government leaders in the region (LETA, 12 April 2012). Its purpose was to represent Latgale's interests and to campaign for solving current regional problems (*Latvijas Avize*, 4 June 2012). While reflecting Latgale's new political visibility in Latvia, Latgale's Party nevertheless adopted the usual practice of allying with national parties more or less in line with its centre-Right alignment for parliamentary elections. In other words, national political ambitions combined with a centrist ideology suggested a situation where local parties were bent on working with rather than against Riga; and this was confirmed by the new party.[19]

By contrast, Harmony Centre party (*Saskanas Centrs*) was a national party which was particularly strong in Latgale, where its vote in parliamentary elections was usually well above its national average, so in effect it acted centripetally. Presenting itself as Social Democratic or centre-Left, it was widely represented in local councils (in 18 of the 21 municipalities in the region), but it was largely restricted by the ethnic divide which overlay the ideological divide in Latvian politics. The main stronghold of Harmony Centre in Latgale is Rezekne where it is unusually well-organised and enjoys high electoral support (48.34% in the local elections of 2013) including among some Latvian voters. Harmony Centre benefits there from a proactive mayor, Aleksandrs Bartasevics, who described his party's voting base as 80% Russians and 20% Latvians, so it had some inter-ethnic appeal; but this local appeal stopped short – indicatively – of Catholics, especially practising ones. Meetings with Roman Catholic Church leaders, he said, were not regular, only for special holiday events, and there was some local government support for church monuments.[20]

The party's main difficulty is not so much its role in Latgale's politics as its general strategy. Its credibility suffers from its fairly close relationship with Moscow, from which the party has apparently received some funding via the Russkii Mir Foundation.[21] It has had a cooperation agreement with United Russia, Putin's party, which became controversial after the Crimea annexation in the 2014 election since its purpose remained mysterious. Then, in October 2017 Harmony Centre announced that its cooperation agreement had ended. The mayor of Rezekne, Bartasevics, with a Russian mother and a father who was a Communist party official in the Soviet period, was distinctly cautious when asked whether it might be in his party's interests to exploit anti-Riga sentiment: "that is not a good form of cooperation", he answered.[22] This caution may have been influenced by a defensiveness on the part of Harmony Centre over its connections with Russia at a time when relations with that country have become increasingly hostile.

NGOs had been one of the beneficiaries of the special development programmes and also the Soros Fund has shown support for their activity. In 2011, Soros provided 75,460 Euros over 17 months for the development of Latgale including NGO support to enhance activity in this sector (LETA, 15 February 2011). In Latgale, NGOs were not nearly so numerous as in Riga which accounted for 44% of such organisations from 2013 (but then Riga also accounted for roughly one third of the national population), but they were nevertheless significant in the public life of the region. Most of them were local rather than regional with a small proportion of only 5% representing national NGOs.[23] They tended to be small there albeit relatively numerous but their presence throughout Latgale was very variable with a strong concentration in the two largest urban populations of Daugavpils and Rezekne. They were weakly represented in border districts like Baltinava and Zilupe (Civic Alliance Latvia 2016, 23). The ethnic divide was evident with separate Russian NGOs in the region as generally in Latvia, with their focus on cultural activities.

A political element has entered the NGO scene in the last few years. Some concern has been expressed based on Security Police and other evidence of an increase in external Russian funding for Russian NGOs, leading to a meeting in Riga in the early summer of 2016 on the security dimension of NGO activity – a new phenomenon – followed by a change in the law on associations to restrict support for non-loyal NGOs in Latvia.[24] Countering this outside influence has involved different activities (e.g. social integration initiatives, events for minority organisations, radio shows) in cooperation with certain ministries like Justice and Defence.[25] Clearly, Latgale has been a priority in this much more security-minded approach to NGO development. Generally, there has been a greater awareness of the importance of civil society in Latvia since the Ukraine crisis and the Crimea annexation.

A number of observations may be made with respect to democratic consolidation. On the positive side, centre-periphery relations are seen to operate centripetally and this tends to embrace the strong localism in the party system in Latgale; while the pragmatism on the part of local authorities was reassuring. From the evidence of NGOs, civil society had been slower to develop than elsewhere in Latvia but it nevertheless made advances especially benefitting from outside assistance. The main concern was the ambiguity on the part of Harmony Centre which was particularly strong in Latgale. It was open to suspicion of covert anti-system tendencies and hence Putin's growing hostile relations with the West – reflected in the Russia factor affecting NGO development – put Harmony Centre in a difficult position. While excluded from national office essentially for reasons of national security, it played an active and largely constructive part in Latgale's local politics. For the time being, therefore, this party should be placed in the category of semi-loyal, a term used in democratisation studies to describe an organisation that is not overtly anti-system, operates within its institutions but reflects a conditional or instrumental acceptance of its rules (Gunther, Diamandouros, and Puhle 1995, 14).

The socio-political

Some serious problems here undoubtedly presented a challenge to the prospects of democratic consolidation. First and foremost there is Latgale's history of socio-economic deprivation. The general story described in the UNDP's Human Development reports during the second decade of Latvian independence, i.e. in the period supposedly moving towards democratic consolidation, is one of continuous backwardness with limited hope for change and improvement. Moreover, Latgale's multi-ethnic society certainly created its own intrinsic difficulties for achieving consolidation.

The 1999 UNDP report showed that Latgale had the worst situation among the Latvian regions for population regeneration with the highest death rate compared with the national average and the lowest birth rate and also a general tendency for the ageing of the population. Widespread poverty and alcoholism and a rising crime rate were linked to these conditions (UNDP 1999, 21–24). These problems persisted. A decade later, the 2008/9 report recorded a poverty which "manifests itself more acutely in Latgale than in other regions" (UNDP 2009, 113). Significant as an obstacle for future efforts to stimulate economic development was a low GDP per capita due to low entrepreneurial activity and low foreign investment (UNDP 1999, 25).

It was not surprising if this state of affairs was reflected in political attitudes and behaviour. The two national referenda of 2003 and 2012 touched on central issues relevant to democratic consolidation. That of 2003 about Latvia's prospective membership of the EU had a "systemic" importance as membership confirmed a Western orientation towards liberal democracies and for which an applicant country had to undergo a fairly tight democratic conditionality. The theme in 2012 was whether to grant Russian official recognition as a second state language. It therefore focussed on inter-ethnic relations; but the issue was very controversial and the referendum made these relations more polarised.

In the 2003 referendum, of the 34 electoral districts the four with majorities against EU membership were all in Latgale. This contrasted with a national vote in favour of 67.5%, with some districts showing very high support for EU membership, in fact over 70% in 20 of them and over 80% in 6 of them. The four exceptions with No majorities in Latgale were (giving the % of No votes in brackets): Rezekne (55.7%), Daugavpils city (67.2%), Daugavpils district (50.3%) and Kraslava (50.4%). But it should be noted that the vote was not actually uniform in Latgale for it was most negative where the Russian population was strong, indicating that Russians in Latgale showed distinctly less support for Latvia's EU membership than ethnic Latvians (Mikkel and Pridham 2005, 186–187).

In the 2012 referendum on the Russian language, support for making this official was only 24.88% nationally but as high as 55.57% in Latgale. Obviously, the different ethnic balance played a major part again. For instance the city of Daugavpils, with its pronounced Russian environment, voted 85.2% for making Russian a state language. The figure for Daugavpils district was 65.79% and for the towns of Rezekne 85.18% and Zilupe 90.25%. This contrasted with the No votes in the regions of Zemgale (87.42%) and of Kurzeme (91.37%) in western Latvia; and it also differed markedly from the No vote of 61.59% in Riga, a city with a higher than average Russian population.[26] Clearly, this was a protest vote influenced by Latgale's socio-economic problems; but obviously Russian ethnic and Russophile cultural influences were also pronounced. Nils Muiznieks, the former Social Integration minister, drew the conclusion from this referendum that there was a need for additional investments concerning economic development in Latgale (LETA, 21 February 2012).

Latgale's "Russian" reputation needs, however, to be put into perspective. The large Russian minority there is relatively well integrated due to a strong presence over several centuries of Old Russians from pre-Soviet times. This tradition has meant that Russians in Latgale are more likely to be Latvian citizens than their co-ethnics in other regions as well the city of Riga (Aasland 1996, 38).[27] Furthermore, there is a high number of mixed marriages in Latgale with a frequent established practice of making children citizens of Latvia – in fact, Latgale has had the largest number of such children who are already citizens (Naturalisation Board of Latvia 2003, 91). Thus, inter-ethnic relations in Latgale feature some positive aspects.

This ethnic character of Latgale originated in the Russification policies both under the Tsarist regime and later Communist rule, the proportion of Russians in the regional population increasing from 27.2% in 1935 to 43.4% in 1989 (compared with 10.6% to 34.0% in the case of Latvia) (Soms and Ivanovs 2002, 17; Peipina 2002, 99). There were parts of Latgale that were very Russified such as certain localities where residents spoke mainly or only Russian such as in the border district of Kraslava (Naturalisation Board of Latvia 2003, 30-31). A local Russian environment was most in evidence in the city of Daugavpils which had a majority Russian population (50.9% in 2015) and where Poles ((14.1%) nearly outnumbered Latvians (18.2%). Daugavpils is an important industrial and transport centre in the region and presents the strongest urban area in the country which is Russified (not absolutely the same as Sovietised but nevertheless something close) also embracing local Latvians among whom it is common to speak Russian in public.[28]

Religious influences have also various relevant effects. There is the special presence in Latgale of Old Believers or dissident Orthodox Russians who by the Second World War provided 14% of the Latgale population compared with 16% Russian Orthodox believers (Soms and Ivanovs 2002, 11). They are likely to resist overtures from Moscow although secularisation effects from the Soviet period have reduced somewhat their religious attachment. While the Orthodox Church leadership in Latvia has demonstrated loyalty to the Latvian state, the Church in Latgale has revealed some pro-Moscow views especially in the Russian environment of Daugavpils (Teraudkalns 2014).[29] It must be remembered that the Kremlin has generally used the Orthodox Church as a channel for its soft power activity abroad.

A form of stability on the Latvian side in Latgale is offered by the Roman Catholic Church. In general, society there is marked by a quite strong religiosity with, according to a 2001 survey, more respondents in whose life religion played an important part and with a much smaller number of admitted atheists than in other regions (Mensikovs 2002, 135). This difference owed much to the strong presence of the Catholic Church for Latvians (as well as Poles) in Latgale were very largely Catholic. By the Second World War 58% of the Latgale population (i.e. essentially Latvian but also Polish) was Catholic compared with 8% Lutheran, in contrast with Latvia as a whole (including Latgale) where the proportions were 24% Catholic (many of them in Latgale) and 56% Lutheran (Soms and Ivanovs 2002, 11).

The Catholic Church has also played an important social role through its sub-cultural networks and its collectivism and mutual assistance activities as well as a radio station and a role in education.[30] It has penetrated areas of rural society in Latgale and has had a unifying effect for different ethnic groups in the region including not just Latvians but also minorities like the Poles, Lithuanians and Belarussians (Runce 2002, 72–73). It is not surprising, therefore, that the Catholic Church exercises some political influence through its social and cultural presence in the region. This influence is indirect for the Church maintains no special links with political parties. Its actual impact on political life obviously varies locally according to the dominant ethnic composition in small town or village life. According to the district council leader in Vilaka, a town with a strong Latvian and Catholic environment, close links between local authorities and the Church did indeed vary from district to district in his part of north-east Latgale. He said that the Church exerted no special direct pressure on politics in his own experience although he himself admitted that he took decisions "looking through a Roman Catholic prism" and that he had constant discussions with Church leaders on local matters.[31]

These different ethnic and religious factors tend on balance to restrain political disaffection within Latgale from pushing to the limits of loyalty to the Latvian state. In spring 2014, at the height of the Ukraine crisis, a survey was carried out by the weekly news magazine *Ir* on the loyalty to the Latvian state of Russians in Latgale taking the city of Daugavpils. The basic conclusion was that the situation in Crimea or Ukraine was seen as different from that in Latgale. One respondent insisted that the strong support for Russian in the 2012 referendum two years before in Daugavpils did not make for a Crimea-type problem as in Latvia there was "a different historical situation, here are different people, there's a different mentality, we cannot be compared with Ukraine" and commented ironically: "How fine we would be joined with Russia!" It was concluded that Soviet nostalgia "lives next to Latvian patriotism" and it was noted that young people spoke freely both Latvian and Russian, a pointer to some optimism about the future (*Ir*, 17–23 April 2014). Obviously, given the timing of this survey, there was bound to be a sensitivity over the question of state loyalty, which might have influenced the answers; but nevertheless the attitudes quoted here tended to confirm the settledness of Latgale's multi-ethnic society referred to elsewhere in this article such as the 2016 SKDS survey detailed in the next section. This reminds us there were positive aspects to Latvian Russians and the state even though their trust in state institutions has usually been rather lower than among ethnic Latvians (Muiznieks 2006).

Available evidence suggests that separatism in Latgale is distinctly a fringe phenomenon and does not pose a serious threat. A top national security official in Riga revealed that in 2012 Russian intelligence services had carried out an investigation which had concluded there was no viable support for separatism in Latgale. He added that after Russia's setback from intervening in eastern Ukraine it was highly unlikely a similar mistake would be made with regard to Latgale (Off the record information given in author interview, September 2016, Riga). It is clear that separatism in Latgale has no mass appeal. A recent National Defence Academy report quoted an SKDS survey conducted in Latgale in January and February 2016, indicating "only 10%" showing a positive attitude to a "Latgale People's Republic" (National Defence Academy of Latvia 2016, 12). This is an idea which had surfaced since the Crimea crisis through social networks and there have been maps of Latvia minus Latgale shown on the internet (www.baltictimes.com/latvian_security_police_investigate_latgale, dated 29 January 2015). This figure of 10% could be worrying if such a minority were really active. The signs are that this idea of a "People's Republic" is a covert initiative from some pro-Russia activists, so it is significant that the same survey also revealed that the vast number of respondents had a low view of their activities while 76% did not even know of the Russian compatriots' organisation run from Moscow. If the 10% are very largely passive, this could well be explained by a certain nostalgia for Soviet times for the same survey interestingly noted a greater sense of belonging to the ex-USSR than to present-day Russia. In the end, much depends on how far people identify the "Republic" idea with Moscow as that would deter ethnic Latvian support. It should be noted that this idea has little or nothing to do with the stronger regional identity evident in Latgale in the past few years.

Any separatist activities however small have been regularly investigated by the Latvian Security Police, who have reported up till now that threats to Latgale's security from this direction are quite minimal or rather are provocations by individuals.[32] Since the shock of the annexation of Crimea, security measures have been strengthened in the region and a special regional committee for Latgale has been established in Daugavpils leading to an increased presence of Security Police officials there.[33] It is quite likely therefore that the idea of Latgale's separatism is one of many aspects of Russia's hybrid warfare approach to the Baltic states, namely of a psychological kind.[34] In short, while the lack of popular support warns against Russian intervention there this does not stop efforts to cause disturbance and suspicion.

In conclusion, this socio-political survey of certain key aspects affecting Latgale's role within Latvia has revealed limits to political alienation despite the dire state of socio-economic deprivation. New admittedly belated efforts by Riga to confront these problems have apparently taken the sharp political edge off persistent criticism about these. The state has at least shown some policy response inadequate though that has so far been. At the same time, the state of inter-ethnic relations in the region shows on balance that these have some positive sides not always evident in the "Russian" image accorded Latgale. While a certain vulnerability to further crises, whether economic or international, is evident, by and large the signs point to state loyalty rather than deep political alienation, the marginal appeal of separatism being one of these.

It could hardly be argued therefore that these "deeper" reaches of Latgale's affairs present a fundamental dilemma for Latvian democracy. The general tendency was for political and social actors to work within that system in parallel with the centripetal behaviour of local government leaders in the region in their relations with the national capital. The evidence above more or less conforms with the view that, while the reduction of political alienation significantly broadens the consolidation of a democracy, a democracy may nevertheless be consolidated despite the existence of pockets of potential opposition for some time (Gunther, Diamandouros, and Puhle 1995, 18).

The external

External actors, meaning primarily international organisations, foreign often neighbouring powers and also international NGOs, may play an influential often supportive role in a new democracy's progress towards its consolidation, although in situations of international tension or conflict negative impacts may also occur (Whitehead 1996; Pridham 1995). But such activity is invariably directed at national governments rather than sub-national authorities. Indirectly, however, regions and local governments may expect to benefit from any strengthening through external pressure of newly democratic institutions in the national capital.

In the case of Latgale there have been two principal external actors of quite different importance: the EU and neighbouring Russia. During recent years it has become ever more apparent that their political intentions conflict over the prospects of liberal democracy as the dominant political system. In this respect, Latgale takes on a special importance for geopolitically it offered Russia an opportunity for countering the pro-West pull of the EU (and NATO) given the region's partial Russophile environment and its socio-economic problems.

Despite the unenthusiastic support for EU membership in the 2003 referendum on prospective membership, Latgale has since accession come to benefit from EU funding programmes and support. This was not at first apparent as EU funds for Latvia were distributed from Riga and not granted directly to the regions; and in doing this national governments for mainly political (patronage and electoral) reasons gave less funds to Latgale than the other regions, both in terms of overall amounts and also financing per 1000 inhabitants (UNDP 2005, 56). Nevertheless, in the course of time Latgale came to appreciate whatever funding it was granted. As we have seen, the two special development programmes for Latgale were driven by EU funding and many local governments in Latgale were the recipients of EU funds for specific projects such as the large new concert hall in Rezekne, to take one of the more notable examples. And local authorities tended rather proudly to advertise their funding successes.[35] The district of Livani in western Latgale benefited enormously from EU funding under the Phare and Interreg programmes for the period 2007–13, allowing it an opportunity to turn into an important development centre having undergone a bad period half a decade before (*Diena*, 2 May 2007). Even modest amounts were appreciated in rural areas where they seemed more valuable than comparative standards would suggest, such as in the Vilaka district in north-east Latgale where a hundred mostly small projects had been funded by the EU in the past eight years.[36] Key interview respondents in 2016, more than a decade after EU membership started, agreed that attitudes towards the EU had become rather more positive since the 2003 referendum due to the impact of EU support for local projects.[37]

In short, local leaders in Latgale showed with time a pragmatic enthusiasm for EU membership. There were other advantages too. The head of the Latgale Planning Region office in Riga emphasised how important membership was for networking as well as funding for it opened up channels for training from other EU countries to strengthen local projects and also project applications.[38] But there was another side to EU membership for the free movement of labour had at the same time encouraged emigration from Latgale especially among young people with its much weaker economic prospects compared with other EU countries and also with the Riga area. The head of Rezekne district had mixed feelings about this new trend: people were lost but there was also return migration for some came back with new skills and started new businesses.[39] But overall this evolution in attitudes towards the EU had a positive influence on public affairs in Latgale, somewhat reducing feelings of neglect by Riga; and, at a stretch, it is possible to argue that it probably reinforced attachment to the political system in a secondary way.

Somewhat by contrast, relations with Russia have tended to work in the opposite direction given Putin's strategic offensive against liberal democracies in European politics. Political elites in Riga have tended to bracket the region with the Russia factor, as did former Prime Minister Valdis Birkavs recently when asked which of the three Baltic States was the most vulnerable geopolitically:

> I suppose that the most vulnerable is Latvia – keeping in mind Latvia's divided society, large number of non-citizens, different information channels for the two segments of society, Latgale as a region with very low population density and deeper historical ties with Russia, anybody can come to this relevant conclusion (*The Baltic Times*, 1–14 December 2016).

In fact, evidence on actual relations between Latgale and Russia reveals a less black-and-white picture than that publicly proclaimed in Riga for any negative effects have been limited though not neutralised by the stabilising factors in Latgale politics and society discussed above. And, as shown, first-order threats like promoting separatism had little effect.

The 2016 SKDS survey quoted earlier identified some relevant differences between Latgale and the rest of Latvia. On the question whether Russia's policies were considered a threat, 48% agreed with this in Latvia but only 26% in Latgale (National Defence Academy of Latvia 2016, 20). This might sound surprising given Latgale's location right next to the Russian border but it is mainly explained by the presence of the large Russian minority in the region and possibly by a pragmatic familiarity of cross-border contacts. One should mention too the influence of the Russian state media which were widely followed especially in border areas of the region. Concern has been shown in Riga over Latgale's information space and there have been plans for LTV to introduce a Russian language channel for Latgale to counter Russian propaganda (*The Baltic Times*, 4 March-2 April 2015; LETA, 2 March 2015). It is also noteworthy that a much stronger concern was expressed in the SKDS survey over socio-economic problems among "the greatest threats" to the inhabitants of the region.

The survey also drew attention to support for Russia's narratives. On the telling question "Are the rights and interests of Russian speakers in Latvia violated on such a scale that Russian intervention is necessary and justified?", Daugavpils stood out with 50.5% agreeing. However, support was only 11.7% in Rezekne, 13.1% in the rest of Latgale compared with 11.6% in the rest of Latvia (National Defence Academy of Latvia 2016, 10). Daugavpils' pronounced Russian environment was decisive in explaining this difference. It was one reinforced by Russian money from across the border for business circles and cultural centres. An academic study at Daugavpils University published in March 2014 concluded however that most residents there would never support reunification with Russia

(Integration and Minority Information Service, Riga, March 13, 2014); and this accorded broadly with evidence above about the very limited support for separatism. The 2016 survey also recorded a strong sense in Latgale of belonging to Latvia (89%) (National Defence Academy of Latvia 2016, 27), much in line with other Latvian regions.

Various Russian-funded projects there had received support from either the Ruskii Mir Foundation (for the Russian Minorities House and a Russian language training centre in Rezekne) or Moscow House in Riga (usually for cultural activities), while the Russian Embassy was discreetly rather active in the region such as in its programme for schools. Of course, there is a grey zone between genuine cultural engagement (a normal function of embassies) and politically motivated activity at the local level. Russian Embassy activities in Latgale were not new, including some apparent involvement in the language referendum of 2012; but they were becoming more intensive and this "makes people nervous" according to a senior civil servant in Riga.[40] And they have become distinctly controversial in Latvia since the Crimea annexation and more divisive in inter-ethnic matters.

There is an increased sensitivity to previously regular activities by the Russian Embassy such as in sponsoring financially celebrations of May 9, the date in Russian eyes for the end of the Second World War, this being different from 8 May set by the Latvian authorities and for that matter Western countries. Given worsened relations with Russia, it is difficult not to view almost any such activity without reference to political motivation. The Russophile mayor of Rezekne regretted there was not more trade with Russia as that would boost the local economy "but politics intervenes". All the same, there was an active twinning arrangement there with Pskov city including cooperation projects on parks and sports,[41] so there remained some normality in cross-border links.

Cross-border activity is not however confined to localities with Russian environments. In Vilaka, 6km from the border in N.E. Latgale, there are close links including regular meetings with local authorities across the border relating to common problems such as environmental ones. Minutes are taken on the Russian side and these are sent to the Interior Ministry in Moscow, the only problem being the one-sided treatment of such matters in the Russian press.[42] Cross-border cooperation projects are now quite common in Latgale with regard to improving infrastructure, promoting entrepreneurship, preserving cultural heritage, promoting tourism and supporting other social and economic ventures in the border area.[43] Generally, it is possible for ordinary people to get free visas if they live within 50 km of the border.

Altogether, one may see an element of implicit conflicting geopolitical tendencies when looking at the impact of EU programmes and Russian projects in Latgale's case, not really surprising in view of its border region status. However, one should beware of reading too much into the outlook of Riga political elites that Latgale risks becoming an arena of East/West conflict – short that is of direct military aggression involving the region. There are grey areas in this picture for not all activity is geopolitically motivated. Indeed, if Riga were intent on using EU policies in this way Latgale would not have been so neglected in the distribution of EU funds in the first years of membership. One should mention too that this article has concentrated on the overt side of the external for its scope does not embrace the significant degree of largely covert hybrid warfare conducted by Russia in Latvia as a whole. As to the relevance of the external to democratic consolidation, one should conclude from the evidence above that these conflicting influences have only to a rather limited extent reinforced or detracted from that process.

Conclusion

This survey of Latgale's politics does broadly confirm the region as problematic within the country's post-Soviet liberal democracy. Its historical socio-economic deprivation, disadvantages as a border region and the proximity of a hostile Russia all emphasise this. While these different factors could have worked against democratic consolidation, that has not basically happened due to the role of regional and local political and social actors as well as forces of stability there even if at times there have been concerns about national security. In other words, the Latgale case study presents a distinctly mixed picture.

In several key respects the situation over time has remained unsatisfactory. The pattern of disinterest on the part of Riga in Latgale's socio-economic problems until recent times made for ill feeling in centre-periphery relations and created a potential for anti-system exploitation even though the behaviour of local governments there and the functioning of the party system have by and large played a positive part favouring democratic consolidation. Divergent voting tendencies in the two referenda of 2003 and 2012 showed that political discontent could express itself rather bluntly against established preferences. These were serious warning signs but it eventually took the shock of the Crimea crisis and Russian intervention in eastern Ukraine to shake complacency in Riga towards Latgale. This mixed picture nevertheless suggested a certain fragility in Latgale's role within Latvia's political system.

It is of course rather significant that these strains and stresses examined in this article occurred within the context of two major crises – economic and international – which could easily have combined to challenge the democratic system, all the more when we consider that Latvian democracy was still deficient because of public alienation and difficult inter-ethnic relations as noted in the introduction. To understand why not, one may turn to the territorial dimension of democratic consolidation focussing on Latgale as a "partial regime" within the political system.

This shows that systemic loyalties in this region are rather strong both to locality and region but also to the Latvian state despite persistent socio-economic deprivation and Russian pressures there. There are elements of local government bringing democracy closer to the people, as witnessed by its positive standing compared with national government. Its actual performance has been highly constrained by limited national financial resources but this difficulty has been alleviated to some extent by alternative resources from the EU. One may summarise positive factors as traditional or historical, functional in the way the political system has operated and also political or policy-focussed in that Latgale's greater self-awareness and also socio-economic needs at last produced a response by Riga.

The most important traditional resource is that Latgale has a long experience as a settled multi-ethnic society. Different ethnic communities there have historically been integrated reasonably well or at least better than in other parts of Latvia where the proportion of non-citizens (largely Russians) is fairly high. The large proportion of non-citizens in Latvia is invariably viewed by international organisations like the EU as the clearest evidence that the country's democracy is not yet fully consolidated; but this applies therefore somewhat less to Latgale. Then, of course, there is the crucial place of religion in the life of the region whether through the Catholic Church on the Latvian side or the Orthodox Church on the Russian side, with its stabilising influences in society.

The functioning of the system in a way conducive to rather than obstructing democratic consolidation has been evident firstly in the state of centre-periphery relations which have operated centripetally rather than centrifugally. A certain pragmatism has been prevalent in relations between local authorities and the national government, whereas antagonism of a sharper kind has flared up at times in some of the media or on the part of fringe extremist groups. Secondly, the political parties in Latgale while including many local examples have clearly behaved in a manner that has integrated them within the national party system. They have nothing in common with the aggressive populist parties increasingly evident in European politics, where they are now a serious threat to de-consolidate liberal democracies, and they have shunned separatist ideas.

The most important political change of late has been the policy attention given by national governments to Latgale's crying socio-economic needs. Ironically, this change has come about through crisis both economic at the end of the last decade onwards and also external with the Ukraine emergency in recent years. The results of this new policy response are not yet fully apparent and they are likely to be limited, but they do represent a new attention to the region of Latgale. The slow if at times reluctant willingness of Riga to confront the region's backwardness has helped to ease Latgale's position within the political system.

At the same time, on external matters, there is a sense that EU – and also NATO – membership from 2004 has provided an additional systemic factor which is pro-West and therefore rivals the efforts of Moscow to steer loyalties eastwards. The Russia factor always had a potential for creating systemic uncertainty. Ironically, perhaps, while this potential has become more of an actuality in the last few years it has at the same time helped to strengthen Riga's concern for Latgale's special socio-economic needs and, thus indirectly acted to help buttress democratic consolidation.

Altogether, one may conclude that Latgale – the obvious weakness in the territorial rooting of Latvia's post-Soviet liberal democracy – has not despite its serious problems and its vulnerabilities as a frontier region become a real threat to democratic consolidation. There is sufficient evidence that democratic consolidation has indeed spread out there from the main urban areas in the country; and that, on balance, Latgale has complemented rather than undermined the advances in democratic consolidation in other "partial regimes" of the Latvian political system.

Notes

1. The theme of the territorial dimension of democratisation began to appear in article form in *World Politics* by Gibson (2005) and Gervasoni (2010); and more recently there is Kelemen (2017). They have focussed on the problems of authoritarian enclaves, using case study material from Latin America.
2. The research visits to Latgale in summers 2016 and 2017 were organised and conducted in cooperation with Gunars Spodris, a friend and social activist in the region; and to him written thanks are here given.
3. One example was the regular weekly demonstrations in the city of Leipzig in the autumn of 1989 which helped to tip the situation against the failing Communist regime in East Germany.
4. Author interview with Monvids Svarcs, Head of Rezeknes Novads, Rezekne, August 2016.

5. This was expressed in 2011 when a new Latgale flag was consecrated for official use by local authorities, the one region to do this. The Latgale flag features a silver griffin on a red shield against a background of three horizontal stripes, two dark blue and one white.
6. Author interview with Liesma Ose, Latvian Community Initiative Foundation, Riga, July 2015.
7. Author interview with Ilmars Mezs, demographer, United Nations Development Programme, Riga, July 2015.
8. Author interview with Liesma Ose, Latvian Community Initiative Foundation, Riga, July 2015.
9. Author interview with Raivis Bremsmits, Director of Regional Policy Department, Ministry of Environmental Protection and Regional Development, Riga, July 2015.
10. Author interview with Raivis Bremsmits, Director of Regional Policy Department, Ministry of Environmental Protection and Regional Development, Riga, July 2015.
11. Author interview with Liesma Ose, Latvian Community Initiative Foundation, Riga, July 2015.
12. Author interview with Juris Vilums, Member of Saeima, Regional Alliance, Riga, August 2016.
13. Author interview with Sergejs Maksimovs, Head of Vilaka *Novads*, Vilaka, August 2016.
14. Author interview with Raivis Bremsmits, Director of Regional Policy Department, Ministry of Environmental Protection and Regional Development, Riga, July 2015.
15. Author interview with Genovefa Barkovska, Historian at Daugavpils University, Daugavpils, September 2016.
16. Author interview with Sergejs Maksimovs, Head of Vilaka *Novads*, Vilaka, August 2016.
17. Author interview with Monvids Svarcs, Head of Rezeknes Novads, Rezekne, August 2016.
18. Author interview with Juris Vilums, Member of Saeima, Regional Alliance, Riga, August 2016.
19. Author interview with Sergejs Maksimovs, Head of Vilaka *Novads*, Vilaka, August 2016.
20. Author interview with Aleksandrs Bartasevics, Mayor of Rezekne, Rezekne, August 2016.
21. Author interview with Aivars Ozolins, political correspondent, *Ir*, Riga, July 2016.
22. Author interview with Aleksandrs Bartasevics, Mayor of Rezekne, Rezekne, August 2016.
23. Author interview with Oskars Zugickis, NGO Support Centre, Daugavpils, August 2017.
24. Author interview with Rasma Pipike, Director of the Civic Alliance Latvia, Riga, July 2016.
25. Author interview with Rasma Pipike, Director of the Civic Alliance Latvia, Riga, July 2016.
26. Integration and Minority Information Service, 20 February 2012; LETA, 19 February 2012.
27. Author interview with Ilmars Mezs, demographer, United Nations Development Programme, Riga, July 2015.
28. Author interview with Ilmars Mezs, demographer, United Nations Development Programme, Riga, July 2015. According to him, half the Latvians in Daugavpils are in this sense Russified. He also noted that in Latgale generally Latvians were under pressure to address shopkeepers in Russian (this not being so in Riga) and that young Latvians were unlike in Riga versed in Russian as this had an advantage in commerce
29. Author interview with Andis Kudors, Director of the East European Research Centre, Riga, August 2017.
30. Author interview with Janis Bulis, Bishop of Rezekne and Aglona, Rezekne, August 2017.
31. Author interview with Sergejs Maksimovs, Head of Vilaka *Novads*, Vilaka, August 2016. There were religious items on his office walls including a crucifix and a picture of the local church with its distinctive twin towers.
32. The source for this information is regular news reports over recent years of the Integration and Minority Information Service, Human Rights Centre, Riga. Abbreviated versions of the annual reports of the Latvian Security Police (also in shorter form in English) are available at: www.dp.gov.lv.
33. Author interview with Arvids Kucins, deputy head of Daugavpils district council, Daugavpils, August 2017.
34. The term "hybrid warfare" embraces a multiplicity of aggressive actions that stop short of direct military attack, including subversion, hostile propaganda, military intimidation, economic pressures, cyber attacks and the systematic use of social networks for weaponising information.

35. During a visit to Rezekne in 2006 the author noticed that the entrance to the town hall had much publicity about local projects funded from Brussels as well as stacks of leaflets about funding possibilities.
36. Author interview with Sergejs Maksimovs, Head of Vilaka *Novads*, Vilaka, August 2016.
37. Author interviews with Aleksandrs Bartasevics, Mayor of Rezekne, Rezekne, August 2016 and with Monvids Svarcs, Head of Rezeknes Novads, Rezekne, August 2016.
38. Author interview with Iveta Malina-Tabune, Head of Administration, Latgale Planning Region, Riga, August 2016.
39. Author interview with Monvids Svarcs, Head of Rezeknes Novads, Rezekne, August 2016.
40. Author interview with Raivis Bremsmits, Director of Regional Policy Department, Ministry of Environmental Protection and Regional Development, Riga, July 2015.
41. Author interview with Aleksandrs Bartasevics, Mayor of Rezekne, Rezekne, August 2016.
42. Author interview with Sergejs Maksimovs, Head of Vilaka *Novads*, Vilaka, August 2016.
43. Author interview with Iveta Malina-Tabune, Head of Administration, Latgale Planning Region, Riga, August 2016.

Disclosure statement

No potential conflict of interest was reported by the author.

References

Aasland, A. 1996. *Latvia: The Impact of the Transformation*. Oslo: Fafo Report 188.
Anderson, M. 1982. "The Political Problems of Frontier Regions." *West European Politics* 5 (4): 1–17.
Cabinet of Ministers. 2015. *Par Ricibas Planu Latgales Regiona Izaugsmei 2015–2017 Gadam, Order no. 230*. Riga: Cabinet of Ministers. 29 April.
Civic Alliance Latvia. 2016. *The Review of the NGO Sector in Latvia, 2015*. Riga: Civic Alliance.
Gervasoni, C. 2010. "A Rentier Theory of Subnational Regimes: Fiscal Federalism, Democracy and Authoritarianism in the Argentine Provinces." *World Politics* 62 (2): 302–340.
Gibson, E. 2005. "Boundary Control: Subnational Authoritarianism in Democratic Countries." *World Politics* 58 (1): 101–132.
Gibsone, K. 2014. "Approaches to Researching Border Regions: Writing the History of Latgalia." In *Via Latgalica, vol. VI*, 10–19. Rezekne: Rezekne University College.
Gunther, R., N. Diamandouros, and H.-J. Puhle, eds. 1995. *The Politics of Democratic Consolidation: Southern Europe in Comparative Perspective*. Baltimore: The Johns Hopkins University Press.
How Democratic is Latvia: Audit of Democracy. 2005. Edited by J. Rozenvalds. Riga: LU Akademiskais Apgads, University of Latvia.
How Democratic is Latvia?: Audit of Democracy 2005–2014. 2015. Edited by J. Rozenvalds. Riga: Advanced Social and Political Research Institute, University of Latvia.
Kelemen, R. D. 2017. "Europe's Other Democratic Deficit: National Authoritarianism in Europe's Democratic Union." *Government and Opposition* 52 (2): 211–238.
Linz, J., and A. Stepan. 1996. *Problems of Democratic Transition and Consolidation: Southern Europe, South America and Post-Communist Europe*. Baltimore: The Johns Hopkins University Press.

Mensikovs, V. 2002. "On Certain Developmental Features in Latgale." In *Regional Identity of Latgale, 3(36)/2002*, edited by University of Latvia, 131–141. Riga: Humanities and Social Sciences.

Mikkel, E., and G. Pridham. 2005. "Clinching the 'Return to Europe': The Referendums on EU Accession in Estonia and Latvia." In *EU Enlargement and Referendums*, edited by A. Szczerbiak and P. Taggart, 160–192. Abingdon: Routledge.

Muiznieks, N., ed. 2006. *Latvian-Russian Relations: Domestic and International Dimensions*. Riga: LU Akademiskais Apgads.

National Defence Academy of Latvia. 2016. *The Possibility of Societal Destabilisation in Latvia: Potential National Security Threats*. Riga: Center for Security and Strategic Research.

Naturalisation Board of Latvia. 2003. *The Role of Regional Aspects in Dealing with Citizenship Issues*. Riga: Naturalisation Board of Latvia.

O'Donnell, G., P. Schmitter, and L. Whitehead, eds. 1986. *Transitions from Authoritarian Rule: Prospects for Democracy*. Baltimore: The Johns Hopkins University Press.

Peipina, O. 2002. "Changes in the Population and the Demographic Structure of Latgale between the National Censuses." In *Regional Identity of Latgale, 3(36)/2002*, edited by University of Latvia. Riga: Humanities and Social Sciences.

Pridham, G. 1995. "The International Context of Democratic Consolidation: Southern Europe in Comparative Perspective." In *The Politics of Democratic Consolidation: Southern Europe in Comparative Perspective*, edited by R. Gunther, N. Diamandouros, and H.-J. Puhle, 166–203. Baltimore: The Johns Hopkins University Press.

Pridham, G. 2000. *The Dynamics of Democratisation: A Comparative Approach*. London: Continuum.

Pridham, G. 2017. "Post-Soviet Latvia: A Consolidated Democracy in the Third Decade of Independence?" In *Latvia, a Work in Progress?: 100 Years of State- and Nation-building*, edited by D. Smith, 189–203. Stuttgart: Ibidem Verlag.

Runce, I. 2002. "Cultural Processes in Latgale: Evaluation of the Role of the Church." In University of Latvia 2002: 66–80.

Soms, H., and A. Ivanovs. 2002. "Historical Peculiarities of Eastern Latvia (Latgale): Their Origin and Investigation." In *Regional Identity of Latgale, 3(36)/2002*, edited by University of Latvia, 5–21. Riga: Humanities and Social Sciences.

Teraudkalns, V. 2014. "Krievu Pareizticiga Baznica Krievijas Publiskaja Diplomatija." In *Krievijas Publiska Diplomatija Latvija: Mediji un Nevalstiskais Sektors*, edited by A. Kudors, 187–214. Riga: LU Akademiskais Apgads.

UNDP. 1999. *Latvia: Human Development Report 1999*. Riga: UNDP.

UNDP. 2005. *Latvia: Human Development Report 2004/2005*. Riga: UNDP.

UNDP. 2009. *Latvia: Human Development Report 2008/2009*. Riga: UNDP.

Vilka, I. 2015. "Decentralisation." How Democratic is Latvia? 2015: 233–248.

Whitehead, L. 1996. *The International Dimensions of Democratisation: Europe and the Americas*. Oxford: Oxford University Press.

Consolidated technocratic and ethnic hollowness, but no backsliding: reassessing Europeanisation in Estonia and Latvia

Licia Cianetti

ABSTRACT
This article contributes to the growing debate on democratic backsliding in Central and Eastern Europe (CEE), by expanding on Béla Greskovits's distinction between backsliding and hollowness, suggesting ways to broaden and specify the concept of hollowness, and discussing the relationship between hollowness and backsliding. Estonia and Latvia provide illustrations of two stable democracies, which nevertheless have consolidated tendencies for an elite-driven and ethnic-majority-driven democratic process hollowed out of its democratic contestation. This is what I call "technocratic" and "ethnic" *hollowness*. This double hollowness consolidated during EU accession, which created a favourable context for well-positioned ethnic majority elites to push forward ethnocentric and neoliberal agendas while restricting the space for debating them. However, far from a symptom of backsliding in the sense of a regression into authoritarianism, double hollowness is in fact central to these democracies' stability. Such stability will have to be destabilised in order to improve their democratic quality.

Introduction

Concern over the state of democracy in Central and Eastern Europe (CEE) has been increasingly voiced in recent years by both academics and policymakers (e.g. Plattner and Diamond 2007; Sedelmeier 2016). While recent developments in Hungary and Poland have made headlines, fears of wider post-accession regional backsliding have prompted a more general reassessment of the success of Europeanisation and democratisation in CEE. This article contributes to the growing debate on democratic backsliding by arguing for the importance of clearly distinguishing between dynamic processes of de-democratisation and static features of low-quality democracies – thus refining the useful distinction between "backsliding" and "hollowness" proposed by Béla Greskovits (2015). Following Greskovits, I argue that the term "backsliding" is useful only if used cautiously to indicate the emergence of worrying signs of democratic de-consolidation (in particular, the chipping away of democratic institutions by self-aggrandising executives). Instead, "hollowness" is a more useful concept to capture structural democratic failings that have to do not with the stability of institutions but with their low popular content.

To use the kind of medical metaphor often employed in the backsliding debate, both democratic "illnesses" need addressing, but their diagnosis and prognosis are different.

This article uses the cases of Estonia and Latvia to enquire in more depth into the nature of "hollowness" (in particular, as it will be discussed below, its "supply-side" aspect), as a specific democratic deficit that cannot be subsumed under the "backsliding" banner. Three key points emerge from the analysis. First, in diverse societies "technocratic" hollowness is compounded by "ethnic-exclusionary" hollowness. The former is the tendency for an elite-driven approach to policymaking, which reduces the room for public debate and opposition, especially in the socio-economic sphere. This is in line with common understandings of hollowness, also in Western democracies. The latter is the tendency to restrict political inclusion along ethnic lines. Conceptualising ethnic exclusion as a form of hollowness is helpful to highlight how it is not only a matter of minority rights (and thus a problem only for minorities), but actually has an effect on democracy as a whole, by narrowing the democratic debate and emptying it of oppositional minority voices.

Second, double hollowness is not the result of post-accession backsliding or imperfect Europeanisation, but has instead consolidated not least as a result of the contradictory incentives of European Union (EU) accession in 2004. With regard to technocratic hollowness, this finding is in line with critical assessments of EU accession. These have highlighted its top-down nature, which favoured the emergence and consolidation of technocratic approaches to policy-making (Ost 2005; Greskovits 2007; Krastev 2007; Mungiu-Pippidi 2007; Rupnik 2007). As for ethnic hollowness, the political and social marginalisation of ethnic minorities has most often been seen not as a facet of democratic settlement, but rather as a symptom of insufficient or half-hearted Europeanisation, that worsened when EU accession conditionalities came to an end (Kelley 2004). However, a deeper look at the direct and indirect effects of Europeanisation on Estonia and Latvia reveals that "ethnic hollowness" – like "technocratic hollowness" – was also helped rather than hindered by the pressures of EU accession.

Third, rather than threatening stability, Estonia and Latvia's double hollowness is a constitutive element of it. Contrary to the expectation that ethnocultural division would make a democratising country particularly prone to instability and backsliding (e.g. Ekiert, Kubik, and Vachudova 2007, 14; Vachudova 2017), the Estonian and Latvian democracies have displayed remarkable stability. This shows a key difference between backsliding and (technocratic and ethnic) hollowness. Backsliding breeds instability and uncertainty: to guard democracy against backsliding its existing institutions must be protected and strengthened. On the contrary, hollowness is part of what sustains a stable (albeit low-quality democratic) status quo. This implies a trade-off: improving the democratic quality of hollow democracies will require the destabilising of existing arrangements in order to open up the space for de-hollowing (substantiating) democracy. While fear of instability has underlined much of the backsliding debate, from the perspective of hollowness stability can be the problem rather than the solution.

Estonia and Latvia: Europeanising and democratising in ethnically divided societies

Estonia and Latvia have remained marginal in the debate about democratic backsliding in CEE. In the seminal 2007 *Journal of Democracy* special issue on this topic, they are mentioned only once, and the assessment was that they are generally doing well notwithstanding some transition "ups and downs" (Mungiu-Pippidi 2007, 8). After that, while worries about CEE democracy increased, Estonia and Latvia were rarely mentioned in the literature on backsliding and, when they were, it was usually to remark on their relative success (e.g. Sitter et al. 2016, 2). Both states have been, by most accounts, good Europeanisers: they are two of the only three former Soviet republics to complete a successful transition to democracy,[1] they have accomplished some of the quickest and most decisive transitions to the market economy, and have generally complied with EU accession demands. Moreover, they are usually seen not displaying the anti-democratic backlash and the emergence of illiberal populist forces experienced by some other CEE countries. In this sense, they have given little reason to worry that their democratic institutions could be at risk.

This level of success and stability was perhaps unexpected, as both countries have sizeable Russian-speaking minorities (about 29% of the population in Estonia and 34% in Latvia, according to the respective 2011 censuses) and their party politics has been to a large extent defined by the divisions between minorities and "titular nations" (Nakai 2014). While other CEE countries have significant minorities, the relative size of the minorities in Estonia and Latvia marked them off as states where the ethnic issue had a higher chance of destabilising democracy, due to the expected risk for inter-ethnic conflict and security threats from the minorities' increasingly authoritarian "kin state" Russia (Hughes and Sasse 2003, 16). Nevertheless, ethnic divisions have not resulted in violent conflict and the chances of inter-ethnic violence remain very low.[2] This stability and the absence of conflict are therefore remarkable.

However, looked at more closely, Estonia and Latvia display a combination of democratic stability, technocratic hollowness, and ethnic exclusion that does not sit well within either a backsliding or a triumphalist narrative of CEE democratisation. Their politics is strongly elite-driven, with low civic participation (Heidmets 2008, 59–61; Rozenvalds 2015, 224) and little open debate about socio-economic policies (Helemäe and Saar 2012; Masso et al. 2012). Some have argued that populism has made little inroads in Estonia and Latvia not due to the restraint of their political class but to the elitist nature of their politics (Jakobson et al. 2012). Moreover, ethnocentrism remains central to both countries' politics, even after some of the harsher policies on citizenship and language use were softened in the years leading up to EU membership (Kelley 2004; Pettai and Kallas 2009). Public discourses that portray Russian-speakers as a potential fifth column are an ordinary feature of public debate and electoral campaigns, and minorities remain underrepresented in parliament, public administration, and (especially) government (Agarin 2010).

After independence, restrictive citizenship and language legislation were passed in keeping with dominant "restorationist" and "nationalising" discourses (Mole 2012). These maintained that the Soviet Union had illegally occupied Estonia and Latvia and so Soviet-era settlers and their descendants had no legitimate claim to political rights, let alone shared ownership of the "restored" independent states. Thus, citizenship was granted only to the descendants of citizens of the interwar Estonian and Latvian republics, which left a large portion of Russian-speakers who were born in Latvia and Estonia or had spent most of their lives in these countries without citizenship.[3] This left a legacy of "non-citizenship" that, although slowly decreasing over time, has affected the minorities' social and political inclusion.[4] Language is the major dividing line between ethnic majority and ethnic (linguistic) minority, and it is the object of extensive legislation regulating language use in, for example, public offices, schools, public and private employment, public and commercial communications, and the media. Through these laws and regulations, language (mother tongue and state language proficiency) became an additional filter that restricts minority access to public life and creates collective privileges for the so-called "titular nations" (Järve 2000, 7). For these reasons, Latvia and Estonia have in the past been referred to as ethnic democracies (Pettai and Hallik 2002; Smooha and Järve 2005), that is, "democrac[ies] that [contain] the non-democratic institutionalisation of dominance of one group" (Smooha and Järve 2005, 21).

While Estonian and Latvian ethnic majority elites have remained broadly in control of the democratic process by occupying all the major positions of power, there are differences between the two countries not captured by the label of "ethnic democracy". In particular, Russian-speakers' political presence – in terms of both representation and grassroots mobilisation – has been higher in Latvia than in Estonia (cf. Cianetti and Nakai 2017, 283). Estonia's Russian-speakers have a more weakly organised civil society, they have a proportionally lower representation in parliament, and the Russian-speakers' vote is mostly collected by the mainstream Estonian Centre Party. Latvia's Russian speakers have shown more capacity for grassroots collective action, the moderate Russophone-led party Harmony gathers most of the Russian speakers' vote, securing higher representation in parliament, and controlling the capital city Riga (whose mayor since 2009 is the Russian-speaker and leader of Harmony Nils Ušakovs). While they are not the focus of this article, these differences must be taken into account when assessing relative ethnic hollowness in the two democracies.

No backsliding, but two faces of hollowness?

Definitions of backsliding have often remained vague and case-specific. Unsurprisingly, a lot of the discussion has been informed by the Hungarian and Polish governments' moves to maximise their power, undermining democratic institutions, marginalising opponents, and attacking media freedom (e.g. Ost 2016; Heller et al. 2017). Used more loosely, "backsliding" has also been associated with electoral gains (though not necessarily victory) by nationalist populist parties (Bútora 2007), and the consequent polarisation of the public debate (Mungiu-Pippidi 2007, 9). Popular disenchantment with democracy (Rupnik 2007), as evidenced by low turnout (Greskovits 2007) and mistrust towards politicians and parties (Krastev 2007, 57), is also often mentioned as part of CEE's democratic malaise. The term backsliding has also been used in relation to Europeanisation to mean the post-accession slowing down or reversal of EU-driven reforms (Sitter et al. 2016), often to do with governance rather than strictly-speaking democracy or liberalism (Dimitrova 2010; Levitz and Pop-Eleches 2010).

While the concern that democracy in CEE might be deteriorating is widespread, there have been few attempts at systematising (rather than merely enumerating) all these disparate "symptoms". Most prominently, Béla Greskovits (2015) proposed a useful distinction between democratic backsliding and democratic hollowing, which is an important step towards putting some order in the CEE "democratic backsliding" frenzy. Backsliding, as noted above, is the more spectacular, headline-grabbing destabilisation of key democratic practices and institutions in an authoritarian and illiberal direction, as in Hungary and Poland. Hollowing is a slower, sometimes imperceptible emptying out of the popular component of democracy. According to Greskovits, we should talk of "hollowness" in CEE rather than "hollowing", because CEE democracies were often already "born with a hollow core" (Bohle and Greskovits 2012; Greskovits 2015, 30).

Adapting the term from Peter Mair's (2006) "hollowing", Greskovits's "hollowness" is intended as the absence of a participatory debate in democratic decision-making, so that institutions are "hollow" from the point of view of participative democracy. In the scholarship on Western democracies, the source of hollowing has been identified in the "twin processes" of citizens' withdrawal from political involvement and political elites' increasing tendency to shield key political decisions from mass democratic participation in favour of "technical" (or "technocratic") solutions (Mair 2006). According to Greskovits, CEE democracies were "born" hollow on both counts (Bohle and Greskovits 2012; Greskovits 2015, 30). For the purpose of conceptual clarity, however, it might be useful to distinguish between "demand-side" hollowness (where citizens are disengaged from politics) and a "supply-side" hollowness (where political elites restrict the scope for meaningful citizens participation and political debate).[5] While recognising that the two are interrelated (Mair 2013, 44), this article's focus is on institutions and elites and thus on the second, "supply-side" aspect of democratic hollowness.

Separating symptoms of backsliding from symptoms of hollowness allows us not only to be clearer about how we define the two terms but also to ask questions about the relationship between the two. However, Greskovits's (2015) exploratory study of this question remains inconclusive: it suggests that a vibrant civil society might have facilitated backsliding in the Hungarian case (see also Greskovits 2017), while Latvia's hollowness might have avoided some of Hungary's excesses but did not prevent backsliding. Thus, in this account, backsliding is not explained by vibrancy of civil society (or by its contrary, hollowness) but rather by the ideology of the actors that manage to mobilise civil society (Greskovits 2015, 35).

This interpretation of the hollowness–backsliding nexus rests on Greskovits's (2015) assessment of Latvia as both hollow *and* backsliding, which sets it apart from Estonia's condition of being particularly hollow but not backsliding. Latvia's high backsliding score (it is the second most severe case of backsliding in Greskovits's ranking) seems to be driven mostly by two key developments. Firstly, the post-crisis electoral success of the far-right party National Alliance, which is compared to the emergence of Jobbik in Hungary (Greskovits 2015, 33–34). Secondly, the eruption of anti-austerity protests in 2009, as the number and intensity of such protests is included in the backsliding index (Greskovits 2015, 31).[6] However, under closer scrutiny, this assessment becomes less convincing.[7]

First of all, while Latvia's party politics is rife with ethno-nationalist claims, this is not a new or even growing feature of Latvian politics. The far-right nationalist National Alliance did not emerge as a new party with a new exclusivist agenda. Rather, it is the latest iteration of several far-right parties and electoral alliances that have had fluctuating electoral success and campaigning strategies since Latvian independence, but have been consistently represented in parliament and have been key partners in almost all governing coalitions.[8] Moreover, National Alliance does not have the monopoly on ethnocentrism, as this has been the electoral currency of moderate centre-right parties as well. While this normalisation of nationalism might be worrying in its own right, it is doubtful whether we should refer to it as backsliding. Backsliding implies a change for the worse, but as ethnonationalism has been a constant feature of Latvian politics since independence, there is no high point from which Latvia would be sliding back.

In this sense, Estonia – which in Greskovits's account is a non-backslider – is rather similar to Latvia. A governmental ethnonationalist party of the "titular" nation also exists (IRL, Union of Pro Patria and Res Publica), which has consistently gained sizeable representation in parliament and has been part of almost all governing coalitions. Ethnonationalist claims have also been often deployed by (ethnic majority) moderate parties in Estonia.[9] The recent emergence of the right-wing Eurosceptic EKRE (Conservative People's Party of Estonia) – which passed the 5% threshold for the first time in 2015, winning seven parliamentary seats – and the possibility of further reinvigoration of the far right in Latvia (Kott 2016) are perhaps signals that there is room for a hardening of ethnonationalist positions. However, these changes have so far not amounted to a significant shift in the countries' party politics and should be understood in the context of deeply entrenched pre-existing ethnonationalism rather than as entirely new developments.

Anti-austerity protests also contributed to boosting Latvia's backsliding score in Greskovits's analysis. This could set Latvia apart from Estonia, where protests have been smaller and rarer. While the rationale for considering anti-austerity mobilisation as a driver of backsliding is not entirely clear, it seems to rest on the idea that popular dissatisfaction might breed instability. This, however, is hardly the case for Latvia, where protests were indeed sizeable, but they were quickly absorbed within the "normal" course of Latvia's party politics (Pryce 2012), including its usual ethnic divisions (Lublin 2013). Moreover, higher (if not long-lasting) anti-austerity mobilisation in Latvia could be a function of civil society vibrancy – and thus a counter to hollowness – rather than an indicator of backsliding (cf. Ekiert and Kubik 2001).

A different picture emerges from this reassessment. First, although – as detailed in the next section – both countries are democratically hollow in the sense that their governments have tended to take a technocratic approach to policy-making, anti-austerity protests in Latvia might show a higher potential for bottom-up challenges to the hollow status quo compared to Estonia (see article by Knott in this issue for other bottom-up challenges in the region). Secondly, ethnonationalism is not a new or emergent feature of these democracies that risks upsetting the status quo. Rather, it is a constituent part of the status quo. As such, it cannot be taken as proof of a dynamic process of backsliding, but is better conceptualised as an additional form of (supply-side) hollowness. That is, a static feature that shrinks the public realm further, by excluding or marginalising a substantial portion of society and by restricting the public debate on issues of identity and belonging. As technocratic hollowness empties democratic institutions of debates about *what* the state is for, ethnic hollowness empties them of debates about *whom* the state is for.

Consolidating technocratic hollowness

The double – technocratic and ethnic – hollowness discussed above is not a result of post-accession backsliding. Rather, it consolidated during Estonia and Latvia's transition to democracy. CEE democratisation process took place in the context of Europeanisation and was influenced by both deliberate acts by European institutions and indirect lesson-drawing by the democratising countries (Schimmelfennig and Sedelmeier 2004; Beyers 2010; Börzel and Risse 2012). The process of EU accession was driven by coalitions between EU institutions and CEE democratisers, which "lengthen[ed] the time horizons of postcommunist politicians, [expanded] the circle of interested reformers, and [deterred] opponents of reform" (Jacoby 2006, 625). EU integration supported CEE democracy- and institution-building (Kelley 2004; Sedelmeier 2008, 2012a) and provided substance to CEE democratisers' political agenda of "return to Europe", giving it an explicit goal and a clear roadmap, as well as expertise and generous financial support.[10] At the same time, conditionalities forced recalcitrant governments to follow through with democratic and good-governance reforms. However, the interaction between domestic and external actors was complex, as the pressures of EU integration were key in shaping the realm of possibilities for the emergent CEE democracies but domestic elites determined the ultimate outcomes (cf. Schimmelfennig and Sedelmeier 2004; McCauley 2011; Spirova 2012; Sedelmeier 2012b).

While external pressures and constraints have certainly helped establish electoral democracies, some have argued that the top-down nature of the EU accession process and the fact that it was based on elite-level coalitions with no need for organised social constituencies also had the negative long-term effect of embedding technocratic practices in the nascent CEE democracies (e.g. Rupnik 2007; Bohle and Greskovits 2012). The need to stick by the EU integration roadmap depoliticised and technicised the democratic process. Thus, at the same time as democratic institutions were being built and consolidated, these were also emptied out of meaningful policy-based contestation (Bohle and Greskovits 2012, 86; Grzymała-Busse and Innes 2003). In this context, democratic elections became a "necessary evil" that should not change the policy course (Mungiu-Pippidi 2007, 15). Thus, the EU accession process helped the successful transition away from authoritarianism, but the top-down approach that characterised it also favoured a technocratic, elite-dominated, "hollow" (at least from a supply-side perspective) version of democracy.[11] This was compounded by the fact that CEE countries democratised in the context of strong neoliberal flows of ideas, which favours technical governance over democratic debate (e.g. Bohle 2006; Schmidt and Thatcher 2013). This affected the options and ideas that were immediately available to the democratising elites.[12] While EU accession was not the only source of this neoliberal "inspiration", it contributed to its persistence (Appel and Orenstein 2016, 319–20).

Technocratic hollowness in Estonia and Latvia

Estonia and Latvia present a strong version of the technocratic hollowness discussed above, as their domestic politics reinforced rather than offset EU accession incentives to de-politicise transition policies, especially in the socio-economic sphere. The effects of neoliberal inspiration were particularly pronounced in Estonia and Latvia, as their democratising elites displayed from the very beginning a strong preference for orthodox neoliberal economic policies (Bohle and Greskovits 2012). The effect of outside inspiration was noted by an Estonian scholar, who remarked that early democratising Estonian elites looked West for inspiration about how to redesign social provisions and what they found was the new fashion of new public management (Toots 2007). The EU was not the only source of such inspiration, but it was an important one. Most importantly, outside "inspiration" and incentives also justified reducing the room for debate on such policies. Indeed, in a period in which EU policymaking increasingly displayed a preference for efficiency over debate (Cafruny and Ryner 2003; Bohle 2006), Estonian and Latvian democratising elites found little contradiction between democratisation and their small-government agenda that showed little patience for debate.

The "neoliberal Baltic capitalism model" – of which Estonia is the most accomplished version – is characterised by a strong belief in an unbridled free market, minimal welfare provisions, low workers' rights, weak unionisation, and non-redistributive taxation (Vihalemm et al. 2011, 24). Notwithstanding some rhetorical differences, there has been a general consensus on economic policies among governing elites.[13] The Centre Party (a mainstream Estonian party which attracts the greatest share of Russophone votes) and the Estonian Social Democrats have moderately leftist agendas but have been in government only as part of ideologically broad coalitions that largely kept to the market economy consensus (Aylott 2014, 9–10). Being consistently excluded from government, Latvia's Russophone party Harmony has had limited occasions to prove its social-democratic credentials.

As with other CEE countries, the process of EU accession provided incentives to depoliticise some key aspects of the politics of democratic transition – especially to do with transition to market capitalism, thus facilitating the consolidation of technocratic hollowness. This is evidenced by the European Commission accession documents, which monitored accession countries' political conditions (democracy, rule of law, human rights, and minority protection), economic conditions (functioning of market economy, and economic integration within the Union), and institutional capacity to implement the *acquis communautaire*. The analysis of the Estonian and Latvian reports from 1998 to 2003 provides substance to the claim made with regard to other CEE countries that while "EU conditionality empower[ed] liberal reform coalitions", it also empowered domestic Europeanising elites to pursue their political agendas without engaging in significant democratic debate (Börzel and Risse 2012, 11).

First of all, while EU conditionalities included both political and economic elements, the latter were clearly prioritised (Hughes 2005; Bohle 2010, 8). For both Estonia and Latvia the accession reports mention several non-economic aspects of democratic transition – for example, rule of law and respect for minority rights – and funds were made available through the PHARE programme for non-economic projects aimed at inter-ethnic inclusion. However, most of the focus was on economic performance and the establishment of a market economy. As accession reports were widely used as a measure of democratisation progress, they contributed to blurring the distinction between "more democracy" and "more free market" (cf. Ost 2005, 2016). Thus, local elites could present small-government economic policies as the necessary recipe to achieve modernisation, prosperity, and – in a conflation typical of the transition period – democracy. In this context, positive results in economic freedom rankings (compiled, among others, by Heritage Foundation, Free Market Foundation, and Cato Institute) were presented in the public discourse as a measure of democratic success (especially in Estonia) or the proof that more neoliberal reform should be done (especially in Latvia).[14]

Secondly, the reports were strongly focused on pushing through specific policy outputs. In particular, economic policies to establish a successful market economy were required, with a strong focus on macroeconomic stability, "especially through the effective control of public finances" (European Commission 1999, 26), "containing government expenditures" (European Commission 2000a, 31), and implementing "structural reforms" – especially privatisation, including of public utilities (European Commission 1998, 17). The need to guarantee adequate salaries and social protection, reduce poverty and inequality, and guarantee adequate healthcare provision in line with the European Social Charter were also suggested (European Commission 2000a, 18, 2002a, 77, 2002b, 86), if much less prominently.[15] Whatever the content of the required (or suggested) policies, this output-driven approach incentivised the idea that democracy is built by passing a set of "optimal policies" with little scope for debate.

Thirdly, the reports advocate for political consensus, especially on economic policies, not least because "[m]acroeconomic stability and consensus about economic policy enhance the performance of a market economy" (European Commission 1998, 17, 1999, 24). So Estonia was repeatedly praised for its "economic consensus" across party lines (European Commission 2000a, 24, 2001, 28), at the same time as one of Latvia's "main weaknesses" was identified in the "lack of political consensus regarding the reform process" (European Commission 2000b, 15) especially on privatisation (European Commission 2000b, 28). The reports repeatedly praised the consistency of economic policies despite changes of government (e.g. European Commission 2002a, 20, 38). The need for a smooth and rapid reform process and the insistence on consensus created an environment in which depoliticisation and technicisation were favoured over lengthy inter-party debate.

Thus, the transition guidelines supported the impression that there was a "democratising elite" that had the trust of the EU and should not be prevented from "doing their job". Estonian and Latvian democratising elites could therefore justify their small-government policy choices as required by the higher aim of re-building and modernising their countries, joining the EU (and later the Eurozone), and "becoming Western". These higher aims meant that their policies should be shielded from opposition and debate: dissent and opposition were impediments to transition rather than part and parcel of democratic politics. An illustration of this was provided by former Estonian prime minister Mart Laar, who claimed in an interview that "in the coming years the reforms will continue to give good results, because they are not dependent upon who is in power" (Arias-King and Laar 2002, 496). Similarly, the Latvian-American economist George Viksnins, who was a key advisor during Latvia's transition to market economy, claimed that, while there had to be a dialogue with the public about new policies, "the reform has to continue despite changes in government" (quoted in Sommers and Bērziņš 2011, 121).

Estonian and Latvian governments presented their unwavering commitment to the free market not only as proof of their commitment to democracy and Europeanisation but also as a source of national pride. So, for example, Trivimi Velliste – Estonian Foreign Minister between 1992 and 1994 – reportedly boasted that "Estonia is the only country in the world whose economic policies have been even tougher than the IMF has demanded" (quoted in Lieven 1993, xvii). In the wake of the financial crisis of 2008, Latvian governments took similar pride in their commitment to textbook austerity and in the Latvian people's alleged readiness for self-sacrifice in the name of the higher good of the country (Åslund and Dombrovskis 2011, 121). This pushed economic grievances even further to the margins of the political debate, making it difficult for them to be mobilised also beyond the transition period. This tradition of free market national pride resulted in little solidarity with the "losers" of these policies when they voiced discontent. As an example of this, in December 2008, in the first months of post-crisis austerity measures, then Latvian president Zatlers suggested that in times of crisis people should not whine.[16] Thus, although the Estonian and Latvian governments' embrace of the free market went beyond EU demands, the EU accession reports' insistence on balancing the budget, privatisation and political consensus provided support to their policy agenda and contributed to delegitimising any opposition to it. This stifled the debate on key policies in the very period in which the democratic foundations of these countries were being laid.

Consolidating ethnic hollowness

While trends towards technocratic hollowness have been noted across CEE (e.g. Ost 2005), in Estonia and Latvia they were compounded by a particularly strong ethnic dimension. There, technocratic hollowness consolidated together with what could be called "ethnic hollowness": a tendency to limit the democratic space as the remit of the ethnic majority, marginalising and delegitimising minority voices. Hollowing and hollowness are generally discussed in terms that highlight the separation between an elite that controls decision-making and a civil society whose participation in decision-making is severely reduced either by disenchantment or by lack of channels through which to affect decisions (e.g. Crouch 2004; Mair 2013). This underplays the fact that hollowing/hollowness can affect different sections of society differently. To put it simply, a democracy can be more or less hollow with respect to civic participation in general, while at the same time being *particularly hollow* with regard to minority voices. The advantage of conceptualising ethnic political exclusion in terms of hollowness is that it shifts the focus from the minority who suffers exclusion to the quality of democratic institutions, which suffers as a result of being emptied out of minority voices.

Ethnic hollowness consolidated as a stable element of Estonian and Latvian democracy at the same time as Europeanisation pressures – at least on the face of it – were pushing in a more inclusive direction. Indeed, although the EU lacks a specific minority *acquis*, it developed a minority rights protection and non-discrimination agenda during the CEE accession round, not least due to fears that ethnonationalism might destabilise the nascent democracies and breed ethnic conflict (Sasse 2005). As part of accession conditionalities, CEE democracies were pressured to improve their minority protection legislation and their minority policies were subjected to scrutiny. In contrast with market reforms, EU and (ethnic majority) democratising elites' agendas did not align on ethnic issues.

As part of the wider debate on EU and other external actors' influence on democratisation, there is an ongoing debate on whether pressures of European institutions (EU, OSCE and Council of Europe) to improve minority rights in CEE were successful (Hughes and Sasse 2003; Kelley 2004; Schulze 2010; Galbreath and McEvoy 2012). Nevertheless, the EU has been generally seen as a moderating force on ethnonational issues, although domestic electoral incentives to adopt nationalist positions can cancel out such leverage (Vachudova 2017). However, the cases of Estonia and Latvia show that ethnic hollowness could consolidate not in spite of but partly because of the pressures of EU accession.

Ethnic hollowness in Estonia and Latvia

Accession conditionalities were successful in pushing Estonian and Latvian governing elites to address some concerns with their minority policies, for example softening language proficiency requirements for employment, simplifying the naturalisation process, and establishing minority integration programmes and dedicated integration agencies (Kelley 2004). However, it has also been noted that (ethnic majority) domestic elites acquiesced to changes to minority policies only to the extent that these did not threaten their position of power – thus the EU accession de facto strengthened majority elites' position by giving them full control of the minority policy agenda (Agarin and Regelmann 2012). Thus, compared to technocratic hollowness, EU accession's incentives for ethnic hollowness were more indirect – they rested not on its explicit demands (which were for minority inclusion) but with implicit messages that provided justifications for majority elites' exclusionary agendas.

First of all, the perception of a double standard in minority protection requirements and monitoring (more stringent for CEE and laxer for Western Europe) weakened the credibility of EU minority policy requirements (Jutila 2009). Ample examples of exclusionary practices in Western Europe and contradictory concepts of minority rights could be brought forward by local majority elites to justify restrictive policies.[17] Thus, while minority exclusion was officially condemned throughout the EU accession process, the ambiguity of the message coming from the EU member states – summarised as "do as I say not as I do" (Galbreath and McEvoy 2012, 55) – implicitly validated domestic elites' lukewarm embrace of minority rights protection.

More directly, the same coalition-building with EU elites that strengthened the hand of Estonia and Latvia's local Europeanisers as technocratic economic reformers, also had the effect of reinforcing ethnic hierarchies as these were the same ethnic majority elites that had successfully pushed forward an ethnocentric restorationist agenda upon independence (Pettai 2007, 17–20; Agarin and Regelmann 2012). As their role as key partners for liberal market reforms was established, majority elites were in a strong position to marginalise minority voices from their democracy-building and modernisation project.

The presence of large communities of Russian-speakers was presented by majority elites as a potential hindrance to a successful transition to democracy and market economy (Norkus 2007, 27). This attitude was not restricted to openly nationalist forces, who regularly presented Russian-speakers as a menace to the survival of the "titular nation". Even the liberal elites – who were also nation-minded but rejected the nationalists' harshest rhetoric – were ambiguous about the role of Russian-speakers in the democratisation process. There was the worry that, if included as citizens early on in the process of democracy and state building, Russian-speakers might have slowed down Europeanisation and democratisation. This was based on the idea that Russian-speakers were "more Soviet-minded" than their ethnic Estonian and Latvian compatriots (Kirch and Kirch 1995, 52), and that they "lack experience with a liberal and legal society" and thus find it more difficult to adapt to the new social and political realities of their countries (Kirch and Kirch 1995, 55). This characterisation of Russian-speakers was in contrast with representations of the "titular nations" as proudly resilient under neoliberal reform. For example, Marju Lauristin and Mati Heidmets – two prominent policy specialists on

Estonian minority integration and by no means nationalists – argued that the "truly complicated task" of democratising Estonia

> was even more complicated, due to the fact that the Estonian and Russian communities were not at the same stage of modern development […] Estonians and Russians occupied quite different positions in the scale of modernisation […] The post-war immigrants in Estonia represented Soviet-type collectivism, including obedience to the party elite, denial of market relations, and paternalism and collectivism in work-place relations. Based on such an historical background, attitudes of Estonians towards the Western world, and people's readiness to accept the capitalist social, political and economic models, have clearly been more positive than those of Russians living in Estonia. (Lauristin and Heidmets 2002, 21)

Seen from this perspective, minority exclusion from the process of democracy building (especially through initial mass disenfranchisement via non-citizenship) appears as perhaps not entirely fair but as having the benefit of ensuring that opposition to transition was minimised during the delicate period of the early 1990s and then of EU accession. Thus, while ethnic exclusion was by no means required by EU accession, it was nevertheless expedient to ensuring the political consensus on reform promoted by EU officials.

The reduction of the debate on socio-economic policies to a choice between a democratic free market future and a repressive socialist past (Lagerspetz 2001, 415) also came with strong ethnic overtones. The bases for this were that in both countries Russian-speakers tended to have a more left-leaning outlook (Bottolfs 2000; Daatland and Svege 2000). This meant that democratising elites could conflate leftist stances on welfare provisions with the ethnic minorities and the Soviet past. Consequently, it was easier to dismiss critics of government socio-economic policies as "Russian revanchists or ignorant populists, regardless of the nature or quality of the critiques" (Sommers and Bērziņš 2011, 121).

Ethnocentric and neoliberal agendas reinforced each other in several ways. Firstly, the survival of the nation was presented as the ultimate goal to which even social welfare could be sacrificed. Consequently, resilience in the face of the harsh economic policies of the transition (and of austerity after 2008) became a matter of national pride. This is what Bohle (2010) called "nationalist social contract" and Kattel and Raudla (2013) "nationalist neoliberalism". Self-reliance, personal responsibility, individualism, competition, and free market could be presented as a matter of Estonian and Latvian national (ethnic) identity. Thus, Russian-speakers' (on average) more left-leaning tendencies were another reason to keep them (and, in Latvia, their parties) at the margins of democratic power.

Secondly, ethnic divisions make ethnic majority elites' position in power more stable and divert attention from socio-economic grievances. In Estonia, "concerned about the Russian threat, Estonians mostly vote for right-wing parties, giving them a free hand to implement radical economic policies with very harsh short-term welfare consequences" (Vihalemm et al. 2011, 29). In Latvia, although the Russian-speakers' party Harmony has been the largest party in the country since 2011, its exclusion from governing coalitions keeps the nationalist and neoliberal parties consistently in power. Harmony's attempts to appeal to austerity's losers with a social-democratic message were met by calls for national solidarity and nationalist retrenching,[18] and were not helped by the war in Ukraine (Ikstens 2015). Thus, in both countries ethnic majority elites can present challenges to their economic policies as "socialist and, thus, backward" (Lauristin and Vihalemm 2009, 20). Ethnic divisions can be stressed to discourage the formation of transversal, cross-ethnic solidarities based on socio-economic status (Cianetti 2015).

Moreover, especially in Estonia, where Russian-speakers have been at a higher socio-economic disadvantage after the transition (Leping and Toomet 2008; Lindemann and Saar 2012), there is also a tendency for majority elites to both individualise and ethnicise social exclusion. Socio-economic exclusion is typically explained as a result of individuals' inability to adapt to the realities of the European market society, backwardness, expecting too much from the state, and lack of entrepreneurial spirit – all characteristics associated with Estonia's Russian-speakers. This rhetoric further delegitimises socio-economic grievances, marginalising people – both "titulars" and Russian-speakers – who find themselves in a weaker socio-economic position (Helemäe and Saar 2012).

Minority rights without minority voices

As shown above, EU accession facilitated, rather than counterbalanced, the exclusivist tendencies of domestic majority elites. Perhaps counterintuitively, this was true even when European institutions intervened directly, using strong prodding and conditionalities, to push for minority-friendly policies – such as simplifying the naturalisation procedure, softening state language requirements for employment, and dropping language requirements for elected officials. The EU monitored Estonia and Latvia's majority–minority relations closely during the accession period, provided PHARE funding for integration programmes, and supported OSCE and Council of Europe in their hands-on work to shape Estonia and Latvia's minority policies. OSCE officials helped to draft policies and the EU supported them with the carrot-and-stick of conditionalities.

However, EU pressures to liberalise minority policies were once again strongly output-driven, following the general approach that the problem of minority exclusion could be "fixed" by forcing governments to pass (or change) certain pieces of legislation. This focus on output – perhaps paradoxically – had a perverse effect on the inclusiveness of the democratic debate. The negotiations between European institutions and local (ethnic majority) governments replaced majority–minority debate. Minorities remained for the most part passive observers of negotiations made on their behalf; policy objects rather than policy makers. Majority elites remained in control of the process, negotiating with external partners and deciding when and how much to budge (Agarin and Regelmann 2012). So, for example, the head of the Estonian Language Inspectorate described policymaking on language policies as a negotiation between the (ethnic majority) government and EU and OSCE officials, assigning no role to minority voices in his account (Tomusk 2009, 23–33).

In fact, external intervention provided a justification for majority elites to exclude minorities from policymaking and reduced the legitimate space for minority grievances to enter the debate. An example of this is the Latvian parliamentary committee's debate over the 1999 Language Law, which set all the key principles on language use in Latvia's public and private spheres. When Russophone MPs complained that the government's draft promoted assimilation rather than integration and unduly restricted Russian language use, the governing parties dismissed their critiques on the bases that OSCE officials had been involved in the drafting procedure so opposition MPs had no grounds to complain.[19] Russophone MPs' request that governmental regulations on how to implement language requirements for employment be discussed in parliament was rejected on the same grounds.[20] Thus, if a policy was deemed satisfactory in the accession monitoring or an issue had not been raised by European officials, that was automatically out of the debate, whatever the reactions and opinions of local minorities.[21]

Therefore, even in the cases in which external intervention resulted in more lenient policies, negotiations de facto reduced the need for ethnic majority elites to engage in a debate with minority representatives. This is not to say that Europeanisation pressures caused minority exclusion. However, by proposing a technocratic, problem-solving approach to tackling minority problems, they paradoxically ended up supporting it, ultimately helping to consolidate ethnic hollowness as a key feature of the Estonian and Latvian democracies.

Conclusions

This article builds on Greskovits' (2015) distinction between "backsliding" and "hollowness" to separate dynamic processes of de-democratisation (for which the concept of backsliding can be useful) from static features of low-quality democracies, which include (but are not necessarily limited to) hollowness. "Hollowness" is a useful concept to subsume the different ways in which democratic institutions can be "empty" of a popular component, but – I argue – it needs to be further developed and nuanced. First of all, demand-side hollowness (that has to do with low citizen participation) should be distinguished from supply-side hollowness (that has to do with the top-down shrinking of the space for participation and debate). The focus of this article has been on the latter.

Drawing from the Estonian and Latvian cases, three key points can be made with regard to supply-side hollowness. First, while hollowness has been most often discussed (both in CEE and in the West) in its "technocratic" aspects, the cases of Estonia and Latvia show that in diverse societies it can be compounded by "ethnic hollowness", in a mutually reinforcing relationship. Conceptually, ethnic hollowness takes us a step further than ethnic exclusion as it moves the focus from what such exclusion does to minorities to what it does to democratic institutions, emptying them out of key dissenting voices. Smooha's (2009) model of ethnic democracy similarly points to the systemic effects of exclusion. However, differently from ethnic hollowness, it does not allow for gradation (while a democracy can be more or less ethnically hollow, it either is or is not an ethnic democracy) and limits comparability to a few democratic-outlier cases. Ethnic hollowness allows for envisaging broader comparisons, as it is most prominent in countries with large ethnic minorities like Estonia and Latvia but elements of it are present to a smaller or larger extent across all democracies, where minority voices are more likely to be absent from the democratic debate (Haddad 2002; Hochschild and Mollenkopf 2009).

Second, ethnic and technocratic hollowness are not the result of post-accession backsliding. On the contrary, in Estonia and Latvia they consolidated in line with EU accession's implicit and explicit incentives. In particular, the explicit incentive to speed up transition and deliver specific policy outputs carried the implicit incentive to limit debate. This empowered the democratising (ethnic majority) elites to limit the role of civil society and opposition, restrict the room for debating policies, and marginalise minority voices. These exclusionary effects remained true even when European officials were pushing for minority-friendly policies.

Third, as they have consolidated as a static (though not necessarily immutable) feature of Estonian and Latvian democracies, technocratic and ethnic hollowness cannot be taken as symptoms of impending backsliding. Indeed, rather than indicators of instability, technocratic and ethnic hollowness are key components of stable (albeit low-quality)[22] democratic systems. This has implications for how we treat the different democratic "syndromes" of backsliding and hollowness, in CEE but also in more advanced democracies. Stabilising and strengthening existing democratic institutions can be a way of preventing backsliding. With hollowness, it is the very stability of institutions that perpetuate a low-democratic status quo. Some destabilisation would be required in order to change that.

To conclude, the findings from Estonia and Latvia seem to mirror Greskovits's (2017) conclusion on the relationship between backsliding and hollowness in Hungary. As in Hungary the vibrancy of civil society (lack of hollowness) supported backsliding, in Estonia and Latvia, by preserving the status quo, hollowness safeguards stability and hinders Hungarian-style backsliding. However, this does not make hollowness desirable. First of all, in the longer-term hollowness might reduce popular stakes in democratic institutions and open up room for anti-democratic reactions – thus, its relationship with backsliding might be more complex than simply impeding it. Moreover, even if that was not the case, there is a trade-off between preserving the kind of low-democratic stability that hollowness can support and improving democratic quality. The latter goal cannot easily be dismissed.

Notes

1. All the major democracy indices give them consistently high marks; see for example Freedom House (where they are classed as "free") and V-Dem (where they are in line with EU average on all main indicators).
2. See for example the assessment of the Minorities at Risk Project (http://www.mar.umd.edu/).
3. It is estimated that about 80% of Estonia's Russian-speakers and 60% of Latvia's were left without citizenship upon independence (Smith, Galbreath, and Swain 2010, 119; Mole 2012, 88).
4. In 2014, 22% of Estonia's Russian speakers and almost 40% of Latvia's were non-citizens. This corresponds to 6.6% of the Estonian total population and 12.7% of Latvia's. A further 24% of Estonia's Russian speakers (7% of population) and 6% of Latvia's (2% of population) are citizens of a third country, mostly Russia (Figures retrieved from Estonian Statistical Database [www.stat.ee] and Latvian Central Statistics Database [www.csb.gov.lv]).
5. Two separate terms for supply-side and demand-side hollowness might in fact be in order.
6. Freedom of the press also worsened – mostly due to ownership concentration, legal limits on language use, and cases of attacks against anti-corruption journalists. However, Latvia's media remain free (https://freedomhouse.org/report/freedom-press/freedom-press-2017).
7. For a different critique see Hanley (2015).
8. Nationalists were only briefly out of government in 2010.
9. For a comparison between the far right in Estonia and Latvia, see Bennich-Björkman and Johansson (2012).
10. Ther (2016) talks about a Marshall Plan for post-communist Europe.
11. For a summary of early critiques of the conflicting logics between Europeanisation and democratisation, see Ekiert (2008).
12. This is the other side of the coin of what Jacoby (2006) called "inspiration" and others called "lesson drawing" (Schimmelfennig and Sedelmeier 2004).
13. On "consensual politics" in Estonia see Lagerspetz and Vogt (1998, 75–78). On how deindustrialisation and financialisation became the undisputable economic policy in post-independence Latvia, see Sommers and Bērziņš (2011).
14. For example: "Eesti — Ida-Euroopa esimene" [Estonia is the first in Eastern-Europe], *Äripäev* 17 February 2005 (http://arileht.delfi.ee/archive/eesti-ida-euroopa-esimene?id=9792836); "Latvija ekonomiskās brīvības reitingā pakāpusies uz 36. vietu" [Latvia's economic freedom rating

climbed to 36th place], *LETA* 2 February 2016 (http://www.delfi.lv/bizness/biznesa_vide/latvija-ekonomiskas-brivibas-reitinga-pakapusies-uz-36-vietu.d?id=47014381).
15. Compared to the pressures for privatising and liberalising, these appeared in the reports less often and more as advisable rather than necessary reforms.
16. Delfi, 29 December 2008 (http://rus.delfi.lv/news/daily/versions/odnorelsovyj-put.d?id=22760833).
17. For example, local policymakers often mention Germany's strict naturalisation policy and its treatment of Turkish settled migrants as proof of the fact that their own governments' minority policies are in line with (or even exceed) European norms (Smith 2003). This was also the case during my own interviews with Estonian and Latvian policymakers in 2013.
18. For instance, in September 2013 National Alliance appealed to the "Latvian parties" to unite against Harmony's electoral advance (Latvian Centre for Human Rights [LCHR], Integration Monitor, 13 September 2013 [http://cilvektiesibas.org.lv/en/monitoring/]).
19. Latvian Centre for Human Rights (LCHR), Integration Monitor, 10 February and 19 March 1999.
20. LCHR, Integration Monitor, 27 June 2000.
21. This stands in contrast with majority elites' pride in "overfulfilling" external requirements of market liberalism.
22. That is, if we define democracy beyond its minimalist electoral form.

Disclosure statement

No potential conflict of interest was reported by the author.

ORCID

Licia Cianetti http://orcid.org/0000-0001-7532-3101

References

Agarin, Timofey. 2010. *A Cat's Lick: Democratisation and Minority Communities in the Post-Soviet Baltics*. Amsterdam: Rodopi.
Agarin, Timofey, and Ada-Charlotte Regelmann. 2012. "Which Is the Only Game in Town? Minority Rights Issues in Estonia and Slovakia During and after EU Accession." *Perspectives on European Politics and Society* 13 (4): 443–461.
Appel, Hilary, and Mitchell A. Orenstein. 2016. "Why Did Neoliberalism Triumph and Endure in the Post-Communist World?" *Comparative Politics* 48 (3): 313–331.
Arias-King, Fredo, and Mart Laar. 2002. "'Just Do It' Interview with Mart Laar." *Demokratizatsiya* 11: 495–508.
Åslund, Anders, and Valdis Dombrovskis. 2011. *How Latvia Came through the Financial Crisis*. Washington, DC: Peterson Institute for International Economics.
Aylott, Nicholas. 2014. "A Question of Priorities: Candidate Selection in Estonian Political Parties." *Journal of Baltic Studies* 45 (3): 321–344.
Bennich-Björkman, Li, and Karl Magnus Johansson. 2012. "Explaining Moderation in Nationalism: Divergent Trajectories of National Conservative Parties in Estonia and Latvia." *Comparative European Politics* 10 (5): 585–607.

Beyers, Jan. 2010. "Conceptual and Methodological Challenges in the Study of European Socialization." *Journal of European Public Policy* 17 (6): 909–920.

Bohle, Dorothee. 2006. "Neoliberal Hegemony, Transnational Capital and the Terms of the EU's Eastward Expansion." *Capital & Class* 30 (88): 57–86.

Bohle, Dorothee. 2010. "East European Transformations and the Paradoxes of Transnationalization." SPS 2010/01. EUI Working Papers. Florence, Italy.

Bohle, Dorothee, and Béla Greskovits. 2012. *Capitalist Diversity on Europe's Periphery*. New York: Cornell University Press.

Börzel, Tanja A, and Thomas Risse. 2012. "From Europeanisation to Diffusion: Introduction." *West European Politics* 35 (1): 1–19.

Bottolfs, Heidi. 2000. "Latvia." In *Politics and Citizenship on the Eastern Baltic Seaboard*, edited by Frank Aarebrot and Terje Knutsen, 77–107. Kristiansand, Norway: Høyskoleforlaget.

Bútora, Martin. 2007. "Nightmares from the Past, Dreams of the Future." *Journal of Democracy* 18 (4): 47–55.

Cafruny, Alan W, and Magnus Ryner, eds. 2003. *A Ruined Fortress? Neoliberal Hegemony and Transformation in Europe*. Oxford: Rowman and Littlefield.

Cianetti, Licia. 2015. "Integrating Minorities in Times of Crisis: Issues of Displacement in the Estonian and Latvian Integration Programs." *Nationalism and Ethnic Politics* 21 (2): 191–212.

Cianetti, Licia, and Ryo Nakai. 2017. "Critical Trust in European Institutions: The Case of the Russian-Speaking Minorities in Estonia and Latvia." *Problems of Post-Communism* 64 (5): 276–290.

Crouch, Colin. 2004. *Post-Democracy*. Cambridge: Polity.

Daatland, Christer D., and Hans Petter Svege. 2000. "The Russian-Speakers in Estonia." In *Politics and Citizenship on the Eastern Baltic Seaboard*, edited by Frank Aarebrot and Terje Knutsen, 255–275. Kristiansand, Norway: Høyskoleforlaget.

Dimitrova, Antoaneta. 2010. "The New Member States of the EU in the Aftermath of Enlargement: Do New European Rules Remain Empty Shells?" *Journal of European Public Policy* 17 (1): 137–148.

Ekiert, Grzegorz. 2008. "Dilemmas of Europeanization: Eastern and Central Europe After the EU Enlargement." *Acta Slavica Iaponica* 25: 1–28.

Ekiert, Grzegorz, and Jan Kubik. 2001. *Rebellious Civil Society: Popular Protest and Democratic Consolidation in Poland, 1989-1993*. Ann Arbor, MI: University of Michigan Press.

Ekiert, Grzegorz, Jan Kubik, and Milada Anna Vachudova. 2007. "Democracy in the Post-Communist World: An Unending Quest?" *East European Politics & Societies* 21 (1): 7–30.

European Commission. 1998. *Regular Report on Estonia's Progress Towards Accession*. Brussels: European Commission.

European Commission. 1999. *Regular Report on Latvia's Progress Towards Accession*. Brussels: European Commission.

European Commission. 2000a. *Regular Report on Estonia's Progress Towards Accession*. Brussels: European Commission.

European Commission. 2000b. *Regular Report on Latvia's Progress Towards Accession*. Brussels: European Commission.

European Commission. 2001. *Regular Report on Estonia's Progress Towards Accession*. Brussels: European Commission.

European Commission. 2002a. *Regular Report on Estonia's Progress Towards Accession*. Brussels: European Commission.

European Commission. 2002b. *Regular Report on Latvia's Progress Towards Accession*. Brussels: European Commission.

Galbreath, David J, and Joanne McEvoy. 2012. *The European Minority Rights Regime: Towards a Theory of Regime Effectiveness*. Basingstoke: Palgrave Macmillan.

Greskovits, Béla. 2007. "Economic Woes and Political Disaffection." *Journal of Democracy* 18 (4): 40–46.

Greskovits, Béla. 2015. "The Hollowing and Backsliding of Democracy in East Central Europe." *Global Policy* 6 (1): 28–37.

Greskovits, Béla. 2017. "Rebuilding the Hungarian Right through Civil Organization and Contention: The Civic Circles Movement." *EUI Working Paper* 37. Fiesole (FI): Robert Schuman Centre for Advanced Studies.

Grzymała-Busse, Anna, and Abby Innes. 2003. "Great Expectations: The EU and Domestic Political Competition in East Central Europe." *East European Politics and Societies* 17 (1): 64–73.

Haddad, Yvonne Yazbeck, ed. 2002. *Muslims in the West: From Sojourners to Citizens*. Oxford: Oxford University Press.

Hanley, Seán. 2015. "East European Democracy: Sliding Back or Hollowed Out?" *Dr Sean's Diary*. https://drseansdiary.wordpress.com/2015/07/21/east-european-democracy-sliding-back-or-hollowed-out/.

Heidmets, Mati, ed. 2008. *Estonian Human Development Report 2007*. Tallinn: Eesti KoostööKogu.

Helemäe, Jelena, and Ellu Saar. 2012. "Estonia – Highly Unequal but Classless?" *STSS: Studies of Transition States and Societies* 4 (2): 49–58.

Heller, Ágnes, Miklos Haraszti, Eva Fodor, Jan-Werner Mueller, David Ost, and Jason Wittenberg. 2017. "A Discussion of Péter Krasztev and Jon Van Til's The Hungarian Patient: Social Opposition to an Illiberal Democracy." *Perspectives on Politics* 15 (2): 542–544.

Hochschild, Jennifer, and John H. Mollenkopf, eds. 2009. *Bringing Outsiders In: Transatlantic Perspectives on Immigrant Political Incorporation*. Ithaca, NY: Cornell University Press.

Hughes, James. 2005. "'Exit' in Deeply Divided Societies: Regimes of Discrimination in Estonia and Latvia and the Potential for Russophone Migration." *Journal of Common Market Studies* 43 (4): 739–762.

Hughes, James, and Gwendolyn Sasse. 2003. "Monitoring the Monitors: EU Enlargement Conditionality and Minority Protection in the CEECs." *Journal of Ethnopolitics and Minority Issues in Europe* 12 (1): 1–37.

Ikstens, Jānis. 2015. "Latvia." *European Journal of Political Research Political Data Yearbook* 54 (1): 181–189.

Jacoby, Wade. 2006. "Inspiration, Coalition, and Substitution: External Influences on Postcommunist Transformations." *World Politics* 58 (4): 623–651.

Jakobson, Mari-Liis, Ilze Balcere, Oudekki Loone, Anu Nurk, Tõnis Saarts, and Raasa Zakeviciute. 2012. *Populism in the Baltic States. A Research Report*. Tallinn: Tallinn University Institute of Political Science and Governance / Open Estonia Foundation.

Järve, Priit. 2000. "Ethnic Democracy and Estonia: Application of Smooha's Model." *ECMI Working Paper* 7. Fensburg: European Centre for Minority Issues.

Jutila, Matti. 2009. "Taming Eastern Nationalism: Tracing the Ideational Background of Double Standards of Post-Cold War Minority Protection." *European Journal of International Relations* 15 (4): 627–651.

Kattel, Rainer, and Ringa Raudla. 2013. "The Baltic Republics and the Crisis of 2008–2011." *Europe-Asia Studies* 65 (3): 426–449.

Kelley, Judith G. 2004. *Ethnic Politics in Europe: The Power of Norms and Incentives*. Princeton, NJ: Princeton University Press.

Kirch, Aksel, and Marika Kirch. 1995. "Ethnic Relations: Estonians and non-Estonians." *Nationalities Papers* 23 (1): 43–59.

Kott, Matthew. 2016. "The Far Right in Latvia: Should We Be Worried?" *Sicherheits Politik Blog*, April 1. http://www.sicherheitspolitik-blog.de/2016/04/01/the-far-right-in-latvia-should-we-be-worried/.

Krastev, Ivan. 2007. "The Strange Death of the Liberal Consensus." *Journal of Democracy* 18 (4): 56–63.

Lagerspetz, Mikko. 2001. "Consolidation as Hegemonization: The Case of Estonia." *Journal of Baltic Studies* 32 (4): 402–420.

Lagerspetz, Mikko, and Henri Vogt. 1998. "Estonia." In *The Handbook of Political Change in Eastern Europe*, edited by Stern Berglund, Hellén Tomas, and Frank H. Aarebrot, 55–88. Cheltenham: Edward Elgar.

Lauristin, Marju, and Mati Heidmets. 2002. "Introduction: The Russian Minority in Estonia as a Theoretical and Political Issue." In *The Challenge of the Russian Minority. Emerging Multicultural Democracy in Estonia*, edited by Marju Lauristin and Mati Heidmets, 19–27. Tartu: Tartu University Press.

Lauristin, Marju, and Peeter Vihalemm. 2009. "The Political Agenda During Different Periods of Estonian Transformation: External and Internal Factors." *Journal of Baltic Studies* 40 (1): 1–28.

Leping, Kristian-Olari, and Ott Toomet. 2008. "Emerging Ethnic Wage Gap: Estonia During Political and Economic Transition." *Journal of Comparative Economics* 36 (4): 599–619.

Levitz, Philip, and Grigore Pop-Eleches. 2010. "Why No Backsliding? The European Union's Impact on Democracy and Governance Before and After Accession." *Comparative Political Studies* 43 (4): 457–485.

Lieven, Anatol. 1993. *The Baltic Revolution. Estonia, Latvia, Lithuania and the Path to Independence.* London: Yale University Press.

Lindemann, Kristina, and Ellu Saar. 2012. "Ethnic Inequalities in Education: Second-Generation Russians in Estonia." *Ethnic and Racial Studies* 35 (11): 1974–1998.

Lublin, David. 2013. "The 2012 Latvia Language Referendum." *Electoral Studies* 32 (2): 385–387.

Mair, Peter. 2006. "Ruling the Void? The Hollowing of Western Democracy." *New Left Review* 42 (43): 25–51.

Mair, Peter. 2013. *Ruling the Void. The Hollowing of Western Democracy.* London: Verso.

Masso, Jaan, Kerly Espenberg, Anu Masso, Inta Mierina, and Kaia Philips. 2012. "Growing Inequalities and Its Impac in the Baltics." *GINI Country Report*. Amsterdam: GINI Project, University of Amsterdam.

McCauley, Darren. 2011. "Bottom-up Europeanization Exposed: Social Movement Theory and Non-State Actors in France." *Journal of Common Market Studies* 49 (5): 1019–1042.

Mole, Richard C. M. 2012. *The Baltic States from the Soviet Union to the European Union: Identity, Discourse and Power in the Post-Communist Transition of Estonia, Latvia and Lithuania.* Oxon: Routledge.

Mungiu-Pippidi, Alina. 2007. "Is East-Central Europe Backsliding? EU Accession is no 'End of History'." *Journal of Democracy* 18 (4): 8–16.

Nakai, Ryo. 2014. "The Influence of Party Competition on Minority Politics: A Comparison of Latvia and Estonia." *Journal on Ethnopolitics and Minority Issues in Europe* 13 (1): 57–85.

Norkus, Zenonas. 2007. "Why Did Estonia Perform Best? The North–South Gap in the Post-Socialist Economic Transition of the Baltic States." *Journal of Baltic Studies* 38 (1): 21–42.

Ost, David. 2005. *The Defeat of Solidarity. Anger and Politics in Postcommunist Europe.* Ithaca, NY: Cornell University Press.

Ost, David. 2016. "Regime Change in Poland, Carried Out from Within." *The Nation*, January.

Pettai, Vello. 2007. "The Construction of State Identity and Its Legacies: Legal Restorationism in Estonia." *Ab Imperio* 3: 1–23.

Pettai, Vello, and Klara Hallik. 2002. "Understanding Processes of Ethnic Control: Segmentation, Dependency and Co-Optation in Post-Communist Estonia." *Nations and Nationalism* 8 (4): 505–529.

Pettai, Vello, and Kristina Kallas. 2009. "Estonia: Conditionality Amidst a Legal Straightjacket." In *Minority Rights in Central and Eastern Europe*, edited by Bernd Rechel, 104–118. London: Routledge.

Plattner, Marc F, and Larry Jay Diamond. 2007. "Is East-Central Europe Backsliding?" *Journal of Democracy* 18 (4): 5–6.

Pryce, Paul. 2012. "The 2011 Parliamentary Election in Latvia." *Electoral Studies* 31: 613–616.

Rozenvalds, Juris, ed. 2015. *How Democratic Is Latvia? Audit of Democracy 2005–2014*. Riga: University of Latvia.

Rupnik, Jacques. 2007. "From Democracy Fatigue to Populist Backlash." *Journal of Democracy* 18 (4): 17–25.

Sasse, Gwendolyn. 2005. "Securitization or Securing Rights? Exploring the Conceptual Foundations of Policies Towards Minorities and Migrants in Europe." *Journal of Common Market Studies* 43 (4): 673–693.

Schimmelfennig, Frank, and Ulrich Sedelmeier. 2004. "Governance by Conditionality: EU Rule Transfer to the Candidate Countries of Central and Eastern Europe." *Journal of European Public Policy* 11 (4): 661–679.

Schmidt, Vivien A., and Mark Thatcher, eds. 2013. *Resilient Liberalism in Europe's Political Economy*. Cambridge: Cambridge University Press.

Schulze, Jennie L. 2010. "Estonia Caught between East and West: EU Conditionality, Russia's Activism and Minority Integration." *Nationalities Papers* 38 (3): 361–392.

Sedelmeier, Ulrich. 2008. "After Conditionality: Post-Accession Compliance with EU Law in East Central Europe." *Journal of European Public Policy* 15 (6): 806–825.

Sedelmeier, Ulrich. 2012a. "Europeanization." In *The Oxford Handbook of the European Union*, edited by Erik Jones, Anand Menon, and Stephen Weatherill, 825–838. Oxford: Oxford University Press.

Sedelmeier, Ulrich. 2012b. "Is Europeanisation through Conditionality Sustainable? Lock-in of Institutional Change after EU Accession." *West European Politics* 35 (1): 20–38.

Sedelmeier, Ulrich. 2016. "Political Safeguards Against Democratic Backsliding in the EU: The Limits of Material Sanctions and the Scope of Social Pressure." *Journal of European Public Policy* 24 (3): 337–351. doi:10.1080/13501763.2016.1229358.

Sitter, Nick, Agnes Batory, Joanna Kostka, Andrea Krizsan, and Violetta Zentai. 2016. "Mapping Backsliding in the European Union." *CEU Centre for Policy Studies - Policy Brief* D6 (1): 1–60.

Smith, David J. 2003. "Minority Rights, Multiculturalism and EU Enlargement: The Case of Estonia." *Journal of Ethnopolitics and Minority Issues in Europe* 4 (1): 1–38.

Smith, David J, David J Galbreath, and Geoffrey Swain, eds. 2010. *From Recognition to Restoration. Latvia's History as a Nation-State*. Amsterdam: Rodopi.

Smooha, Sammy. 2009. "The Model of Ethnic Democracy: Response to Danel." *Journal of Israeli History* 28 (1): 55–62.

Smooha, Sammy, and Priit Järve, eds. 2005. *The Fate of Ethnic Democracy in Post-Communist Europe*. Budapest: Open Society Institute.

Sommers, Jeffrey, and Jānis Bērziņš. 2011. "Twenty Years Lost: Latvia's Failed Development in the Post-Soviet World." In *First the Transition Then the Crash. Eastern Europe in the 2000s*, edited by Gareth Dale, 119–142. London: Pluto Press.

Spirova, Maria. 2012. "European Integration and Minority Politics: Ethnic Parties at the EP Elections." *East European Politics* 28 (1): 76–92.

Ther, Philipp. 2016. *Europe Since 1989. A History*. Princeton, NJ: Princeton University Press.

Tomusk, Ilmar. 2009. *Keele Ja Poliitika II (Language and Politics 2)*. Tallinn: Estonian Language Inspectorate.

Toots, Anu. 2007. "Sotsiaalne Ebavõrdsus Kui Tabu, Rutiin Ja Mootor [Social Inequality as Taboo, Routine and Engine]." *Sirp*, September 28.

Vachudova, Milada Anna. 2017. "*Party Positions, EU Leverage and Democratic Backsliding in the Western Balkans and Beyond*." Paper presented at rejected Europe. Beloved Europe. cleavage Europe?, Budapest, European University Institute, May 2017.

Vihalemm, Peeter, Mare Ainsaar, Mati Heidmets, Triin Vihalemm, Vello Pettai, Erik Terk, and Marju Lauristin, eds. 2011. *Estonian Human Development Report 2010/2011. Baltic Way(s) of Human Development: Twenty Years on*. Tallinn: Eesti KoostööKogu.

Index

Note: *Italicized* numbers indicate figures, **bold** indicate tables and those followed by 'n' indicate endnotes.

accession *see* European Union
adoption rights 80–1, 87–90, 94–5, 96n11
Alliance for Family 92
Almond, G. A. 63
Amendment to the Act on Slovak state citizenship 112
American Discovery Corporation 67
Amnesty International 35
ANO (political party) 87–8, 90, 94–5
anti-Americanism 104
anti-Roma: racism 104; rhetoric 115; violence 103, 115
anti-Semitism 104, 116
authoritarianism 106; Caesarean politics and 60–1, 63; in Central and Eastern Europe (CEE) 21–38; democratisation and 123–5; populism and 106, 110; populist governments 28–31, 35–7; right-wing 103, 105; wartime 101, 104–6, 115

Babiš, A. 94, 108
backsliding 147–9; de-democratisation and 15; defined 37n1; democratic 21–2, 24–5, *26*, 27–8, 75, 101–2, 108, 144–5; post-accession 23, 31–4, 145
ballot box revolution 68
Bartasevics, A. 131
Bertelsmann Stiftung social justice index 49
Birkavs, V. 137
Bochsler, D. 13
Bohle, D. 5, 155
Borisov, B. 30, 55–6
Börzel, Tanja A. 32–3, 37n2
BSP *see* Bulgarian Socialist Party (BSP)
Bulgaria: distribution of minority parties in 55; distribution of nationalist in 55; early transition period (1989 – late 1990s) 50–2; political disempowerment of minorities in 48–9; post accession (2007 to present) 54–6; pre-accession period (late 1990s – 2007) 52–4; public attitudes over time 47–8; rise of identity politics in 13–14, 28, 42–57, 81; towards polyarchical democracy 46–56; weak subcultural pluralism in 13, 42, 44–6, 52, 54, 56, 57
Bulgarian Orthodox Church 56; *see also* Orthodox Church
Bulgarian People's Union 54
Bulgarian Socialist Party (BSP) 52, 55, 56
Bustikova, L. 13–14

Caesarean politics 60–75; authoritarianism and 60–1, 63; in Hungary 60–75
Canovan, M. 7
Čaputová, Z. 94, 108, 117n2
Cardinal Laws 68
catch-all strategy 10, 83, 90
Catholic Church 105, 140; Czech 86, 88, 94; Latvia 140; political influence 134; Roman 131, 134; Slovak 90, 92, 96n14
Central & Eastern Europe (CEE) 121; authoritarian footprint in 21–38; backsliding and hollowness 158; Communist regimes 121; "democratic backsliding" 147; democratisation 144, 146–7; process of democratic changes in 28–35; state-society compact in 1–15
Charter of Paris 51
Charter of the United Nations 51
Christian Democratic Movement (*Kresťanskodemokratické hnutie*, KDH) 107
Christian Democrats 75n1, 87, 88, 90, 92–3, 95n7, 96n18
Chrzanowski, M. 66
Cianetti, L. 2, 14–15
Citizens' Rights Directive 83
COE *see* Council of Europe (COE)
cohabitation 80, 83, 92
"compassion deficit" 110
Conference of Slovak Bishops 92, 96n18
"consensual politics" 158n13
Constitutional Court of Hungary 67–9, 75
Constitutional Tribunal (Poland) 70
Copenhagen Criteria 6
Council of Europe (COE) 6, 46, 51, 52–3, 55–6, 156

INDEX

credible accession perspectives 33
Crimea annexation in the 2014 131
Crimea crisis of 2014 128
Czech Catholic Church 86, 88
Czech Parliament 86–7
Czech Republic 102; adoption rights in 87–8; backlash against LGBT rights in 88–90; comparing accommodation and backlash 89–90; LGBT rights in 80–95; passing the bill on registered partnership 86–7; public opinion on LGBT rights 86, 89; same-sex marriage rights in 88

Dahl, R. 42–4, 47, 56
DAHR *see* Democratic Alliance of Hungarians in Romania (DAHR)
Decade of Roma Inclusion (2005–2015) 54
de-democratisation 15, 37n1, 144, 157
Deegan-Krause, K. 115
defection 84
democracy 101–17; functions of 24; liberal 2, 7, 8–9, 12, 22, 60–1, 63, 71, 73, 81, 103, 107, 114; measures of 24; nationalist persistence in Slovak politics 113–16; "The people" in Eastern and Central Europe 111–13; populist 62, 71; quality of 12, 22–37, 37n1; Slovakia in context of Central Europe 107–11; Slovak People's Party 103–7; trends in Central and Eastern Europe (1990–2016) 25–8
Democracy Barometer 21, 22–4, 27, 36
Democratic Alliance of Hungarians in Romania (DAHR) 50, 51–4
democratic backsliding 21, 28, 101–2, 117n1, 144–9; Caesarean politics 75; defined 37n1; Hungary and Poland 108; prominently-cited explanatory factors 22, 28; relies on measures of democracy 24
democratic consolidation: challenges 132; democratic transition 121; EU accession 8; in Hungary and Poland 63; political development 1; structural tasks of 122; territorial dimension of 123–5, 139; threats to 140
democratic deconsolidation 13, 21, 35, 60, 144
democratic developments 22–3, 28
democratic pluralism 43
democratisation: authoritarianism and 123–5; challenges in 43; de-democratisation 15, 37n1, 144, 157; Estonia 145–7; Latvia 145–7; postcommunist 4; for sexual minorities 81; territorial dimension in 121, 122, 123–5, 140n1
Department for Protection of National Minorities, Romania 52
Diamond, L. 23
Duka, D. 86

Eastern Europe 104; LGBT rights in 80–95; people's democracies 3–6
ECJ *see* European Court of Justice (ECJ)
ECtHR *see* European Court of Human Rights (ECtHR)
Ekiert, G. 35
Employment Equality Framework Directive 83
Estonia: democratisation 145–7; ethnic hollowness 154–6; Europeanisation 145–7; technocratic hollowness 150–3
Estonian Centre Party 147
Estonian Social Democrats 151
ethnic conflicts 43, 46, 146, 153
ethnic hollowness 153; Estonia 154–6; "ethnic-exclusionary" 145; Latvia 154–6
Ethnic Power Relations Dataset 48
ethnocentrism 146, 148
ethnonationalism 14, 149, 153
Eurobarometer 63
Europe 104
European Charter of Human Rights 85
European Commission 151
European Court of Human Rights (ECtHR) 70, 83–4
European Court of Justice (ECJ) 70, 82, 83–4, 93–4, 95n5, 109
Europeanisation: and corruption 107; and democratisation 8, 144, 149, 154; Estonia 145–7; post-accession backsliding 145
European Regional and Development Fund 129
European Social Survey 49
European Union (EU) 145; accession 1–4, 7–9, 11, 22–4, 32–6, 49, 52, 54–7, 84, 144–6, 150–7; consequences of financial crisis 34–5, *34*; immigrants who were enforced on Slovakia 101–2; political integration 31–4, *32*; post-accession backsliding 31–4; role in minority accommodation 84–5
exclusionary identity politics 61–4, 71–3
external actors: in democracy 22, 30; European Union 21, 153; Latgale 136–8

"far-right movement party" 104
Fico, R. 22, 30, 92–3, 102, 108–10, 113–16
Fidesz-KDNP alliance 14, 27, 28, 30, 60, 63–9, 72–5, 75n1
Final Act of Helsinki 51
Financial Supervision Authority (KNF) 66
foreign influence 42, 44, 51, 56
Framework Convention for the Protection of National Minorities (FCNM) 53–4
Francis (Pope) 93
Freedom and Solidarity (SaS) party 92, 115
Froese, P. 90
Fundamental Law 68, 112

gender-based violence 55–6
gender equality 43
GERB (political party) 55
Gersdorf, M. 70
global financial crisis (2008) 13, 21, 22, 28, 32, 34–5, *34*, 37, 64
Globsec Policy Institute 109

Greater Romania Party (PRM) 50, 53
Greskovits, B. 5, 144, 147–9, 157–8
Guasti, P. 13–14

Hale, H. E. 62
Hanley, S. 108
Harmony Centre party *(Saskanas Centrs)* 130
Harris, E. 14, 107, 111, 117n2
Haughton, T. 115
Havlík, V. 105, 115
Heidmets, M. 154
Helsinki Foundation for Human Rights 67
Hiers, W. 113
Hitler, A. 107
hollowness 147–9; backsliding and 158; ethnic 153–6; technocratic 149–53
human traffickers 72
Hungarian Democratic Alliance of Romania 50, 56
Hungary 102; anti-immigrant rhetoric 102; Caesarean politics in 60–75; democracy in 63–4; domestic dynamics 13; EU disciplinary proceedings 31; transparency of government communication 27; vibrancy of civil society 158; violent demonstrations 75n3
hybrid regimes 23
"hybrid warfare" 135, 138, 141n34

identity politics: challenge of 2–3; effect of 9; exclusionary 61–4, 71–3; longevity of 1–15; polarisation on 82; polyarchical theory of 44–6; rise in Bulgaria 13–14, 28, 42–57, 81; rise in Romania 13–14, 28, 42–57, 81; salience of 9–12
IMF *see* International Monetary Fund (IMF)
individual liberties 24, 27, 33, 34, 35
intermediary actors 121, 125, 129–32
International Monetary Fund (IMF) 71, 152
Islamization of Europe 72; *see also* Europe
Istanbul Convention (2011) 55

Jakubiak, A. 66
Jankoľa, M. 110
Journal of Democracy 145
Juon, A. 13

Kaczyński, J. 22, 60, 63–6, 72–5
Kaliňák, R. 108
Karolewski, I. P. 14
Kattel, R. 155
Kelley, J. 52
Kiska, A. 93
Klaus, V. 86
Klaus Jr., V. 88
KNF *see* Financial Supervision Authority (KNF)
Kolev, K. 13
Kotleba, M. 91, 115
Kuciak , J. 108

Latgale: external actors 136–8; flag 141n5; and historical legacy problems 125–7; intermediary actors 129–32; socio-political problems 132–6; structural/institutional needs 127–9
Latin America 123
Latvia: democratisation 145–7; ethnic hollowness 154–6; Europeanisation 145–7; post-Soviet democracy 121–3; technocratic hollowness 150–3
Lauristin, M. 154
legal framework 82–4, 93–4
Levitz, P. 32
LGBT rights 43, 57, 80–95, *89*, *91*; accommodation 80–95; anti-discrimination for 81, 83–5, 89, 91, 94–5; backlash against 80–2, 85, 88–92, 94; expansion of 93–4; legal framework of 82–4, 93–4; politicisation of 81, 82, 85; role of the EU in minority accommodation 84–5; theoretical framework of 82–4
liberal democracy 9, 12, 61, 73, 81, 103, 114; in CEE 63; EU's technocratic implementation of 12; Latvia 121; liberals and 71; market economy and 10; nationalists 107; pluralism and 15; political agenda 22; political decision-making 8; post-authoritarian/totalitarian regime 123; postcommunist citizens 2; rise of "people *versus* elites" 7; transformation 60

"Machine of Narrative Security" 72
mainstream right 90
majoritarianism 3, 6, 8, 12, 24, 30, 36, 46, 48, 50, 52–3, 56–7, 71; Bulgarian 55; CEE countries 43; culture and identity of 44; dominant 45; ethnic 15; national 11; in parliament 27; repressive 43; Romanian 49, 51; tyranny of 45; undemocratic 42
Malova, D. 115
Mareš, M. 105, 115
Mečiar, V. 22, 110
Merkel, W. 23
Mészáros, L. 67
Mezs, I. 141n28
migration crisis 72, 102, 106; advantage of 114; Central European political establishment 117; Christian refugees 109; ĽSNS 103; migrants in the Media 110; Slovak politics 103
Mihálik, J. 110
Minkenberg, M. 102, 104–5
minority rights: acceptance of 44; European Union 85; expansion of 82; non-constitutional infringements 28; pluralism and 56; politics of 82; protection 36, 51, 153; tolerance and 42; without minority voices 156–7
Morlino, L. 23
Most-Híd (political party) 92
Movement for a Democratic Slovakia (*Hnutie za Demokratické Slovensko* (HZDS)) 110

Movement for Rights and Freedoms 50, 51
Munich Agreement 107

Năstase, A. 30
National Alliance 148
national identity 1, 45, 51–2, 107, 110, 112; democratic political process 13; Eastern European politics 8; into politics 9, 15; and state sovereignty 4
nationalist neoliberalism 155
nationalist populism 114
nationalist social contract 155
National Movement Simeon the Second (NDSV) 52–3
national security 3, 129, 132, 139
National Union Attack 50, 55
National Unity Party 50
Nations in Transit 2018 107
nativism 2, 15, 105, 106
NATO 102, 104, 121, 136, 140
Nazi Germany 122
NDSV *see* National Movement Simeon the Second (NDSV)
Neighbourhood Policy 38n16
"neoliberal Baltic capitalism model" 151
Népszabadság 67
NGOs 72, 74, 129–31, 136
Ninova, K. 56

ODS (political party) 88, 90
Offe, C. 11
Orbán, V. 22, 27–8, 30, 36, 60, 63–75, 75n4, 109
Orthodox Church 133, 140
Otherness Initiative 90

Pamporov, A. 49
pan-Slavism 104
Pappas, T. S. 62, 71
Paroubek, J. 86
Party Manifesto Project 50
party state capture 67–71
patronalism 61–2, 65, 67, 73
patronal politics 64–7
People's Party Our Slovakia (ĽSNS) 101–4; extreme rhetoric 113; of extreme right 105–6; extremist 117; non-parlia-mentary 110; politically isolated 116; success 101
PHARE programme 151
Piotrowicz, S. 76n7
Pirro, A. 104, 106
PiS (political party) 13, 14, 60, 62–70, 72–5
Pit'ha, P. 88
pluralism *see* subcultural pluralism
Poland 102; Caesarean politics in 60–75; democracy in 63–4
polarisation 63–4, 80, 82, 86, 88, 114, 147
politics: Caesarean 60–75; competition 30–1, 33; volatility 55
polyarchical democracy 44–56

Pop-Eleches, G. 32
Popescu-Tăriceanu, C. 30
PO-PSL government 69
populism 106; authoritarianism and 106, 110; definition of 2, 28–30, 38n10, 106; nationalist 114; radical right 106, 113; rise of 2, 7, 15, 28, 113, 117; role in democracy 7, 12, 22, 31, 36, 37n8, 43, 71; sources of 7, 38n11, 38n12
populist democracies 62, 71
postcommunist elites 5, 70
postcommunist transition 2, 5, 11, 101, 111, 117
"post-Soviet cultural problem" 127
Prawo i Sprawiedliwość (Law and Justice) *see* PiS (political party)
Pride Parade in Bratislava 90, 91
Pridham, G. 5, 14
PRM *see* Greater Romania Party (PRM)
pro-liberal influence 42–4
PSD *see* Social Democratic Party (PSD)
public discourses 146, 151
public opinion 7, 45, 47, 50, 72, 83, 84, 86, 89–91, 92, 95, 96n13
public sphere 24, 25, 27, 33, 36

radical right 2, 85, 88, 90, 102, 104, 106, 117n4
"rainbow families" 87, 89
"rainbow plague" 80
Raudla, R. 155
refugee crisis 54, 72
registered partnership 81–3, 86–94, 95n6
re-interpretation 84
re-monopolization 62, 67
right-wing authoritarianism 103, 105; *see also* authoritarianism
Roman Catholic Church 131, 134
Roman Catholicism 122, 126
Romania: distribution of minority parties in 55; distribution of nationalist in 55; early transition period (1989 – late 1990s) 50–2; political disempowerment of minorities in 48–9; post accession (2007 to present) 54–6; pre-accession period (late 1990s – 2007) 52–4; public attitudes over time 47–8; rise of identity politics in 13–14, 28, 42–57, 81; towards polyarchical democracy 46–56; weak subcultural pluralism in 13, 42, 44–6, 52, 54, 56, 57
Rossi, M. 109
rule of law 2, 4, 23–5, 27, 30–5, 37n6, 43, 67–70, 73, 75, 84, 124
Ruskii Mir Foundation 138
Russian Empire 126
Russkii Mir Foundation 131

Sakskoburgotski, S. 28
salami tactics 87
same-sex partnership 80–95

SaS *see* Freedom and Solidarity (SaS) party
Sata, R. 14
Saxe-Coburg Gotha, S. 52
Schimmelfennig, F. 32–3, 37n2
Schumpeter, J 4, 61
Second World War 115, 134, 138
Šefčovič, M. 108
sexual minorities *see* LGBT rights
sexual orientation, discrimination against 56, 80, 83
Simeonov, V 56
Simicska, L. 64, 75n4
SLD (Alliance of the Democratic Left) 64
Slechtova, K. 88
Slovak Catholic Church 90, 92
Slovak Constitution 104
Slovak-Hungarian relationships 92, 112
Slovakia: in context of Central Europe 107–11; democracy 103; disproportional backlash in 91–2; expansion of LGBT rights in 93–4; failed referendum against LGBT accommodation in 2015 92–3; international allies and funding 93; law on registered partnership 92; LGBT rights in 80–95; nationalist persistence in politics 113–16; public opinion on LGBT rights 90–1; Slovak People's Party 103–7
Slovak National Party (Slovenská Národná Strana, SNS) 104, 107, 114, 116
Slovak State 101
Slovak Togetherness (neo-Nazi political movement) 103
SMER party 92–4, 102, 108–10, 113, 115–16
Social Democratic Party (PSD) 53–4
Social Democrats 86–8
Social Europe 117n2
social justice 49
socio-politics 102, 111, 116, 121, 132–6
Soehl, T. 113
Southern Europe 123
sovereignty: of the community 71; national 2, 6, 11, 13, 14, 86, 95, 110, 113, 117; restoration of 114; state 4, 93–4
Soviet Union 122
Spodris, G. 140n2
state-society compact: in Central and Eastern Europe (CEE) 1–15; postcommunist 6–9; renegotiation of 2, 3, 5

subcultural pluralism 13, 42, 44–6, 52, 54, 56, 57
Svarcs, M. 140n4
Szydlo, B. 68

Tarlev, V. 30
technocratic hollowness 149–50; Estonia 150–3; Latvia 150–3
"ten (10) Commandments" programme 106
Teraz website 103
Tilly, C. 44
Tiso, J. 105
TOP 09 (political party) 87, 95n7
Toplánek, M. 30
Trading Economics website 108
transparency 23, 24–5, 27, 30–1, 33, 36, 127
Tudor, C. 53
tyranny of the majority 45

ultranationalist and extreme right parties **115**
Union of Democratic Forces 52, 54, 55
United Patriots 50
U.S. State Department 35, 67
Úsvit (Dawn of Direct Democracy) 88

Vachudova, M. A. 108
vacuum effect 3
Vajna, A. 67
Velliste, T. 152
veto rights 65, 86, 88; *see also* LGBT rights
Viksnins, G. 152
Visegrád (V4) countries 101

wartime authoritarianism 101, 104–6, 115; *see also* authoritarianism
Washington Consensus 5
Waszczykowski, W. 73
Weber, M. 61
Welzel, C. 49
Wimmer, A. 113

Zaslove, A. 105
Zeman, M. 86, 88, 108
Ziobro, Z. 65, 66, 70
Zybertowicz, A. 72

Printed in the USA
CPSIA information can be obtained
at www.ICGtesting.com
LVHW072325160224
772060LV00007B/903